A WRITER'S PLAN

SUZANNE S. WEBB
Texas Woman's University

WILLIAM E. TANNER
Texas Woman's University

Theodore Lownik Library
Illinois Benedictine College
Lisle, Illinois 60532

WITHDRAWN

HARCOURT BRACE JOVANOVICH, PUBLISHERS

San Diego New York Chicago Atlanta Washington, D.C.
London Sydney Toronto

To John F. Adams and
Philip Mahone Griffith

808
.042
W368w

COPYRIGHTS AND ACKNOWLEDGMENTS

For permission to use the selections reprinted in this book, the authors are grateful to the following publishers and copyright holders:

p. 2 THE HEART OF A WOMAN by Maya Angelou, as it appeared in *Essence,* January 1984. From *The Heart of a Woman* by Maya Angelou. Copyright © 1981 by Maya Angelou. Reprinted by permission of Random House, Inc.

p. 61 HORROR MOVIES: WHY FEAR IS FUN by Mary Ann Bachemin in *Teen,* March 1982. Reprinted by permission of Petersen Publishing Co.

p. 177 GUMPTION in *Zen and the Art of Motorcycle Maintenance* by Robert M. Pirsig. Copyright © 1974 by Robert M. Pirsig. By permission of William Morrow & Company. Titled "Gumption" by the editors.

p. 226 HOW TO MAKE A TERRARIUM by Nancy Bubel. Reprinted by permission from *Blair & Ketchum's Country Journal.* Copyright © December 1978, Historical Times, Inc.

p. 277 WHERE FUTURE JOBS WILL BE in *World Press Review,* March 1981. This article was excerpted from the news magazine *The Economist* of London. Reprinted with permission from *World Press Review,* March 1981.

p. 324 THE FAMILY NUMBERS GAME by Richard Wolkomir in *American Way,* May 1982. Reprinted by permission of *American Way,* inflight magazine of American Airlines, copyright 1982 by American Airlines, and by permission of the author.

p. 373 GETTING DOWN TO BUSINESS: HOW PERSONAL COMPUTERS CAN AID THE PROFESSIONAL by Danny Goodman. From *Chicago,* September 1983. Reprinted by permission of Danny Goodman.

Copyright © 1985 by Harcourt Brace Jovanovich, Inc.

All rights reserved. No part of this publication may be reproduced or transmitted in any form or by any means, electronic or mechanical, including photocopy, recording, or any information storage and retrieval system, without permission in writing from the publisher.

Although for mechanical reasons all pages of this publication are punched and perforated, only those pages imprinted with an HBJ copyright notice are intended for removal.

Requests for permission to make copies of any part of the work should be mailed to: Permissions, Harcourt Brace Jovanovich, Publishers, Orlando, Florida 32887.

ISBN: 0-15-597898-5
Printed in the United States of America

PREFACE

A Writer's Plan offers a controlled approach to the writing process for students who need an introductory course to improve writing and reading skills before undertaking the usual sequence of college English courses. The first unit, "Writing: A Plan," leads students through the entire writing process. In subsequent units, students continue to use the controlled writing process while learning to modify it to develop their own personal writing processes.

Beginning with the first unit and continuing throughout the book, students take increasing responsibility for their writing and the evaluation of their writing. This textbook not only increases instructor-student interaction during writing but reduces the amount of time the instructor must spend grading student work. The textbook encourages students to accept responsibility for their own writing by instructing them to seek the instructor's help *during* writing instead of relying on the instructor to mark repeated errors in completed papers. The plan casts the instructor in the role of mentor and expert rather than grader.

Every unit has the same plan. This approach guides the students' progress from understanding to applying basic concepts. Each unit includes instruction on more efficient reading and a reading selection with exercises designed to measure reading comprehension and to develop ideas for writing. Each unit also includes a writing assignment, a discussion of the writing process, and exercises on paragraph development as well as ones on grammar, spelling, and vocabulary. Units 4 and 8 include sections on the organization of the essay. Controlled exercises in each section help students use the concepts in the plan. For example, the text introduces the concept and plan for a three-part paragraph in the first unit. Then each further unit contains a paragraph development section, including a worksheet on which students write in the three parts of a paragraph. This guides the students' growth in writing well-developed paragraphs.

Theodore Lownik Library
Illinois Benedictine College
Lisle, Illinois 60532

iii

Key features of *A Writer's Plan* merge recent theories about language and writing with more traditional approaches that have proved successful in the classroom.

- Each unit augments and reinforces the writing process until the student is thoroughly familiar with it.
- Complex grammatical and rhetorical concepts are made accessible to introductory writing students.
- The treatment of the organization and development of paragraphs proceeds from a controlled pattern to an open-ended plan.
- Each writing assignment coordinates with the paragraph section and emphasizes the mode of development introduced in each of the readings.
- Discussion of the writing process helps students to recognize that their problems are similar to those of other writers.
- Audience evaluation exercises encourage students to write for a specific audience.
- Study questions lead students through explanations of grammatical concepts and help students consider ideas from three perspectives: static (What is it?), dynamic (How does it change?), and relative (What is it like?).
- Peer evaluation becomes a learning experience and leads each student to revisions before the instructor sees the completed essay.
- The plan relieves the instructor of time spent grading essays and frees vital time for teaching and conferences.

For the convenience of both students and instructors, *A Writer's Plan* is perforated and punched. Students may hand in certain sections and may easily reassemble the complete text with exercises in a standard three-ring binder.

ACKNOWLEDGMENTS

We particularly wish to thank Mary E. Whitten, North Texas State University, for her careful reading of the manuscript and the many valuable suggestions she offered throughout the writing of this book. We are also grateful to Tommy J. Boley, University of Texas at El Paso, for his incisive view of the needs of inexperienced writers.

Without Matt Milan of Harcourt Brace Jovanovich, *A Writer's Plan* would not exist. We thank him for recognizing the value of a text that places the student in the midst of the writing process and for encouraging us to write it. Gene Carter Lettau—for her sustained enthusiasm, sensible advice, and careful editing—is due our sincere appreciation. We also thank the others at HBJ who successfully completed the various tasks of publication: Marji James, Kim Turner, and Merilyn Britt.

Finally, we would like to thank those closest to us: Dick Webb, for taking over as ''mother'' and for the use of the computer to write this book; Aaron Webb, for cheerfully eating TV dinners; and—for encouragement and patience—Martha Elizabeth Willingham Tanner, Betty Aline Tanner Lindsey, and Glenda Joyce Tanner Vasicek.

CONTENTS

UNIT TWO   *Writing: Reentered*   60

UNIT THREE   *Writing: Reconsidered*   121

UNIT ONE
WRITING
A PLAN

1.1 GETTING STARTED BY READING

Writing and reading are two skills you can develop at the same time. When you improve your reading, you improve your writing; when you improve your writing, you improve your reading. Writers write no better than they read though some readers may read better than they write. Since reading and writing are closely connected, improving one helps you improve the other.

The instruction in this course brings writing and reading together to help you develop these skills. Guided practice leads to improvement in both, but without such practice, improvement in either is not possible. Books and teachers can point you in the right direction and keep you out of blind corridors, but neither can substitute for the practice you must do with guidance.

Improvement in reading and in writing always comes slowly; your improvement rate will depend upon your regular practice of reading and writing. To improve your skills in reading and writing, you must attempt uses of language that you have not yet developed. Without such attempts you cannot progress or improve beyond your present level.

When you first encounter new ways to express ideas, you can expect to increase the number and kinds of errors that you make. Taking risks, however, leads you to discoveries about language—reading and writing—that are not otherwise possible. Making mistakes when learning a skill is part of learning any skill. On the one hand, you cannot improve without making mistakes; on the other, you cannot improve if you keep making the same mistakes over and over. If your mistakes are the result of experimentation, they should not discourage you. The advice and instruction in this course, if practiced, can help you reduce chronic errors and improve through taking risks.

Understanding the close connections between writing and reading explains why you will begin this unit, and every unit, with reading. As you read the following selection, you are preparing yourself to write. To do that, you will need to notice specific details in the selection: For instance, who is telling the story?

Once you have decided who is telling the story, you will want to understand how she feels about people that she tells about. How does she feel about the people who are close to her? Her mother? Her son? Her boyfriends? The three main events that she describes are a third thing to look for in reading this selection.

As you read, take a pencil with an eraser and write notes to yourself in the margin and underline details that impress you or that answer the questions above. If you make a mistake or change your mind, you can erase your comment or your underlining. Reading with a pencil is one way to become actively engaged with the text; what you underline and write will remain in your memory far more easily than if you read without being involved with what you are reading.

During your reading, then, look for answers to the following questions:

1. Who tells the story?
2. How does she feel about the people who are close to her? Her mother? Her son? Her boyfriends?
3. What three events does she describe in the selection?

1.2 NARRATION

Maya Angelou   *from "THE HEART OF A WOMAN"*

California, 1959

I decided to leave Los Angeles and move to New York City with my son, Guy. I called my mother in San Francisco.

"I'd like to see you. I'm going to move to New York and I don't know when I'll come back to California. Maybe we could meet somewhere and spend a couple of days together."

Copyright © 1985 by Harcourt Brace Jovanovich, Inc. All rights reserved.

She didn't pause. "Of course, we can meet, of course, I want to see you, baby." Six feet tall, thirty-one years old, with a fourteen-year-old son, and I was still called baby. "How about Fresno? That's halfway. We could stay at that hotel. I know you read about it."

"Yes. But not if there's going to be trouble. I just want to be with you."

"Trouble? Trouble? But, baby, you know that's my middle name. Anyway, the law says that hotel has to accept Negro guests."

Vivian Baxter sensed the possibility of confrontation and there would be no chance of talking her out of it.

In 1959, Fresno was a middling town with palm trees and a decidedly Southern accent.

The Desert Hotel lobby had been decorated with welcome banners for a visiting sales convention. Large florid men mingled and laughed with portly women.

My entrance stopped all action. Every head turned to see, every eye blazed, first with doubt, then fury. I wanted to run back to my car and race to Los Angeles. I straightened my back and forced my face into indifference and walked to the registration desk. "Good afternoon. Where is the bar?" The young man dropped his eyes and pointed behind me.

The crowd made an aisle and I walked through the silence, knowing that before I reached the lounge door, a knife could be slipped in my back or a rope lassoed around my neck.

My mother sat at the bar wearing her Dobbs hat and tan suede suit.

"Hi, baby," her smile was a crescent of white. "Jim?" I knew she'd already have the bartender's name and his attention. The man grinned for her.

"Jim, this is my baby. She's pretty, isn't she? Baby, you're looking good. How was the drive? How's Guy? Is he happy about the move?" After a drink and some talk, we started for our room. Again in the noisy lobby the buzz of conversation diminished, but Mother never noticed. She switched through the crowd, up to the desk.

"Mrs. Vivian Baxter Jackson and daughter. You have our reservation."

It was a statement. The clerk slowly pushed a form across the counter. Mother opened her purse, took out her gold Sheaffer and signed us in.

Copyright © 1985 by Harcourt Brace Jovanovich, Inc. All rights reserved.

"The key, please." Again using slow motion, the clerk slid the key to Mother.

The hotel's color bar had been lifted only a month earlier, yet she acted as if she had been a guest there for years.

When we got to our room, she said, "Sit down, baby. I'm going to tell you something you must never forget . . . Animals can sense fear. You know that human beings are animals, too. Never, never let a person know you're frightened. And a group of them . . . absolutely never. Now, in that lobby you were as scared as a rabbit. I knew it and all those white folks knew it. If I hadn't been there, they might have turned into a mob. But something about me told them, if they mess with either of us, they'd better start looking for some new asses, 'cause I'd blow away what their mammas gave them."

She laughed like a young girl. "Look in my purse." I opened her purse.

"The Desert Hotel better be ready for integration, 'cause if it's not, I'm ready for the Desert Hotel."

Under her wallet, half hidden, lay a dark-blue German Luger.

"But now, let's talk. Why New York? You were there in '52 and had to be sent home. What makes you think it has changed?"

"I met a writer, John Killens. I told him I wanted to write and he invited me to New York. I've met his wife and children. I'll go to New York, stay with them for a couple of weeks, get an apartment and send for Guy."

"And where will he stay for two weeks? Not alone in that big house. He's only fourteen."

"I've made arrangements with a friend. And after all, it's only two weeks."

We both knew that she had left me and my brother for ten years to be raised by our paternal grandmother. We looked at each other and she spoke first.

"You're right. It is only two weeks."

There was a knock at the door. She had called room service earlier. A uniformed Black man opened the door and halted in surprise at seeing us. He deposited the tray and turned.

"Good evening, you all surprised me. Sure did. Didn't expect to see you. Sure didn't."

Copyright © 1985 by Harcourt Brace Jovanovich, Inc. All rights reserved.

"Who did you expect? Queen Victoria?"

"No. No, ma'am. I mean . . . Our people . . . in here . . . It's kinda new seeing us . . . and everything."

"This is for you." She gave him a tip. "We are just ordinary guests in the hotel. Thank you and good night."

"Mom, you were almost rude."

"Well, baby, I figure like this. He's colored and I'm colored, but we are not cousins. Let's have a drink." She smiled.

During the next two days, Mother showed me off to some old card-playing friends she had known twenty years earlier.

When it was time to leave, we hugged in the empty lobby of the hotel; the convention had ended the day before our departure.

"Take care of yourself. Take care of your son, and remember, New York City is just like Fresno. Just more of the same people in bigger buildings. Black folks can't change because white folks won't change. Ask for what you want and be prepared to pay for what you get." She kissed me and her voice softened to a whisper. "Let me leave first, baby. I hate to see the back of someone I love."

We embraced again and I watched her walk, hips swaying, into the bright street.

Brooklyn, New York, a Few Weeks Later

I picked up Guy at the airport, and when he walked into the house I saw that he was already too large for the living room. We had been separated a month and he seemed to have grown two inches taller and years away from me. He looked around.

"It's OK. It looks like every other house we've lived in."

I wanted to slap him. "Well, it's a little better than the street."

"Oh, Mother, come now. That wasn't necessary." The superiority in his voice was an indication of how he had been hurt by our separation.

I grinned. "OK. Sorry. How about the desk? You always said you wanted a big office desk. Do you like it?"

"Oh sure, but you know I wanted a desk when I was a little kid. Now . . . ."

The air between us was burdened with his aloof scorn. I understood him too well.

Copyright © 1985 by Harcourt Brace Jovanovich, Inc. All rights reserved.

When I was three my parents divorced in Long Beach, California. They sent me and my four-year-old brother, unescorted, to our paternal grandmother in Stamps, Arkansas, for a ten-year stay. Our reunion with Mother in California was a joyous festival, but under and after the high spirits was my aching knowledge that she had spent years not needing us. Now my angry son was wrestling with the same knowledge.

He remained standing, hands in his pockets, waiting for me to convince him of the stability of my love. Words were useless.

"Your school is three blocks away, and there's a large park almost as nice as the one on Fulton Street."

At the mention of the San Francisco park, a tiny smile tried to cross his face, but he sent it away.

" . . . and you liked the Killens children. Well, they live around the corner."

He nodded and spoke like an old man. "Lots of people are different when they're visiting than when they're at home."

"Guy, you know I love you, and I try to be a good mother. I try to do the right thing, but I'm not perfect"—his silence agreed—"it's not my intention . . ."

He was studying my face, listening to the tone of my voice.

"Mom . . ." I relaxed a little. "Mom" meant closeness, forgiveness. "Mom, I know. I know you do the best you can. And I'm not really angry. It's just that Los Angeles . . ."

"Did Ray do anything . . . mistreat you?" My friend Ray had stayed with Guy.

"Oh no, Mom. He moved about a week after you left."

"You mean you lived alone?"

Shock set my body into furious action. Tears surfaced and clouded my vision. Guy lost half his age and suddenly he again was a little boy of seven who slept with a butcher's knife under his pillow one summer at camp.

"My baby. Oh honey, why didn't you tell me when I phoned? I would have come back."

Now his was the soothing voice. "You were trying to find a job and a house. I wasn't afraid."

Copyright © 1985 by Harcourt Brace Jovanovich, Inc. All rights reserved.

"But Guy, you're only fourteen. Suppose something had happened to you?"

He stood silent and looked at me, evaluating my distress. Suddenly, he crossed the room and stopped beside my chair. "Mom, I'm a man. I can look after myself. Don't worry. I'm young, but I'm a man." He stood, bent and kissed me on the forehead. "I'm going to change the furniture around. I want my desk facing the window."

The Black mother perceives destruction at every door, and even she herself is not beyond her own suspicion. She questions whether she loves her children enough—or more terribly, does she love them too much? If she is unmarried, the challenges are increased. Her singleness indicates she has rejected, or has been rejected by her mate. Yet she is raising children who will become mates. Beyond her door, all authority is in the hands of people who do not look or think or act like her and her children. Teachers, doctors, sales clerks, librarians, policemen, welfare workers are white and exert control over her family's moods, conditions and personality: yet within the home, she must display a right to rule which at any moment, by a knock at the door, or a ring of the telephone can be exposed as false. In the face of these contradictions, she must provide a blanket of stability, which warms but does not suffocate, and she must tell her children the truth about the power of white power without suggesting that it cannot be challenged.

"Hey, Mom, come and see."

Every piece of furniture was in a new place, and the room looked exactly the same.

"Like it? After dinner, I'll play you a game of Scrabble. What are we having for dinner? Does the television work?"

My son was home and we were a family again.

New York, 1960

One Monday morning, a mound of cardboard boxes stood against my office wall. I opened them all. Each contained a beautiful piece of luggage and a note: "Best Wishes to My Bride." I carried pleasure to my desk.

I was going to marry Thomas Allen. He was forty-three and a hardworking bail bondsman who lived in Brooklyn also. He was kind to me and generous to Guy. I knew I wasn't in love with him, but I was lonely and I would make a good wife. I

Copyright © 1985 by Harcourt Brace Jovanovich, Inc. All rights reserved.

had only one regret. We didn't talk. He treated my work at the SCLC as just another job. After the most commonplace greetings, our conversations were mostly limited to my shouting in his bedroom and his grunts at my dining room table. Our lives would be quiet.

That same Monday morning, one of my SCLC office mates told me that over the weekend she had heard a South African freedom fighter speak. He was so thorough and so brilliant that even the biggest fool in the world had to see that apartheid was evil and would have to be brought down. His name was Vusumzi Make (pronounced *Mah*-kay).

I was interested in hearing him. Working late prevented that on the next few occasions. But I met him at a gathering at John Killens' about ten days later. "He's the representative of the Pan-Africanist Congress," John had said. "That's the radical organization, but he's coming over with Oliver Tambo, head of the African National Congress. The ANC is to the PAC what the NAACP is to the Black Muslims. The two get along, though."

I had not met such a man. Vusumzi Make was intense and contained. And he didn't seem to know that he was decidedly overweight. John's introduction of him was probably apt. He was a warrior, sure of his enemies and secure with his armament.

After Oliver Tambo spoke, John intoduced Mr. Make to the group, and my love no longer was in the hands of Thomas Allen.

I saw Make twice more at public gatherings in the next few days. The third time, Make said, "Miss Angelou, I intend to change your life. I am going to take you to Africa."

"Mr. Make, I am going to be married in two months. So your plan is impossible."

"I owe it to our people to save you. When you see your bloody fiancé, tell him that I'm after you and that with me every day is Saturday night and I'm Black and I'm dangerous."

The next night Thomas took me to see a movie. It was deadly boring. I got up on the pretext of wanting a soft drink and I sat in the lobby smoking and wondering what Make was doing. Patrice Lumumba was in New York. Rosa Guy, the writer,

Copyright © 1985 by Harcourt Brace Jovanovich, Inc. All rights reserved.

was going to meet him and his assistant Thomas Kanza. Abbey Lincoln and her husband, Max Roach, were performing in the Village. Malcolm X was speaking at a public meeting in Harlem, and somewhere Make was showering his listeners with glittering words. Guy was attending a youth rally in Washington Square Park. The world was on fire.

Later, sitting in the car, I told Thomas we were living in exciting times and that because of the United Nations, Africans and oppressed people from all over the world were making New York the arena where they fought for justice.

"I haven't lost anything in Africa and they haven't lost anything in our country," he said. "They can all go back where they came from as far as I'm concerned. Anyhow, I get all the excitement I need in my job and I don't want to hear about politics at home."

It was a long speech for Thomas and a disastrous one for our relationship.

The next days brought bouquets of mixed flowers and vases of red roses to cover my desk "From Vusumzi Make to Maya Angelou Make."

Thomas chose the same time to have more wedding presents delivered. "Tom to Maya."

I refused Make's daily invitations to lunch and declined Thomas' offer to visit his apartment.

Thursday morning I agreed to meet Make for lunch a few blocks from my office. I would explain to him why he had to accept my rejection.

He stood as I entered and began talking before I sat down. My coming showed I had courage, a virtue which we both knew was a prerequisite in the struggle. He had talked to my friend Paule Marshall, by telephone, and told her that his intention was to marry me and take me to Africa. I couldn't focus on the menu, but we ordered lunch. He continued talking.

He had been jailed for political action in South Africa. When the government released him, the police took him to an isolated desert area near South-West Africa [Namibia] and left him there, hundreds of miles from the nearest human beings. He walked out of South Africa and kept on walking. He took his first breath of freedom when he crossed into Ethiopia.

Copyright © 1985 by Harcourt Brace Jovanovich, Inc. All rights reserved.

"I was the first Pan-Africanist Congress member to escape. But, Miss Angelou, when I left exile without water or food, I intended to reach Ethiopia. When I knew I was coming to the U.S., I came with the intention of finding a strong, beautiful Black American woman, who would be a helpmate, who understood the struggle and who was not afraid of a fight. I heard about you and you sounded like the one. I met Guy and I was impressed with his manliness and intelligence, obviously your work, and then I saw you."

He reached across the table and took my hand. "You are exactly what I dreamed on my long march. Needing to be loved. Ready to fight and needing protection. And not the protection of a bloody bail bondsman."

Oh Lord, that reminded me.

"Mr. Make, I agreed to have lunch with you to tell you I am going to marry the bloody bail bondsman."

"You are breaking my heart. I am an African with large things to do . . . I need you. I want to marry you."

"I'm sorry." And God knew I meant that.

"I shall finish at the UN tomorrow. On the next day, I shall fly to Amsterdam. Then I shall go to Copenhagen, then London. My desire for you is total, Miss Angelou. I want your mind and your spirit and your body. After all, I may be an African with a mission, but I am also a man." He stopped talking and I waited in silence for a second before I excused myself and went to the toilet.

A woman bumped into me on her way out. She saw the tears on my face.

"Hey, are you OK? You sick? You sure you don't need any help?"

I shook my head and thanked her.

After an agonizing few minutes, I called Abbey Lincoln from a pay phone. She answered.

"Just wanted to make sure you were there."

"What's happening?"

"Nothing yet, I'll call back."

"Are you all right?"

"Yeah. Really. I'll call you in a few minutes."

Copyright © 1985 by Harcourt Brace Jovanovich, Inc. All rights reserved.

Make stood again as I reached the table. I sat down.

"Mr. Make, I'll do it. I'll do it. I'll go with you."

His face broke open.

"I'll marry you, Miss Angelou. I'll make you happy. We will be known as the happiest family in Africa." He came around the table and pulled me to my feet to kiss me. I noticed other customers for the first time and drew away.

Make laughed, turning to the tables of Black people openly watching us.

"It is all right. She has just said she'll marry me."

Applause and laughter.

"This is the joining of Africa and Africa-America! Two great peoples back together again."

I tried to sit back down.

"No. I claim my engagement kiss."

Shaken by the physical touching, we took our seats again. The woman who had offered to help me in the toilet came to our table.

"Honey, I should have known you weren't crying out of sadness." She smiled. "You all have a drink with us. We've been married eighteen of the best years of my life."

A man's voice shouted across the room, "Ernestine, just offer the folks a drink and come on back and sit down."

The woman grinned. "See how nice we get along? He orders. I obey. Sometimes."

Make and I laughed as she strutted back to her table.

Copyright © 1985 by Harcourt Brace Jovanovich, Inc. All rights reserved.

Notes

1.3 UNDERSTANDING WHAT YOU READ

After you have finished reading the Angelou selection, glance over these questions. Then see if you noted or underlined passages that will help you answer the questions. Write your answers in the blanks.

1. a. How would you describe the narrator?

   _____

   b. Is she someone you would like to know?

   _____

   c. Give two reasons for your opinion.

   _____

   _____

2. a. Is her family like your family? How?

   _____

   b. If not, how does your family differ?

   _____

3. a. Do the three events in this narrative cause changes in the people involved?

   _____

   b. If so, identify the changes.

   _____

   _____

   _____

1.4 DISCOVERING IDEAS FOR WRITING

By jotting responses to the following six questions as you think about them, you will discover ideas for an essay of your own. When you write it, you should use these notes.

Copyright © 1985 by Harcourt Brace Jovanovich, Inc. All rights reserved.

1. Have you ever felt like an outsider from having moved or changed schools?

   _____

   _____

   _____

2. How did you feel when you first came to college?

   _____

   _____

   _____

3. Can you imagine people feeling different about being an outsider than you felt?

   _____

   _____

   _____

4. What kinds of changes can you think of that can occur in relationships between parents and children?

   _____

   _____

   _____

5. Have you seen a relationship with a close friend or relative change?

   _____

   _____

   _____

6. Do you think your parents may have felt like outsiders at some time? Would they have felt as you did, or would their feelings have been different?

   _____

   _____

Copyright © 1985 by Harcourt Brace Jovanovich, Inc. All rights reserved.

Notice that these questions look at relationships with other people in several organized ways. Some of the questions ask you to think about a relationship by telling what it is, others explore how relationships change, and still others help you understand what else a relationship you have had may be like. These key questions can be used with all sorts of subjects and can help you discover what to write in your own essay. Keep the key questions in mind and use them.

1. What is it?
2. How does it change?
3. What else is it like?

Copyright © 1985 by Harcourt Brace Jovanovich, Inc. All rights reserved.

Notes

1.5 UNDERSTANDING WRITING

Most people go to work on days when they really do not feel like working. Many successful writers write when they do not feel like writing. Writing is work.

To be successful at acquiring writing skills, you will first have to understand that writing is work. In college and after you will frequently be called upon to write at times when you would rather be doing almost anything else. You may feel at those times that you cannot think of anything to write; if you could, whatever you wrote nobody would want to read anyway. Every published writer has shared your frustration. If you were to write only when you feel like it or have something important to say to the entire world, you would seldom write anything.

Understanding that you will not always be inspired to write shows you the value of imitating the habits of proven writers. You have already encountered one: writing is work, and since it is, you should approach writing like any other job. You do it whether you want to or not. A second reason as well as the second principle to be introduced here is that the act of writing helps you to discover what you want to say. One famous writer, E. M. Forster, illustrated this principle when he puzzled, "How can I know what I think before I see what I say?"

Two important principles for you to borrow from professional writers, then, are these insights:

1.   You must write even when you would rather not.
2.   The act of writing will help you know better what you think.

These two principles, when adopted and applied consistently to your writing, will help you to write better.

1.6 WRITING—NARRATION

In a narration, a writer presents events in a time order. In other words, you just tell a story (narrative) as Maya Angelou does. Telling a story, though, may not be as easy as it seems at first because you may not be able to think of everything that you need to include in your draft.

For this assignment you are to draft a narrative. When writing a draft, you should not worry about sentence structure, spelling of words, paragraph development, or even logic, though, of course, it would be silly to ignore these entirely. Writing a draft is spilling words on the page that you alone will read. In doing this uninhibited composing, you will begin to discover what you want to say as well as begin to have some ideas about how you want to say it. Some of what you write in a draft will appear in your final version; you will change most drafts several times as you shape

Copyright © 1985 by Harcourt Brace Jovanovich, Inc. All rights reserved.

your narrative for an audience other than yourself. During drafting, put your ideas on paper as fast as you can write because you may never capture them again.

WRITING ASSIGNMENT

Choose one of the following.

1. Draft a narration of approximately 350 words telling of events that made you or someone you cared about feel like an outsider.
2. Draft a narration of approximately 350 words telling of events leading to a change in a relationship you were a part of.

The writer's role: All writing, from the first draft to the final version, is the responsibility of the writer. Here, you are the writer, and you cannot expect your reader—even if your reader is your writing instructor—to read anything you have written until you have written it as well as you can. This responsibility should not keep you from asking advice from your instructor as you write. In fact, it should encourage you to ask your instructor such questions as ''How can I fix this sentence?'' or ''What do I do to develop this paragraph?'' Ask such questions while you are writing your essay because these questions are not the same as asking your instructor to read and evaluate a draft.

The evaluation your instructor does will be helpful to you in other ways, but it will not help you solve a writing problem at the moment it arises. Your instructor can usually answer these questions quickly; the answers can help you get past your difficulty at the same time that you learn how to handle such situations the next time they come up. Your instructor wants to help you improve your writing and will be able to help you more efficiently if you ask specific questions at the time you need to know the answers.

During the writing of an essay, you should write much more than your instructor—or anyone else—will ever read. At first, you may write no more than 300 words at a time, but with practice and effort you can learn to write more without padding.

As you learn to write, you will learn that your first draft is not your final version. You will learn to think of the early drafts of your writing as practice, and from that practice you will learn to keep only your very best writing in your final version. If you were learning to play the piano, you would practice many hours by yourself without your piano teacher's coaching. Learning to write, like learning to play the piano, requires practice your instructor will not supervise. This practice—or preliminary drafts your instructor will NOT read—will teach you the value of rewriting, and you will learn that revision is more than correcting spelling and punctuation errors.

Of course, your instructor will want to have all versions of your essay before evaluating your final version in case there is a need to look more closely at the process you used to write it. Since this assignment is your first essay in this writing course,

Copyright © 1985 by Harcourt Brace Jovanovich, Inc. All rights reserved.

a summary of your responsibilities as a writer will guide you through writing your narration before you can reasonably expect your instructor to read it. In this course, before you submit any essay to your instructor, you should follow the advice given here.

SUMMARY OF WRITER'S RESPONSIBILITIES

This draft is your first version of your narration which will be changed several times before your instructor reads it. When you submit your narration for your instructor's evaluation, you will submit all versions at the same time. To make the evaluation of your writing as meaningful as possible and to reduce the amount of time it will take your instructor to evaluate your writing, clearly label this version as "FIRST DRAFT" and all later versions as "REVISION 1," "REVISION 2," and so on.

You cannot reasonably expect your instructor to read every word you write in this course, or indeed any of your writing, until you have made it the very best you can by working through several versions. But if you follow these instructions exactly, your instructor will be able to evaluate your best writing, to spot faults you did not know to ask about, and to suggest ways for you to improve your writing.

1.7 THE WRITING PROCESS

As you wrote your narration, you may have changed words, altered sentences, and rearranged it as you worked. Such activities are normal for trained writers because they know that writing involves thinking of something to write, writing it, and, most important, rewriting it.

At the point where inexperienced writers too often stop writing, experienced writers continue because they know how to reenter their writing so that rewriting can take place, and they do so. Inexperienced writers hesitate, though, to disturb their writing once it is on paper. *A major step in learning to write is to overcome this hesitation.*

Learning specific ways to reenter your writing will help you overcome any hesitation you have about changing what you have written. Reentering your writing allows you to improve it by revising your ideas and the ways you express them. Revision is rethinking, rephrasing, and rearranging.

One useful way to reenter your writing is to identify the sentences you have written. Underlining each sentence in a color pen or pencil will create a visual impact enabling you to see the number and length of the sentences you have in each paragraph. Once you have identified your sentences, rethink their effectiveness by asking the following questions.

Copyright © 1985 by Harcourt Brace Jovanovich, Inc. All rights reserved.

1. How many sentences does my narrative have?

   Sentence total: _____

2. How many words does my narrative contain?

   Word total: _____

3. Do all my sentences have subjects and verbs?

   Number with no subject: _____

   Number with no verb: _____

   Number with subject and verb: _____

4. Do more than half my sentences begin with ''I''?

   Number beginning with ''I'': _____

   Others: _____

5. What is the average length of my sentences?

   Divide total number of words _____ by total number of sentences _____

   for your average sentence length. _____

6. Do I need to make any of my sentences longer? _____

   Do I need to make any of my sentences shorter? _____

7. How many sentences do I have in each paragraph?

   Paragraph 1 _____

   Paragraph 2 _____

   Paragraph 3 _____

   Paragraph 4 _____

   Paragraph 5 _____

8. Do I have too many paragraphs? _____

   Do I have too few paragraphs? _____

Copyright © 1985 by Harcourt Brace Jovanovich, Inc. All rights reserved.

9. Does my narrative have a time order that my reader can follow? _____

10. How should I change my narrative in light of my responses to the above questions? _____

_____

When you have completed the evaluation of your narrative, revise it by making the changes suggested by the answers you gave to the questions. Label the new version clearly REVISION 1. When you have done everything you can do yourself to improve your narration, you need to get a response to what you have written from someone else. If you ask a friend or relative, you may not get a productive response because he or she may not be able to separate personal feelings about you from feelings about the work you have done.

You are better off to ask someone in your class who can help you see faults and gaps in your writing that you may not see yourself. To see if you have been successful in conveying your true opinion in your writing, ask two members of your class to be your editors, to read your narrative, and to decide from your writing how you feel about the events you report.

After you review the comments from your two editors, you may want to rewrite your narrative considering their responses. Before you make any revisions ask yourself: Have I been successful in communicating what I intended? If you have, there is no need for change or revision. However, very few writers can get it just right the first time. If your editors' understanding of what you have written is different from what you intended, but you think you have communicated successfully, you may not have told your audience everything they need to know to understand what you have in mind. To revise, ask yourself ''What must I include in my narrative to help my reader follow the events logically and understand them the way I do?''

EXERCISE 1

Writing students must learn to evaluate their own writing as well as the writing of others. To offer honest opinions and constructive criticism of a classmate's writing serves a twofold purpose. First, you assist a classmate with a particular piece of writing. Second, by judging the writing of your classmate, you learn to read your own writing through the eyes of an evaluator rather than focusing only on your own intentions. Ask two classmates to edit your narration. When you have received their comments and completed your revision, attach both evaluation forms to REVISION 2 so your instructor will know the kind of assistance you received.

Note to peer editor: In your evaluation focus on more than spelling and punctuation. Those are properly proofreading activities. Instead, focus your attention on the

Copyright © 1985 by Harcourt Brace Jovanovich, Inc. All rights reserved.

ideas or feelings the writer communicates. Do not ask the writer what was meant. Instead, determine what you think was meant according to what the writer actually wrote. After you have decided what you think, complete the Editor's Evaluation by offering two or three things you liked about this piece of writing and two or three suggestions for possible improvement. Sign your name and date the form before attaching your Editor's Evaluation to the narration. Then return both to the writer so that the instructor can see your comments when the writer submits the draft and revisions.

Copyright © 1985 by Harcourt Brace Jovanovich, Inc. All rights reserved.

EDITOR'S EVALUATION

Writer's Name _____

Title _____

I liked . . .   I think you could improve if . . .
1.   1.

2.   2.

3.   3.

Editor _____

Date _____

Copyright © 1985 by Harcourt Brace Jovanovich, Inc. All rights reserved.

Notes

1.8 PARAGRAPH POWER

A paragraph is a conventional form which writers find useful to help their readers follow a sequence of ideas or thoughts. You can easily find this courtesy to the reader because writers usually indent paragraphs about a half inch from the left margin if handwritten or five to seven spaces if typewritten. Sometimes, though, writers leave a small but noticeable blank space between paragraphs instead of indenting. Either way makes locating the beginning of a paragraph easy for a reader. Experienced writers organize and develop paragraphs in many different ways; however, inexperienced writers who do not generate paragraphs easily will find it helpful to learn some proven patterns for successful paragraphs.

You will notice from reading Maya Angelou's account that the number of sentences in her paragraphs range from *one* to as many as *nine*. Although there is no set number of sentences a paragraph should contain, paragraphs in college writing usually contain four to seven sentences. This number of sentences usually allows you to explain your ideas sufficiently.

Many of Maya Angelou's paragraphs are short because she is writing dialogue. As such they are effective. However, the typical paragraph you will write will not be the short paragraphs found in dialogue. Rather, you will most often be explaining a concept, describing an object, or relating an event. When you explain, describe, or relate in writing, you will want to supply enough information so your reader will be satisfied and will understand fully. To satisfy your reader's expectations, you should find and include details which will help you develop your paragraphs.

Paragraphs often develop by the addition of details to a general statement. Details are bits of information. When you combine these specifics, these bits of information, with each other in systematic ways, they form paragraphs. One effective way to develop a paragraph is to describe something by stating several positive, negative, and neutral characteristics, features, or details of that thing. Of course, you can develop a paragraph by giving only positive or negative or neutral characteristics rather than combining all kinds in a single paragraph. Maya Angelou writes a number of paragraphs developed in exactly this way. Look at the paragraph beginning ''I was going to marry Thomas Allen.''

(1) I was going to marry Thomas Allen.   **(2)** He was forty-three and a hardworking bail bondsman who lived in Brooklyn also.   **(3)** He was kind to me and generous to Guy.   **(4)** I knew I wasn't in love with him, but I was lonely and I would make a good wife.   **(5)** I had only one regret.   **(6)** We didn't talk.   **(7)** He treated my work at the SCLC as just another job.   **(8)** After the most commonplace greetings, our conversations were mostly limited to my shouting in his bedroom and his grunts at my dining room table.   **(9)** Our lives would be quiet.

Copyright © 1985 by Harcourt Brace Jovanovich, Inc. All rights reserved.

The first sentence introduces Thomas Allen, and the next lists neutral characteristics—his age and occupation. The third sentence gives positive features: He is kind and generous. The fourth sentence predicts the future of the relationship based on those positive features stated in the third sentence. Sentence five prepares you for negative characteristics which sentences six, seven, and eight specify. Sentence six expresses deep concern about a lack of communication. Then, sentence seven explains the kind of communication needed (Thomas needs to treat his fiancée's work at SCLC as important). Sentence eight contains negative details about how the lack of communication reveals itself, in shouting and in grunts. The final sentence sums up the relationship and indicates a response to the neutral, positive, and negative qualities presented by stating, ''Our lives would be quiet.''

A summary of this analysis appears on Paragraph Analysis Worksheet #1. The visual arrangement of the details on this worksheet helps you to see the organization of the paragraph at a glance.

EXERCISE 1

As a class activity, examine this paragraph to discover which details are positive, negative, or neutral. As you decide where the details belong, jot them in the boxes provided in Paragraph Analysis Worksheet #2.

(1) I had not met such a man. **(2)** Vusumzi Make was intense and contained. **(3)** And he didn't seem to know that he was decidedly overweight. **(4)** John's introduction of him was probably apt. **(5)** He was a warrior, sure of his enemies and secure with his armament.

EXERCISE 2

As a class activity, examine the paragraph and classify the kinds of details you discover. As you decide what kinds of details are used, jot them in the boxes of Paragraph Analysis Worksheet #3. When you are finished, compare the number of details in each column.

(1) The Black mother perceives destruction at every door, and even she herself is not beyond her own suspicion. **(2)** She questions whether she loves her children enough—or more terribly, does she love them too much? **(3)** If she is unmarried, the challenges are increased. **(4)** Her singleness indicates she has rejected, or has been rejected by her mate. **(5)** Yet she is raising children who will become mates. **(6)** Beyond her door, all authority is in the hands of people who do not look or think or act like her and her children. **(7)** Teachers, doctors, sales clerks, librarians, po-

Copyright © 1985 by Harcourt Brace Jovanovich, Inc. All rights reserved.

PARAGRAPH ANALYSIS WORKSHEET #1

	Positive	Negative	Neutral
1.			*named Thomas Allen*
2.			*age 43* *bail bondsman* *lives in Brooklyn*
3.	*kind and generous*		
4.	*positive attitude of narrator*		
5.		*one regret*	
6.		*they didn't talk*	
7.		*Thomas needs to show more understanding of her work*	
8.		*shouts in the bedroom grunts at the table*	
9.	*Their lives would be quiet*		

Copyright © 1985 by Harcourt Brace Jovanovich, Inc. All rights reserved.

PARAGRAPH ANALYSIS WORKSHEET #2

	Positive	Negative	Neutral
1.			
2.			
3.			
4.			
5.			

licemen, welfare workers are white and exert control over her family's moods, conditions, and personality; yet within the home, she must display a right to rule which at any moment, by a knock at the door, or a ring of the telephone can be exposed as false.   **(8)** In the face of these contradictions, she must provide a blanket of stability, which warms but does not suffocate, and she must tell her children the truth about the power of white power without suggesting that it cannot be challenged.

EXERCISE 3

Think of yourself or someone else you wrote about in your narrative (Section 1.6). Close your eyes and think of that person in a particular place dressed for a particular

Copyright © 1985 by Harcourt Brace Jovanovich, Inc. All rights reserved.

PARAGRAPH ANALYSIS WORKSHEET #3

	Positive	Negative	Neutral
1.			
2.			
3.			
4.			
5.			
6.			
7.			
8.			

Copyright © 1985 by Harcourt Brace Jovanovich, Inc. All rights reserved.

activity. If possible, remember the sound of the voice. Think of a time you want to recall—yesterday, last year, or even ten years ago. Once you get the image in your mind, think two or three minutes about this person keeping your eyes closed. When you have done that, list four positive features of that person or yourself. (These can be things you like about the person or yourself.)

1. _____

2. _____

3. _____

4. _____

List four negative features of that person. (These can be things you dislike about the person.)

1. _____

2. _____

3. _____

4. _____

List four neutral features of that person. (These can be things that you neither like nor dislike about the person.)

1. _____

2. _____

3. _____

4. _____

EXERCISE 4

Combine the positive, negative, and neutral characteristics you have discovered in the previous exercise into a paragraph of four to seven sentences. Write this paragraph specifically to fit into the next revision of your narrative (Section 1.6). This paragraph could either replace one you have already written, or it could be inserted at the appropriate place.

Copyright © 1985 by Harcourt Brace Jovanovich, Inc. All rights reserved.

1.9 SENTENCE POWER

THE SOUND AND LOOK OF AN ENGLISH SENTENCE

A sentence **is** a form through which writers **express** thoughts, ideas, and information. The previous group of words—from the word ''A'' (that **begins** with a capital letter) to the period after the word ''information''—**is** a sentence. Ordinarily, a group of words which **has** both a subject and a verb and **conveys** at least one complete thought **is** a sentence. Sometimes, though, a sentence **has** only a verb. (Verbs in the preceding sentences appear in **boldface** type.) Unless a writer deliberately breaks with established rules, a sentence begins with a capital letter and ends with a period, exclamation point, or question mark. In speech, many utterances convey complete thoughts that are recognizable as sentences only because they derive their meaning from a specific situation.

An utterance such as ''hot''—when a baby means ''my soup is too hot''—is a virtual sentence because it conveys the baby's meaning from context (an adult, probably a mother or father, observes the baby's behavior and understands what the baby means from the situation—the context). The word ''hot,'' which has meaning in context, does not satisfy the conventional form of written sentences because a written sentence must have a verb. In fact, some sentences have a single word which is a verb.

Example 1	Go.
Example 2	Sit.

Notice that these one word sentences are commands. If a sentence is not a command, it will have both a subject and a verb, the two basic divisions of sentences.

Example	Mother sat.

The simple subject *mother* and the simple verb *sat* express an idea and satisfy the most basic requirements for a sentence by having both a subject and a verb.

The two-word sentence in the example above may be expanded by adding more information to the single idea.

Example 1	My mother sat at the bar.
Example 2	My mother sat beside her friend at the bar.
Example 3	My mother sat at the bar beside her friend Mildred.

In this instance, the simple subject *mother* and the word *my* which modifies *mother* are the **complete subject** *my mother*. The verb and all the words which grammatically belong to it are called the **complete predicate**. In the third example, the complete predicate is ***sat at the bar beside her friend Mildred***. Notice that the complete predicate has a verb (in boldface type) as well as other words that are not verbs. These words belong to the verb in sense and in form, and they complete it.

Copyright © 1985 by Harcourt Brace Jovanovich, Inc. All rights reserved.

EXERCISE 1

Test your sentence sense. Classify the following sentences by writing *yes* in the blank before a complete sentence and *no* in the blank before an incomplete sentence.

_____1.   Mother opened her purse.

_____2.   Mother never noticing.

_____3.   She switched through the crowd.

_____4.   You have our reservations.

_____5.   The clerk slowly pushing a form across the counter.

   Did you identify sentences one, three, and four as sentences? If so, you have correctly recognized one important kind of English sentence which can be lengthened by adding a series of verbs. (The verbs in the following example are in boldface.)

Example   Mother **opened** her purse, **took** out her gold Scheaffer and **signed** us in.

The complete subject *mother* is followed by twelve words which make up the complete predicate (the verb and all the words that belong to it). **Opened, took,** and **signed** are verbs.

EXERCISE 2

Write the complete predicate for each of the following sentences.

1.   Mother opened her purse. _____

2.   Mother took out her gold Scheaffer. _____

   _____

3.   She signed us in. _____

EXERCISE 3

Write *yes* in the blank before a complete sentence; write *no* in the blank before an incomplete sentence (usually called a fragment).

_____1.   Yolanda lives in Greenwich Village and earns extra money by accepting speaking engagements around the country.

Copyright © 1985 by Harcourt Brace Jovanovich, Inc. All rights reserved.

_____2. A uniformed Black man opened the door and halted in surprise at see-
ing us.

_____3. He deposited the tray and turned.

_____4. I refused Make's daily invitations to lunch and declined Thomas's offer
to visit his apartment.

_____5. He stood as I entered and began talking before I sat down.

You probably identified each of the items in Exercise 3 as a sentence. As you worked
through the exercise, you may have noticed that the sentences vary in length, but
each has two or more verbs.

EXERCISE 4

Write five sentences that use at least two verbs each and no more than three. (*Hint:*
Using two or more well-chosen verbs in a sentence is an excellent way to make your
writing more interesting.) To help yourself develop the habit of using interesting verbs,
do not use the following common verbs: **is**, **am**, **are**, **was**, **were**, **have**, **has**, **had**.
Try for variety in your writing by selecting verbs that Maya Angelou used which
impressed you. Draw a box around each verb you use.

Example   *The parole board* ⟦*struggles*⟧ *over each prisoner's record and*
⟦*releases*⟧ *a few deserving ones*.

1. _____

_____

_____

2. _____

_____

_____

3. _____

_____

_____

4. _____

Copyright © 1985 by Harcourt Brace Jovanovich, Inc. All rights reserved.

_____

_____

5.   _____

_____

_____

Subjects usually come before the verb in a sentence, though they may not. The two parts of a sentence are the complete subject and the complete predicate. Once you have identified the complete predicate, you locate the subject by looking for the word or words that fit with the verb. There are no definite rules for finding subjects and predicates, but once you understand the concept of a sentence, you can learn to identify them. In the following controlled exercise, you can identify the subject as the second word of the sentence by starting each sentence with the word "do" or "does."

Example   Mother **sits**.
                  ***Does* Mother *sit*?**

EXERCISE 5

Rewrite the sentences into questions using "do" or "does." Draw a box around the subject. Check your answers in class.

Example   They struggle over the decision.
                  ***Do* | they | *struggle over the decision*?** _____

1.   You deposit the tray.

     _____

2.   He stands as I enter.

     _____

3.   Yolanda lives in Greenwich Village.

     _____

4.   We earn extra money.

     _____

Copyright © 1985 by Harcourt Brace Jovanovich, Inc. All rights reserved.

5.   I refuse Make's daily invitations.

This way of finding subjects works only for special sentences, but once you learn to recognize subjects you will have little trouble locating them in any sentence you come across. When you can locate them in special sentences by using "do" or "does," then try to identify subjects in the following sentences. This time the subject may not be the second word, but if you have grasped the idea of subject, you will begin to see the connection between the verb and its subject. Do not expect the subject to be the first word of a sentence because many times it comes later in the sentence.

EXERCISE 6

Draw a box around each subject you find. (*Hint:* There may be more than one subject in a sentence.) Check your answers in class.

Example   The ⬚couple⬚ sat quietly.

1.   She saw the tears on my face.
2.   The woman grins.
3.   Every head turned to see.
4.   During the next two days, Mother showed me off.
5.   One Monday morning a mound of cardboard boxes stood against my office wall.
6.   I saw Make twice more at public gatherings.
7.   The law says that hotel has to accept Negro guests.
8.   You mean, you lived alone.
9.   Her singleness indicates she has rejected, or has been rejected by, her mate.
10.   You know that's my middle name.

Copyright © 1985 by Harcourt Brace Jovanovich, Inc. All rights reserved.

Notes

SENTENCE SENSE

My stopped entrance all action

The preceding group of words is a scrambled form of a sentence which appears in ''The Heart of a Woman.'' Few people would understand this word group as a complete thought because the usual and expected order of words in an English sentence has been mixed up. Most of the time we expect words to be used in a specific and regularly occurring order, in ''slots.'' If words appear in slots where we are unaccustomed to seeing them, they do not make good sense. In English you have to put the words in the right places. We usually expect a subject to appear first in a sentence, followed by the verb and, often, an object.

Subject + Verb + Object = Sentence

When arranged in that order, words in a group form a sentence. The group of words above scrambles the order of the subject and the verb, but the form of those words has not changed to comply with the forms we expect in those slots. If we changed the forms to look like words we ordinarily expect in those slots, the sentence would more nearly make sense:

My stop entranced all action.

However, we do not really understand this sentence because the words do not ''fit'' together.

EXERCISE 7

Rearrange the following word groups into good sentences. Change word forms as necessary and add the appropriate end mark. Check your answers in class.

Example   Answers your class in check.
   Check your answers in class.

1. My stop entranced all action

2. An aisle crowd the made

3. I just with you to be want

4. A knock there at was the door

Copyright © 1985 by Harcourt Brace Jovanovich, Inc. All rights reserved.

5. Pushed slowly across the counter a form the clerk

_____

_____

_____

Jango Broper fribbed the spicklet of blandigong.

The preceding sentence is a jabberwocky sentence; that is, it has the pattern of a sentence, but the "words" are made up—though they follow the forms of real words. When you read a jabberwocky sentence, you sense that you could understand it if you could only know what the words mean. You sense a sentence as much by the word forms and sentence pattern as by the meanings of the words in it. Consider the following sentence from "The Heart of a Woman":

Vivian Baxter sensed the possibility of confrontation.

Notice that it has exactly the same pattern as the jabberwocky sentence.

EXERCISE 8

Draw a line from each word in the jabberwocky sentence to the corresponding word in Angelou's sentence.

Jango Broper fribbed the spicklet of blandigong.
Vivian Baxter sensed the possibility of confrontation.

Did you discover that the words in both sentences come in exactly the same order? They do.

EXERCISE 9

Write your own sensible sentences following the patterns of these jabberwocky sentences.

Example   She gronks the blinches.
            She organizes the demonstrations. _____

1. The Gorch prinded an umugle and cribble manked through the revich. _____

_____

2. The jorpy smiggle veeps the lala but tigs behind the lakang. _____

_____

Copyright © 1985 by Harcourt Brace Jovanovich, Inc. All rights reserved.

3. He didn't meggle, but sranged the dorp in the wih. _____

_____

_____

4. When frapper hibbled a plabble, the bommer meeped the cuption. _____

_____

5. Freep the blanger, Joe, and don't prog the vrang! _____

_____

_____

Copyright © 1985 by Harcourt Brace Jovanovich, Inc. All rights reserved.

Notes

RECOGNITION OF SENTENCES

In the spoken language, a listener could consider almost any utterance you might make a virtual sentence because in a particular situation the meaning might be clear. Writers, though, maintain forms of sentences. As a writer, you need to develop sentence sense so that you will recognize when you have written a sentence and when you have not. The most common test is to locate a subject and a verb. You cannot have a sentence without a verb, and usually you have both a subject and a verb. This test, though, is not a sure test of a sentence. In later lessons, you will learn specific ways to identify sentences and to avoid writing incomplete sentences. At this time you can rely on the rule of thumb which serves well in many instances: A sentence is a group of words that expresses a complete idea and has the form required for a sentence. (*Hint:* Meaning and sense alone do not provide a reliable test for a sentence. Your sentences must have form *and* sense.)

When you write or read a group of words that you do not recognize as containing a complete idea, you probably do not have a sentence. Sometimes, though, you will sense completeness when you do not technically have a sentence. For instance, "How about Fresno?" has a sense of completeness because of its meaning (sense). You can sense completeness from the context, but "How about Fresno?" is not a sentence in the strictest sense because it does not have a verb.

EXERCISE 10

Write *yes* in blanks before complete sentences and *no* in blanks before incomplete sentences.

_____   1.   Six feet tall, thirty-one years old, with a fourteen-year-old son.

_____   2.   And a group of them . . . absolutely never.

_____   3.   If I hadn't been there.

_____   4.   Because I'd blow away what their mammas gave them.

_____   5.   In the face of these contradictions, she must provide a blanket of stability.

_____   6.   Not alone in that big house.

_____   7.   Just more of the same people in bigger buildings.

_____   8.   Hands in his pockets, waiting for me to convince him of the stability of my love.

Copyright © 1985 by Harcourt Brace Jovanovich, Inc. All rights reserved.

——————— 9.   A little boy of seven who slept with a butcher's knife under his pillow one summer at camp.

——————10.   The Black mother perceives destruction at every door.

If you wrote *no* before all except numbers five and ten, you correctly identified them, and you have an excellent sentence sense. If not, you will learn in future lessons ways to test for complete sentences.

Copyright © 1985 by Harcourt Brace Jovanovich, Inc. All rights reserved.

SENTENCE COMBINING

These following five short sentences contain the information in the one longer sentence, "Mother opened her purse, took out her gold Sheaffer, and signed us in."

> Mother opened her purse.
> Mother took out her pen.
> The pen was gold.
> The pen was a Scheaffer.
> Mother signed us in.

Practice in combining short sentences into longer ones will help you discover ways to arrange your ideas into longer sentences. More important, it will aid in developing your sentence sense.

EXERCISE 11

Combine the short sentences in each group into a longer sentence. Be sure to include in your longer sentence all of the information contained in all of the short sentences. Take this opportunity to experiment and to play with several different arrangements as you fit the information together. While sharing your best version with the class, decide if you like your version or another one better.

Example a. I met a writer.
  b. The writer's name was John Killens.
  c. I wanted to write.
  d. I told him.
  e. The writer invited me to his home.
  f. His home was in New York.

I met a writer named John Killens who invited me to his home in New York when I told him I wanted to write.

When I met John Killens, the writer, and told him I wanted to write, he invited me to his New York home.

1. a. The year is 1959.
  b. Fresno was a town.
  c. The town was middle-sized.
  d. The town had palm trees.
  e. The town had a Southern accent.

———————————————————————————————

———————————————————————————————

Copyright © 1985 by Harcourt Brace Jovanovich, Inc. All rights reserved.

_____

_____

2. a. Maya Angelou is a woman.
    b. Maya Angelou is Black.
    c. Maya Angelou writes narratives.
    d. The narratives are autobiographical.
    e. Maya Angelou appears on talk shows.

_____

_____

_____

_____

3. a. Guy was fourteen.
    b. Guy became a little boy.
    c. The little boy was seven.
    d. He went to camp.
    e. The camp was in the summer.
    f. The little boy slept.
    g. The little boy had a knife.
    h. The knife was a butcher knife.
    i. The knife was under his pillow.

_____

_____

_____

_____

_____

_____

Copyright © 1985 by Harcourt Brace Jovanovich, Inc. All rights reserved.

CLASSIFICATION OF SENTENCES BY PURPOSE

English sentences fulfill the four basic purposes for speaking and writing: telling, demanding, asking, and reacting. Declarative sentences make statements (telling); imperative sentences give commands (demanding); interrogative sentences ask questions (asking); and exclamatory sentences express strong feelings such as urgency or excitement, or even hate, love, joy, or fear (reacting).

Declarative (telling)	When I was three my parents divorced in Long Beach, California.
Imperative (demanding)	Take care of yourself.
Interrogative (asking)	What are we having for dinner?
Exclamatory (reacting)	This is the joining of Africa and Afro-America!

Declarative sentences end with a period. Imperative sentences may end with either a period or an exclamation point (!) depending on the degree of urgency expressed in the command. Interrogative sentences end with a question mark (?), and exclamatory sentences with the exclamation point (!).

SENTENCE	END PUNCTUATION	
Declarative	.	(period)
Imperative	. or !	(period *or* exclamation point)
Interrogative	?	(question mark)
Exclamatory	!	(exclamation point)

EXERCISE 12

Identify whether sentences below are declarative (D), interrogative (questions: Q), imperative (commands: C), or exclamatory (E). Then punctuate them using the appropriate end punctuation mark: period, question mark, or exclamation point.

Example   Did the elevator arrive
          _Q_ Did the elevator arrive **?**

_____ 1.   She didn't pause

_____ 2.   Where is the door

_____ 3.   Look in my purse

Copyright © 1985 by Harcourt Brace Jovanovich, Inc. All rights reserved.

——— 4. I am ecstatically happy

——— 5. Does the television work

——— 6. You know I wanted a desk when I was a little kid

——— 7. Take care of your son, and remember, New York City is just like Fresno

——— 8. Vusumzi Make was intense and contained

——— 9. Her singleness indicates she has rejected, or been rejected by, her mate

———10. Why didn't you tell me when I phoned

EXERCISE 13

Write five declarative sentences.

1. _____

_____

2. _____

_____

3. _____

_____

4. _____

_____

5. _____

_____

EXERCISE 14

Write five interrogative sentences.

1. _____

Copyright © 1985 by Harcourt Brace Jovanovich, Inc. All rights reserved.

2. _____

3. _____

4. _____

5. _____

EXERCISE 15

Write five imperative sentences. If you can change one of your declarative or interrogative sentences into a command, do so.

1. _____

2. _____

3. _____

4. _____

5. _____

Copyright © 1985 by Harcourt Brace Jovanovich, Inc. All rights reserved.

EXERCISE 16

Write five exclamatory sentences.

1. _____

   _____

2. _____

   _____

3. _____

   _____

4. _____

   _____

5. _____

   _____

Copyright © 1985 by Harcourt Brace Jovanovich, Inc. All rights reserved.

1.10 PROOFREADING POWER

Use your sentence sense to determine where sentences begin and end in the following passage. Put the proper end punctuation at the end of sentences, and capitalize the first word of each sentence. Compare your corrections with the original which you can find in the reading selection. (*Hint:* Your version may differ from the original without being wrong. If it does, do you prefer your version to Angelou's? Why?)

i was going to marry Thomas Allen he was forty-three and a hardworking bail bondsman who lived in Brooklyn also he was kind to me and generous to Guy i knew i wasn't in love with him, but i was lonely and i would make a good wife i had only one regret we didn't talk he treated my work at the SCLC as just another job after the most common-place greetings our conversations were mostly limited to my shouting in his bedroom and his grunts at my dining room table our lives would be quiet

that same Monday morning one of my SCLC office mates told me that over the weekend she had heard a South African freedom fighter speak he was so thorough and so brilliant that even the biggest fool in the world had to see that apartheid was evil and would have to be brought down his name was Vusumzi Make

1.11 DICTATION

Your instructor will choose a passage of approximately 100 words and read it aloud as you write what is read. As each sentence is read, you must concentrate and maintain silence. Do not ask your instructor to repeat because any sound other than the instructor's voice reading will break not only your concentration but that of others. Your instructor will repeat key words and phrases during the dictation, allow sufficient time for you to write what has been read, and will reread the entire passage a second time at a faster rate so that you can check what you have written and fill in any gap you may have.

You will want to write on every other line so that you will have space to correct your dictation upon the final reading in case you have made a mistake. Your instructor will show you the dictated passage and ask you to compare your version, or perhaps a classmate's version, to the original. Be especially alert when you check the dictation because this exercise will help you develop your sentence sense by translating spoken into written language.

Copyright © 1985 by Harcourt Brace Jovanovich, Inc. All rights reserved.

1.12 WORD POWER

PREFIXES

Words are made with bases. You can attach prefixes and suffixes to many of them. Prefixes are syllables that you can attach to the beginnings of base words. Suffixes are syllables which you can attach to the ends of base words. When you attach prefixes and suffixes to base words, the meanings of the base words change. If you know the meanings of prefixes and suffixes, you can add them to base words and increase the variety of words you use in your writing as well as understand them when you encounter them in your reading.

EXERCISE 1

Find the words in Angelou's narrative with the prefixes listed below and draw a box around each prefix. Then, make a list of the words with those prefixes. Each prefix appears in the selection at least once, but it may not always appear six times. (*Hint*: Just because a word begins with the letters of a prefix does not always mean it contains that prefix. When in doubt, use your dictionary.)

1. **ad-** (Latin) means "near, next to." The prefix always appears as *ad-* when it has this meaning.
   (Old English) means "towards." Sometimes *ad-* takes other forms with this meaning such as *ac-* before *c*, *k*, or *g*, af- before *f*, *ag-* before *g*, *al-* before *l*, *ap-* before *p*, *as-* before *s*, and *at-* before *t*.

   Example [ac] cept

   _____   _____

   _____   _____

   _____   _____

2. **con-** (Latin) means "with, together, thoroughly." Use *con-* except before *m*, *b*, and *p* which require *com-* or *l* which requires *col-*.

   _____   _____

   _____   _____

   _____   _____

3. **contra-** (Latin) means "against, contrasting."

   _____   _____

Copyright © 1985 by Harcourt Brace Jovanovich, Inc. All rights reserved.

_____   _____

_____   _____

4. **de**- (Latin) means "do the opposite of, reverse of, remove from, reduce."

_____   _____

_____   _____

_____   _____

5. **dis**- (Latin) means "not, opposite of, exclude from."

_____   _____

_____   _____

_____   _____

6. **en**- (Latin) means "put into or onto." Use *em*- before *m, b, p*.

_____   _____

_____   _____

_____   _____

7. **ex**- (Latin) means "out of, not, former."

_____   _____

_____   _____

_____   _____

8. **for**- (Old English) means "concerning exclusion or omission, completely."

_____   _____

_____   _____

_____   _____

9. **in**- (Latin) means "not, within."

_____   _____

Copyright © 1985 by Harcourt Brace Jovanovich, Inc. All rights reserved.

_____   _____

_____   _____

10. **intro**- (Latin) means "in, into, inward."

_____   _____

_____   _____

_____   _____

11. **per**- (Latin) means "through."

_____   _____

_____   _____

_____   _____

12. **pre**- (Latin) means "earlier, in front of."

_____   _____

_____   _____

_____   _____

13. **pro**- (Latin) means "earlier, anterior, supporting."

_____   _____

_____   _____

_____   _____

14. **re**- (Latin) means "again, backward."

_____   _____

_____   _____

_____   _____

15. **sub**- (Latin) means "under, secondary."

_____   _____

Copyright © 1985 by Harcourt Brace Jovanovich, Inc. All rights reserved.

_____   _____

_____   _____

16. **tele-**   (Greek) means ''distant.''

_____   _____

_____   _____

_____   _____

17. **un-**   (Old English) means ''not, opposite of.''

_____   _____

_____   _____

_____   _____

EXERCISE 2

Select a word from each prefix category in the preceding exercise, and write a sentence using that word. Draw a box around the word where it appears in the sentence. Use a word you are not familiar with to increase your word power.

Example   *Most parents* boxed(*accept*) *their children's moody behavior.*

1. _____

_____

2. _____

_____

3. _____

_____

4. _____

_____

5. _____

Copyright © 1985 by Harcourt Brace Jovanovich, Inc. All rights reserved.

6. _____

7. _____

8. _____

9. _____

10. _____

11. _____

12. _____

13. _____

14. _____

15. _____

16. _____

Copyright © 1985 by Harcourt Brace Jovanovich, Inc. All rights reserved.

17. _____

    _____

EXERCISE 3

For each prefix in Exercise 1, write a word that does *not* appear in Angelou's narrative. You will need to use your own creativity for this, but if you get stuck, you can look the prefix up in a good college dictionary.

1. _____   10. _____

2. _____   11. _____

3. _____   12. _____

4. _____   13. _____

5. _____   14. _____

6. _____   15. _____

7. _____   16. _____

8. _____   17. _____

9. _____

Copyright © 1985 by Harcourt Brace Jovanovich, Inc. All rights reserved.

Notes

SPELLING

The words in the following exercise contain prefixes studied in the vocabulary exercises. Study the list and observe the various forms of the prefixes *ad-*, *en-*, *con-*, and *in-*. Learning to spell these words will help you master the various forms of common prefixes. Your teacher may select a list for a spelling test and ask you to identify the basic form of the prefix. Notice that adding the prefix does not affect the spelling of the base word and that no letters are dropped from the prefix. In some cases, though, the last letter in one prefix changes to make the new word easier to say.

EXERCISE 4

Here is the original form of the prefix and the base word. Combine these two elements to form a new word. Use your dictionary if you need to.

Example   in- + rigate   =   _____ *irrigate* _____

1. ad- + tend   = _____

2. ad- + propriate   = _____

3. ad- + paratus   = _____

4. ad- + parent   = _____

5. ad- + fect   = _____

6. ad- + cept   = _____

7. ad- + cess   = _____

8. ad- + custom   = _____

9. ad- + company   = _____

10. ad- + quisition   = _____

11. ad- + knowledge = _____

12. ad- + similate   = _____

13. ad- + sure   = _____

14. ad- + gregate   = _____

Copyright © 1985 by Harcourt Brace Jovanovich, Inc. All rights reserved.

15. ad- + grandize = _____

16. ad- + gravate = _____

17. ad- + gressive = _____

18. con- + mit = _____

19. con- + missioner = _____

20. con- + mittee = _____

21. con- + pare = _____

22. con- + pel = _____

23. con- + pass = _____

24. con- + municate = _____

25. con- + pete = _____

26. con- + puter = _____

27. con- + bine = _____

28. con- + bat = _____

29. con- + bustion = _____

30. en- + bark = _____

31. en- + balm = _____

32. en- + bezzle = _____

33. en- + blem = _____

34. in- + proper = _____

35. in- + possible = _____

36. in- + polite = _____

37. in- + mense = _____

Copyright © 1985 by Harcourt Brace Jovanovich, Inc. All rights reserved.

38. in- + merse = _____

39. in- + balance = _____

40. in- + mobile = _____

41. in- + moral = _____

42. in- + becile = _____

43. in- + bibe = _____

44. in- + legal = _____

45. in- + legitimate = _____

46. in- + logical = _____

47. in- + rational = _____

48. in- + regular = _____

49. in- + resistible = _____

50. in- + responsive = _____

Copyright © 1985 by Harcourt Brace Jovanovich, Inc. All rights reserved.

UNIT TWO

WRITING
REENTERED

2.1 GETTING STARTED BY READING

Before you read "Horror Movies: Why Fear Is Fun," review the three key questions introduced in Unit One: What is it? How does it change? What else is it like? You will find that if you seek answers to specific questions, you will remember more details when you finish reading. These three key questions can help you frame additional questions for any reading that you might do. As you read this assignment, look for answers to the following specific questions, which were framed from the three key questions.

1.   What emotions do people experience when viewing horror movies?
2.   How do horror movies make people feel these emotions?
3.   Why do people go to horror movies? (Find three or more reasons.)

You read Unit One with a pencil in your hand. That is an excellent way to become engaged with what you are reading. Some people, though, think taking notes as they read slows them down and causes them to forget what they are reading when they are writing notes or underlining passages. People who feel this way prefer to read without a pencil. To discover whether you prefer to read with or without a pencil, try reading the following selection *without* taking any notes at all until after you have completed reading the selection.

2.2 ANALYSIS

Mary Ann Bachemin   *"HORROR MOVIES: WHY FEAR IS FUN"*

The movie poster reads:

> The nightmare isn't over yet.
> More of the night he came back.

The movie is *Halloween II.*

The dimly lit theater is packed with people, over half of them under 25 years of age. And each one is anxiously anticipating two hours of terror, suspense, ghosts, ghouls and gore.

Suddenly the lights are lowered, the curtains open and as promised, the nightmare begins. . . .

Chances are, you know the feeling. You're on the edge of your seat, scared stiff, caught somewhere between panic and pleasure, enthralled in a thriller that lures you into a world of haunts and horrors.

It's like riding the big roller coaster at an amusement park. It's frightening and at the same time it's fun. You're daring yourself to do something, yet you know (or at least hope) that you'll come out the winner.

This feeling is a common one. But the question still remains——Why? What drives people, especially kids, to fork out $4 or $5 to be scared silly?

''Why?'' asks Stephen King, author of *Danse Macabre* (Everest House, 1981). ''Some of the reasons are simple and obvious. To show that we can, that we aren't afraid, that we can ride this roller coaster.

''Which is not to say that a really good horror movie may not surprise a scream out of us at some point, the way we scream when the roller coaster twists through a complete 360-degree turn or plows through a lake at the bottom of the drop,'' he explains. ''And horror movies, like roller coasters, have always been the province of the young. After all, by the time one turns 40 or 50, one's appetite for double twists or 360-degree loops may be considerably depleted.''

Copyright © 1985 by Harcourt Brace Jovanovich, Inc. All rights reserved.

In addition to having an appetite for the horrifying, teens are frequently the subjects of these tales of terror. Take, for example, the movie *Carrie,* a thriller based on the novel by Stephen King, about a teen with mysterious powers that enable her to annoy and eventually destroy almost everyone around her.

Other young subjects of scare include Regan in *The Exorcist* and Damien in *The Omen.* Even Walt Disney has ventured into the fright field with the film *The Watcher in the Woods.*

But can all this attention on terror have negative effects? Or might we find being scared out of our seat a positive release?

According to Dee Shepherd-Look, a professor of psychology at California State University, Northridge and a licensed clinical psychologist, horror movies serve different purposes for different kinds of people.

"Horror movies are a tremendous catharsis for rage, anger and other destructive feelings," says Dr. Shepherd-Look. "Society demands that we suppress these emotions even when they're justifiable. But frightening films allow us to let those feelings out without actually doing anything destructive."

You see, the horror film deliberately appeals to what's worst in us. It puts us in touch with our negative emotions. It frightens us, makes us uncomfortable and some are even gross enough to turn us off to popcorn permanently.

On the other hand, these terrifying tales provide us with a means of channeling our fears and anxieties. They say the very things we're afraid to say and force us to confront emotions that society says we should keep hidden.

Actually, they affect us on two levels. On top is the "gross out" level which stands for our surface reaction to what is taking place. It's how the films affect us visibly. We scream, we shudder, we're frozen in fear.

Yet, it's the second level that touches us far more profoundly. It delves into our souls and touches on the feelings and emotions that no one else knows. It plays upon and expresses fears that exist in all of us. In short, it gives us "the creeps."

But can these same films, many of which are violent in nature, cause us to act destructively after viewing them?

Says Dr. Shepherd-Look, "Whether our reaction to a horror movie is positive or

Copyright © 1985 by Harcourt Brace Jovanovich, Inc. All rights reserved.

negative depends on several factors; among them are our personality, behavior patterns, upbringing and how well-socialized we are.

"A fairly well-adjusted young person can constructively reduce his or her anger and rage through a horror film," she explains. "However, the adolescent who has a tendency toward violence anyway may be triggered to exhibit his or her emotions after seeing violent behavior. And this holds true not only for horror films but for violence on television and in books."

Then there are those of us who don't go to see horror movies simply because we don't enjoy them. They make us uncomfortable, tense and afraid. So, if seeing old television reruns of *The Blob* and *Frankenstein* are enough to keep you awake at night, it's safe to assume you should stay away from chillers like *Ghost Story* or *Friday the 13th*.

"I go to see scary movies because they're exciting and fun to watch," says 17-year-old Jenny from Houston, Texas. "Sure they're frightening and sometimes really gross, but you know it's not real.

"I don't dwell on what I've seen because it's only make-believe," she adds. "And it sure is fun to talk about it with your friends afterwards!"

"Horror creates excitement for teens," states Dr. Shepherd-Look. "Often it's not the horror itself, but the suspense and excitement beforehand that they crave.

"It's a way of coping with what scares them without experiencing these things firsthand," she adds.

Apparently, there's a horror film for almost everyone, one that's able to touch each of us in the place where we're most vulnerable.

No longer is the action confined to far-away Transylvania. Now there's horror in the hospital (*Coma*), on a train (*Terror Train*), at the prom (*Prom Night* and *Carrie*) and even at home (*The Amityville Horror*). Although nature thrillers (*The Fog* and *Prophecy*) and earth invaders (*Alien* and *Invasion of the Body Snatchers*) are still big at the box office, the mass murderer is the latest fright figure to burst upon the screen. And he or she is wreaking havoc all across America (*The Texas Chainsaw Massacre*, *Halloween*, *Halloween II*, *My Bloody Valentine* and the list goes on and on!).

Whatever scares you—insanity, storms, snakes or the supernatural—there's a fright

Copyright © 1985 by Harcourt Brace Jovanovich, Inc. All rights reserved.

film to play upon that fear; a picture that'll allow you to experience what you dread most within the safe confines of a movie theater; a film able to stretch familiar subjects to almost ridiculous proportions.

And when all is said and done, you realize that no matter what your problems, they're not now and probably never will be . . . this bad. After all, isn't it comforting to know that no matter how mad your dad may sometimes get at you, he's an absolute angel compared to the madman Jack Nicholson portrays in *The Shining*?

But at the same time, horror movies touch on the one topic which evokes fear in almost everyone. That subject is death.

"Our culture has a tremendous fear of death," says Dr. Shepherd-Look. "This is probably because death represents the unknown. It's difficult to feel comfortable with something we can't fully understand."

"Movies that overflow with death and destruction allow us to deal with death without ever really being a part of it," she continues. "It's not real, so we can look at it and respond to it on a make-believe level. This is especially important to teens since they're developmentally at a stage where they're beginning to confront death and are even trying to understand it."

Yet even though horror films focus on death and dying, they don't celebrate it. They aren't merely vehicles for exhibiting pain, terror, violence and tragic deaths.

Stephen King contends that horror movies "don't love death, as some have suggested. They love life. They don't celebrate deformity. But by dwelling on deformity, they sing of health and energy. By showing us the miseries of the damned, they help us to rediscover the smaller joys of our own lives."

And so the credits roll, the lights go on and the young audience begins to slowly file out of the theater. Some are still visibly shaken, but most are talking excitedly about what they've just witnessed.

The mood is almost euphoric. Each young viewer has learned another lesson in terror and has lived to tell about it.

They've sat through scenes that would scare the pants off their parents, teachers and even their 6'3", 235-pound uncle.

How can this be, you ask?

Copyright © 1985 by Harcourt Brace Jovanovich, Inc. All rights reserved.

Says the undisputed master of the horror story, Stephen King, ''In the final sense, the horror movie is the celebration of those who feel they can examine death because it doesn't yet live in their own hearts.''

The nightmare isn't over yet. In fact, it never will be. There'll always be a market for horror. But the choice will always be yours as to whether or not you dare to entertain these dreadful dreams!

Copyright © 1985 by Harcourt Brace Jovanovich, Inc. All rights reserved.

Notes

2.3 *UNDERSTANDING WHAT YOU READ*

When you finish reading, try to answer the questions below without looking at the selection again. Once you have tried all the questions, you can then reread the selection with a pencil in hand to answer any questions that you could not answer after the first reading.

1. Choose two or three reasons why you go to horror movies? _____

    _____

    _____

    _____

    _____

    _____

2. What experiences in life are similar to those in horror movies? _____

    _____

    _____

    _____

    _____

    _____

3. How do you feel after you have seen a horror movie? Does the feeling differ from how you felt while you were watching the movie? Why do you think you

    feel this way? _____

    _____

    _____

    _____

    _____

    _____

Copyright © 1985 by Harcourt Brace Jovanovich, Inc. All rights reserved.

2.4 DISCOVERING IDEAS FOR WRITING

Jot your answers and reactions to the following questions that are designed to help you discover ideas and material to use in writing your own essay. These questions are patterned on the three key questions that you used to help you understand the reading selection.

1. What do you like or dislike about attending sporting events or cultural activities with a large audience? _____

    _____

    _____

2. What kinds of people have you noticed in the audience (crowd) of a sporting event or a cultural event? _____

    _____

    _____

3. How does the audience (crowd) at a sports event differ from other audiences you have been in? _____

    _____

    _____

4. In what ways have your preferences for sports and/or cultural events changed since you were in junior high school? _____

    _____

    _____

5. How does your preference for attending events differ from that of your college roommate? _____

    _____

    From people you work with? _____

    _____

Copyright © 1985 by Harcourt Brace Jovanovich, Inc. All rights reserved.

From the dean of your college? _____

_____

_____

6. How do you decide to attend a sports event or a cultural event rather than another kind of event such as an automobile show, a religious service, a state or

county fair? _____

_____

_____

Copyright © 1985 by Harcourt Brace Jovanovich, Inc. All rights reserved.

Notes

2.5 UNDERSTANDING WRITING

Every published writer has faced a deadline without having written a word. If you have found yourself with an assignment due which you had not started, you were in a similar situation. You undoubtedly promised yourself then that you would never let things get so out of hand again. But they probably have. If so, you are like most other writers, most of whom procrastinate until they feel the pressure of time. Unlike student writers, professional writers create pressure for themselves by accepting contracts which have deadlines. When copy promised to an editor is late, professional writers may feel guilty. Such agreements and the commitments they carry offer ample pressure.

In reality, students have similar pressures. For instance, by having enrolled in a writing class, you will find yourself faced with situations similar to those of professional writers. Assignment due dates become your deadlines and provide the pressure of time. Like professionals, you too have commitments to your peer editors and your teacher.

If you want to learn to write, you must learn to edit writing because part of learning to write is learning to make judgments about writing—both your own and others. Making judgments and decisions about writing and modifying a draft after consideration of them is editing. Because learning to edit requires practice and because practice in editing requires cooperation between an editor and a writer, every member of your writing class should provide copy on time so that scheduled editing activities can proceed. During the editing activity, you will edit copy of a classmate at the same time that your copy is being edited by your peer editor. If you do not have your drafts and revisions—your copy—ready on time, you will jeopardize your own progress as well as impede the progress of others in your class.

A considerate student will honor a commitment and will produce copy—drafts and revisions—on time. To do so, you first fix in your mind the date your assignment is due. Even though you know the date, you may procrastinate and feel guilty for not keeping to a schedule you develop for yourself. Most conscientious students, like most successful professionals, still manage to meet deadlines, even if it means staying up all night.

To avoid such drastic measures, many professional writers schedule specific times for daily writing and write for a specified length of time or until they have written a specified number of pages whether they feel like it or not. Because professional writers find scheduling writing sessions helpful, especially when the schedule has a deadline, you probably will too. Review your daily routine and select a definite time each day for writing. Once you have established the time, prevent any intrusion into your writing session. If you miss your writing session or you have interruptions one day, promise yourself to get back on your schedule the very next day. Then, keep your promise.

Copyright © 1985 by Harcourt Brace Jovanovich, Inc. All rights reserved.

2.6   *WRITING—ANALYSIS*

Your answers to the preceding questions helped you identify the main reasons you attend sports or cultural events. As you answered the questions, you gathered the information about yourself you can now organize into an essay. As you write your draft, you will tell yourself why you attend the events you do, how you choose one event over another, and in what ways your behavior differs from that of others.

When you complete your draft, you will have likely written an analysis. If so, you may have discovered that in an analysis you divide your information into its main parts and organize your writing around the main points. An analysis, then, is the process of dividing information into the main points that it contains. To write an analysis, you report what those divisions (main points or parts) are.

WRITING ASSIGNMENT

Choose one of the following:

1. Write a paper of approximately 350 words analyzing why you attend cultural or sporting events with large audiences.
2. Write a paper of approximately 350 words in which you analyze particular types of spectators or groups in the audience that you have observed at a sporting or cultural event.

Reminder: Follow the same process for composing and evaluating an essay that you learned in Unit 1. Before your instructor reads your essay, you should have completed the entire writing process: discovering ideas for writing, drafting those ideas, revising your draft for your audience (your peer editor), revising after consideration of your peer editor's suggestions, proofreading your paper to find any error you may have missed during the other parts of the process.

Finally, submit all versions of your writing to your instructor. Be sure to attach all Editor's Evaluation forms to your drafts and revisions. Remember to keep all versions of this essay and to submit them in the order you wrote them when your instructor collects this assignment, but do not expect that your instructor will read all of them for every assignment. The drafts and revisions are evidence of how you developed the present form of the essay and the instructor may want to look at them in case some part of your writing process has gone awry.

2.7   *THE WRITING PROCESS*

Perhaps comparing learning to write to learning to play the piano will help you see that writing skills can be learned. If you were taking music lessons, you would expect to practice, yet you would not expect your instructor to listen. In practicing a

Copyright © 1985 by Harcourt Brace Jovanovich, Inc. All rights reserved.

musical selection, you might well play one passage over and over before you could perform it with ease and be willing to play the entire selection for your instructor's comments. In fact, you would never expect your music instructor to listen to the practice necessary to make your playing sound smooth and effortless, nor would you play for an audience until you decided your performance would be the best you could do.

Thinking of the writing process in a similar way may be helpful to you. When learning to write, you should expect to do much writing that you do not want your instructor to see. Even if your instructor did look at all of your writing, it would not necessarily help you develop your writing skills, and the amount of work it would take for the instructor to look at all the writing everyone in the class produced would be staggering. One of the most important ways to improve your writing is to learn to evaluate it yourself.

You will benefit in at least two ways by learning how to evaluate your own writing. First, you will become an independent and more effective writer. Second, your instructor will have more time to address those writing problems you cannot solve yourself. You can develop this skill if you try different ways to express your ideas; then, you can select the most effective one for your particular purpose. The judgments you make when you choose the best version from among those you have written will give you confidence to view your writing critically and help you see it through the eyes of your reader (your audience). The goal you will strive to reach is to be able to make such judgments independently whenever you write.

Answering the following questions will help you to rethink the ideas in the analysis you have written and give you specific ways to reenter your writing so you can make necessary changes in it. After you evaluate your analysis by answering these questions, you can rewrite your ideas. When you have produced other versions, you can select whichever works best. (*Hint*: Rewriting does not mean that you change every word. Sometimes you change only a word or a phrase; at other times, you change entire sentences or even paragraphs. To make these changes easier, try writing on every other line so you will have space for your changes.)

1. Do I have a verb in each sentence? (*Hint*: Circle all the verbs in your analysis.)
2. How many "to be" verbs do I have? (*Hint*: "To be" verbs include *am*, *are*, *is*, *was*, *were*, *be*, *been*, *being*. Put a check over each in your essay.) *Tip*: During rewriting, skilled writers reduce the frequency of "to be" verbs to make their writing precise and interesting.
3. How many "to be" verbs can I change to a more precise verb? (*Hint*: When you change the verb, you may have to adjust other parts of your sentence.)
4. How many sentences do I prefer with the new verbs?
5. How many sentences begin with the subject as the first, second, or third word?
6. Would adjectives before some of my subjects make my ideas more precise?
7. Do my paragraphs average four to seven sentences?
8. Do my paragraphs contain a thesis sentence? (*Hint*: Underline the thesis sentence in a color different from the one you used for writing.)

Copyright © 1985 by Harcourt Brace Jovanovich, Inc. All rights reserved.

9. Does my analysis contain the right information so that my reader can understand my feelings and observations?

   a. Have I omitted necessary information?

   b. Have I made points that are not important to my ideas?

   c. Have I maintained a logical relationship between my ideas and my illustrations?

10. How should I change my analysis in light of my responses to the above questions?

EXERCISE 1

Study each of the pairs below to see if the revision improves the original. The revision is an attempt to make a more precise and interesting version. Do you agree? Check the one you prefer in each pair, and be prepared to defend your choice in class.

____1. a.   Horror movies are terrifying to me.

____   b.   Horror movies terrify me.

____2. a.   This feeling is a common one.

____   b.   Most people feel this way.

____3. a.   Horror movies are a tremendous catharsis for rage, anger, and other destructive feelings.

____   b.   Horror movies make possible a tremendous catharsis for rage, anger, and other destructive feelings.

____4. a.   This is particularly important to teens since they're developmentally at a stage where they're beginning to confront death and are trying to understand it.

____   b.   Teens benefit in important ways from make-believe because they have developed enough to begin to confront death and to try to understand it.

____5. a.   The nightmare isn't over yet. In fact, it never will be. There'll always be a market for horror. But the choice will always be yours as to whether or not you dare to entertain these dreadful dreams.

____   b.   The nightmare continues, and it always will continue because a market for horror will always exist. You can choose whether or not you dare to entertain these dreadful dreams.

Copyright © 1985 by Harcourt Brace Jovanovich, Inc. All rights reserved.

2.8 PARAGRAPH POWER

Most acceptable paragraphs in college writing contain a topic sentence. A topic sentence expresses the central or controlling idea of a paragraph. Often, it is the first sentence in the paragraph, and the writer positions it there to help the reader follow ideas presented in an orderly and coherent manner.

One useful pattern which will help you present your ideas in an orderly manner, then, begins with a topic sentence expressing the central idea. Next in this pattern, the writer limits or restricts the topic sentence through the addition of details closely related to that sentence. Many writers then provide one to three illustrations or examples of that limited idea.

EXERCISE 1

Identify the topic sentence in the following paragraph by writing it in the blank space indicated below by the word *topic*. Next, write the sentence which limits the topic in the blank labeled *restriction*. Finally, fill in the illustrations in the blank labeled *illustration*.

You see, the horror film deliberately appeals to what's worst in us. It puts us in touch with our negative emotions. It frightens us, makes us uncomfortable and some are even gross enough to turn us off to popcorn immediately.

Topic _____

_____

_____

Restriction _____

_____

_____

Illustration _____

_____

_____

The preceding paragraph contains all three parts of this pattern paragraph. You can vary the pattern successfully, though, in a number of ways. For example, you can follow the topic sentence with one or two restrictions and no illustration, or you can

Copyright © 1985 by Harcourt Brace Jovanovich, Inc. All rights reserved.

follow it with one or more illustrations and no restriction. When the writer includes no restriction, he or she may believe the restriction to be so obvious that the reader can easily supply it by looking at the illustrations. However, in college writing you should include the restriction to make your idea as clear as it can possibly be.

EXERCISE 2

Perform the following operations to analyze these two paragraphs. First, underline the topic sentence in each paragraph. Next, draw a wavy line under any restrictions. Finally, draw a box around illustrations. (Do not break sentences apart for this exercise.)

Paragraph One

Then there are those of us who don't go to see horror movies simply because we don't enjoy them. They make us uncomfortable, tense and afraid. So, if seeing old television reruns of *The Blob* and *Frankenstein* are enough to keep you awake at night, it's safe to assume you should stay away from chillers like *Ghost Story* or *Friday the 13th*.

Paragraph Two

No longer is the action confined to faraway Transylvania. Now there's horror in the hospital (*Coma*), on a train (*Terror Train*), at the prom (*Prom Night* and *Carrie*) and even at home (*The Amityville Horror*). Although nature thrillers (*The Fog* and *Prophecy*) and earth invaders (*Alien* and *Invasion of the Body Snatchers*) are still big at the box office, the mass murderer is the latest fright figure to burst upon the screen. And he or she is wreaking havoc all across America (*The Texas Chainsaw Massacre*, *Halloween II*, *My Bloody Valentine*, and the list goes on and on!).

EXERCISE 3

For this assignment, choose any form or any aspect of group entertainment that evokes a response in you. Your response may be positive or negative, but you should write about the one you had in mind in Section 2.4. If you do, you can include this paragraph in a revision of your analysis. As you write this paragraph use your responses from Discovering Ideas for Writing (Section 2.4).

Write a pattern paragraph of at least fifty words—but strive for a hundred or more—following the pattern of topic-restriction-illustration-illustration. (T-R-I-I). If you wish,

Copyright © 1985 by Harcourt Brace Jovanovich, Inc. All rights reserved.

you may rewrite a paragraph you produced in your draft of your analysis. (*Hint*: An illustration may be a detail or an example. The detail or example illustrates the idea the topic and restriction have specified. *Detail* and *example* fall under the general heading *illustration*.)

A graphic design can help you visualize the pattern of a paragraph. In the graphic design for a T-R-I-I paragraph, write your topic, restriction, and illustrations in the appropriate spaces. This controlled exercise will help you produce a paragraph that has at least four sentences with an orderly (unified) development.

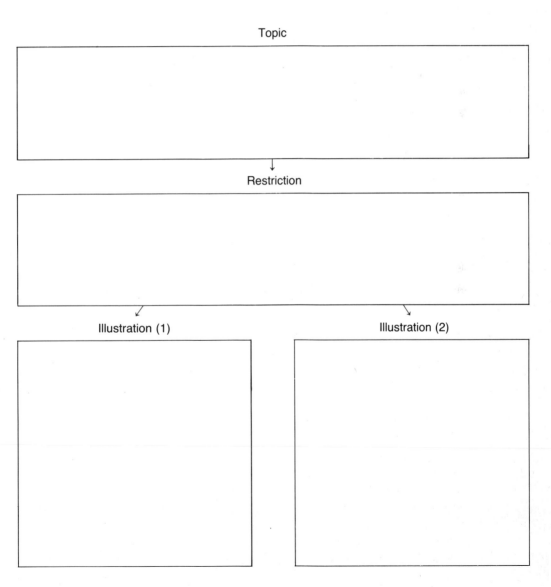

Topic

Restriction

Illustration (1)   Illustration (2)

Copyright © 1985 by Harcourt Brace Jovanovich, Inc. All rights reserved.

2.9 SENTENCE POWER

VERBS

Every complete sentence must have a verb. If a sentence is a single word, then that word will be a verb. Verbs are often defined as "action" words. You may think of such action words as "dance" or "drink" as verbs at first, but we use these words as nouns sometimes. Compare different uses of the same words in the examples below. (The target words appear in bold print.)

Verb	Melinda and George **dance** at Gilley's.
Noun	The **dance** begins at 9:45 pm.
Verb	Don Meredith **drinks** Lipton tea.
Noun	Tea is a refreshing **drink**.

These examples help you see that a definition is not always a reliable guide when you want to identify verbs, nouns, or indeed any other part of speech. The truth is that most words can fill several different slots in sentences depending on how they are used in the sentence.

To identify what part of speech a word is, you first have to determine the function of the word in a particular sentence. Indeed, the use of the word in the sentence determines whether it is a noun, a verb, or some other part of speech. Unless you understand a word's function within a sentence, you cannot know its part of speech; but if you do understand, you will always be able to locate the verb in a sentence.

The way a word functions in a sentence is the only reliable test for identifying which of the eight parts of speech a word is. When you have grasped the idea that words change their part of speech according to function, you have made a major step toward understanding how language works. This understanding helps you evaluate the correctness of your own sentences.

EXERCISE 1

In this controlled exercise you can learn to locate verbs by changing statements into questions. Sometimes you may need to change the *form* of the second word in the statement when you change the statement to a question, but that change does not affect this exercise. This test for verbs works when the subject is the very first word in the sentence and is not a verb like *am, is, are, was, were*. To use this test for verbs, change each sentence by starting with "do," "does," or "did." Then, the third word in the question will be the verb in the original sentence.

Rewrite each sentence as a question. Then draw a box around the verb of the original sentence.

Example   You locate verbs by changing statements into questions.
Do you locate *verbs by changing statements into questions*?

Copyright © 1985 by Harcourt Brace Jovanovich, Inc. All rights reserved.

1.   Films focus on death and dying.

   _____

   _____

2.   Films help us to discover the smaller joys of our own lives.

   _____

   _____

3.   They make us uncomfortable, tense, and afraid.

   _____

   _____

4.   Society demands that we suppress these emotions.

   _____

   _____

5.   Films allow us to let those feelings out.

   _____

   _____

6.   It puts us in touch with our negative emotions.

   _____

   _____

7.   It frightens us.

   _____

   _____

8.   They say the very things we are afraid to say.

   _____

   _____

Copyright © 1985 by Harcourt Brace Jovanovich, Inc. All rights reserved.

9.   Horror creates excitement for teens.

_____

_____

10.   Movies touch on one topic.

_____

_____

The preceding exercise has helped you identify verbs. A bonus from learning to identify verbs is that knowing the verb of a sentence allows you to find the subject. In the questions you wrote, the second word is the subject. So you can use this *do-does-did* test for verbs to identify subjects as well as verbs in sentences with this particular structure. This structure is very common for English sentences. Soon you can perform this test for verbs and subjects easily by rephrasing a sentence in your mind without rewriting the sentence into the form of a question. Next you will learn to pick the subject from among modifiers that many times belong to it in sentences with this structure.

This test for verbs and subjects works only when a sentence has the exact structure of those in the preceding exercise. With practice and understanding of this test, you can rearrange any sentence into this structure. When you can do that, you will have mastered the principles of finding most subjects and verbs. Admittedly, as sentences become more sophisticated, the task becomes more challenging and will likely be more interesting to you as you continue to gain mastery and to improve your writing skills.

Copyright © 1985 by Harcourt Brace Jovanovich, Inc. All rights reserved.

Notes

SIMPLE TENSES

Find the verbs in each of these three sentences. Then, write each verb in the space provided.

1. The horror film appeals to us. _____

2. The horror film appealed to us. _____

3. The horror film will appeal to us. _____

As you wrote the verbs, did you notice that they are all slightly different? The first ends in *-s*; the second ends in *-ed*; and the third adds another word, *will*.

1. Copy the sentence that fits with "now."

   Now _____

2. Copy the sentence that fits with "yesterday."

   Yesterday, _____

3. Copy the sentence that fits with "tomorrow."

   Tomorrow, _____

As you copied the sentences, did you notice the time relationship between the verb and those introductory words?

"Now" reinforces present time.
"Yesterday" reinforces past time.
"Tomorrow" reinforces future time.

In grammar, the time relationship indicated in the verb is called *tense*. The three simple tenses are present tense, past tense, and future tense. The sentence with "now" is present tense, the one with "yesterday" is past tense, and the one with "tomorrow" is future tense. These reinforcing words are only a guide or rule of thumb to help you learn to recognize tenses. Although they will work with many verbs, you cannot always rely on them to test for tense. They can help you recognize tense until you can rely on your own language sense.

EXERCISE 2

Some of the verbs in this exercise appear in **boldface** type. Decide the tense of these verbs and write the name of the tense of the verb in the blank. (*Hint*: When in doubt, put "now," "yesterday," or "tomorrow" at the end of the sentence.)

Copyright © 1985 by Harcourt Brace Jovanovich, Inc. All rights reserved.

Example   ___*future*___   Horror films **will entertain** teens for generations to come. ***tomorrow***

_____ 1. The movie **haunts** us.

_____ 2. It **frightened** us.

_____ 3. Frightening films **will allow** us to let feelings out without actually doing anything destructive.

_____ 4. The roller coaster **twists** through a complete 360-degree turn or **plows** through a lake at the bottom of the drop.

_____ 5. These terrifying tales **provided** us with a means of channeling our fears and anxieties.

_____ 6. A picture **will allow** you to experience what you dread most within the safe confines of a movie theater.

_____ 7. Actually, they **affect** us on two levels.

_____ 8. Horror movies **touch** on the one topic which evokes fear in almost everyone.

_____ 9. Stephen King **contends** that horror movies "don't love death," as some have suggested.

_____10. By showing us the miseries of the damned, horror movies **will help** us to rediscover smaller joys.

Review the previous exercise and notice the verbs you identified as present tense. Most of them end with the suffix -*s*. If a verb ends with an -*s* the verb is singular in number (singular or plural). (Unlike nouns, you add -*s* to make a verb **singular**.)

Did you find a present tense verb that did not end in -*s*? If not, look again at sentence number 8. Notice that the subject "movies," is plural; it is a *noun* that ends in -*s*. The subject and the verb must match: when the subject is singular, the verb is singular; when the subject is plural, the verb is plural. Usually there is no problem in getting the subjects and verbs to match. The only time a mistake might occur is in the present tense when the subject is *he*, *she*, or *it*, or a noun these pronouns can replace. (*He*, *she*, *it* are third-person singular pronouns which can replace *Michael* [Michael = he], *Elizabeth* [Elizabeth = she], *movie* [movie = it].) Otherwise, the singular and plural forms of verbs are always identical. (*To be* is a special case.)

Any slip in matching these third-person singular subjects (he, she, it, etc.) and third-person singular verbs (all of which must end in -*s*) is considered a major gram-

Copyright © 1985 by Harcourt Brace Jovanovich, Inc. All rights reserved.

matical error and can have a severe effect on the perceptions people have about your intelligence regardless of the justice of that prejudgment. In some kinds of speech it is acceptable to ignore agreement between the subject and the verb. It is **never** acceptable in college writing and is always considered an error.

To make this error is to make an error in what people call *agreement*. The third-person singular of the verb and of the subject, like all others, must agree. Therefore, generally speaking, a rule of thumb is that if you have an *-s* on your subject, you cannot have one on your verb. If you have an *-s* on your verb, you cannot have one on your subject.

When you need to discuss more than one of anything, make the noun plural. Most nouns form plurals by adding *-s*. There are other ways some nouns become plural which will be discussed later.

EXERCISE 3

Identify the verb in each sentence and write it in the blank. Next, rewrite the sentence and change each verb to the present tense. (*Hint*: Remember the "do-does-did" test to help you locate the verb. When words change for the sentence to make sense, those words will be verbs. A second test for a verb is to begin the sentence with "now," "yesterday," or "tomorrow.")

Example   *giggled*   She giggled nervously from fear.
                She giggles nervously from fear.

1. _____ That terrifying tale provided us with a means for channeling our fears and anxieties.

   _____

   _____

2. _____ The second level touched us profoundly and developed our emotional maturity.

   _____

   _____

3. _____ It delved into our souls and touched on feelings and emotions.

   _____

   _____

Copyright © 1985 by Harcourt Brace Jovanovich, Inc. All rights reserved.

4. _____ Horror will create excitement for teens.

   _____

   _____

5. _____ The movies celebrated deformity.

   _____

   _____

6. _____ It helped us discover the smaller joys of our own lives.

   _____

   _____

7. _____ A horror film stretched familiar subjects almost to ridiculous proportions.

   _____

   _____

8. _____ She continued with her opinion about horror movies.

   _____

   _____

9. _____ He showed why we liked fear.

   _____

   _____

10. _____ The young viewers learned another lesson in terror and lived to tell about it.

    _____

    _____

Copyright © 1985 by Harcourt Brace Jovanovich, Inc. All rights reserved.

NOUNS

Fill the blank slot of the pattern sentence with words from this list: **sign**, **carport**, **fence**, **ruin**, **pony**.

The ten-year-old _____ stands at the end of the street.

Now read the same sentence and fill the blank slot with these words: **understand**, **friendship**, **education**, **fear**, **job**, **longing**, **mysticism**, **faith**, **emptiness**. You probably see that none of the words from the second list completes the sentence sensibly. Now, use the words in the second list in this sentence:

The _____ I feel remains my secret.

Any single word that can fit in the blank slot in either of the above pattern sentences will be a noun. However, there are several kinds of nouns, only one of which will make sense in any particular slot. Nouns that fill the slot in the first sentence name concrete things that can be counted. They are called concrete nouns. (In the second pattern sentence, the noun is also the subject of the sentence. Try the "do-does-did" test.)

Another kind of noun names ideas, emotions, and other concepts. Any word that sensibly completes the second sentence is an abstract noun that designates an idea, a feeling, or some other concept. Unlike the nouns that complete the first sentence, these nouns name what cannot ordinarily be counted. Here, the words that fill the slot are abstract nouns which also function as the subject of the sentence. (Try the "do-does-did" test here, too.) Both abstract and count nouns can be referred to as common nouns.

EXERCISE 4

Complete each statement by supplying the official name of a person or a place. Be certain to capitalize each name used to fill a slot.

1. Ms. _____ taught me second grade at _____

   _____ .

2. Mr. _____ lives next door to my parents in _____

   _____ , _____ .

3. Dr. _____ vaccinated me for polio.

4. Rev. _____ married my cousin.

5. President _____ struggled with inflation daily.

Copyright © 1985 by Harcourt Brace Jovanovich, Inc. All rights reserved.

6. Mrs. _____ , my mother's best friend, sent me a box of homemade cookies.

7. I graduated from _____ in _____

_____ , _____ .

The names you used to fill the slots in Exercise 4 are known as proper nouns, a third kind of noun. Like other nouns, proper nouns function as subjects. (Try the "do-does-did" test here to discover which proper nouns occupy the subject slot.) Frequently, proper nouns that are the official name of a person or a place will be more than a single noun. For instance, most people have at least three names. For example, one authority on fear with three names is James David Stafford. Every name on your own official documents is a proper noun. When a multiple-name proper noun is a subject, all of them function as a unit.

Example   James David Stafford understands about fear.
Rephrased   He understands about fear.

He, a pronoun, replaces the proper nouns *James David Stafford*, the subject of the sentence. In the rephrased example, *he* is the subject. (Try the "do-does-did" test.)

EXERCISE 5

Place a check above each proper noun you find.

1. Take, for example, the movie *Carrie*, a thriller based on the novel by Stephen King, about a teen with mysterious powers that enable her to annoy and eventually destroy almost everyone around her.

2. Other young subjects of scare include Regan in *The Exorcist* and Damien in *The Omen*.

3. Even Walt Disney has ventured into the fright field with the film *The Watcher in the Woods*.

4. According to Dee Shepherd-Look, a professor of psychology at California State University, Northridge, and a licensed clinical psychologist, horror movies serve different purposes for different kinds of people.

5. "Horror movies are a tremendous catharsis for rage, anger and other destructive feelings," says Dr. Shepherd-Look.

6. "I go to see scary movies because they're exciting and fun to watch," says 17-year-old Jenny from Houston, Texas.

Copyright © 1985 by Harcourt Brace Jovanovich, Inc. All rights reserved.

7. No longer is the action confined to faraway Transylvania.

8. Now there's horror in the hospital (*Coma*), on a train (*Terror Train*), at the prom (*Prom Night* and *Carrie*) and even at home (*The Amityville Horror*).

9. After all, isn't it comforting to know that no matter how mad your dad may sometimes get at you, he's an absolute angel compared to the madman Jack Nicholson portrays in *The Shining*?

10. Stephen King believes that horror movies "don't love death as some have suggested."

In Exercise 4 you supplied several proper nouns which function as subjects and as other parts of a sentence. In Exercise 5 you identified proper nouns which function as subjects and as other parts of a sentence. Any noun, regardless of its type, can function in several different slots in sentences, and you will learn to identify nouns in each of the slots they occupy.

EXERCISE 6

Identify each noun used as a subject by drawing a box around count nouns, a circle around abstract nouns, and a triangle around proper nouns. Of course, nouns here occupy various slots, but for this exercise strive to identify only nouns that function as subjects. (*Hint:* Notice that some sentences may have two or more subjects.)

Example   Dr. McGraw feels that patients can benefit from anger and rage.

1. The dimly lit theater is packed with people.

2. Suddenly the lights are lowered, the curtains open and as promised, the nightmare begins.

3. "Why?" asks Stephen King, author of *Danse Macabre* (Everest House, 1981).

4. One's appetite for double twists or 360-degree loops may be considerably depleted.

5. Mysterious powers enable her to annoy and eventually destroy almost everyone around her.

6. Even Walt Disney has ventured into the fright field with the film *The Watcher in the Woods*.

7. Society demands that we suppress these emotions even when they're justifiable.

Copyright © 1985 by Harcourt Brace Jovanovich, Inc. All rights reserved.

8. A fairly well-adjusted young person can constructively reduce his or her anger and rage through a horror film.

9. ''Horror creates excitement for teens,'' states Dr. Shepherd-Look.

10. Nature thrillers (*The Fog* and *Prophecy*) and earth invaders (*Alien* and *Invasion of the Body Snatchers*) are still big at the box office.

Copyright © 1985 by Harcourt Brace Jovanovich, Inc. All rights reserved.

PRONOUNS

A noun does not function as a subject in the following sentence:

He understands about fear.

The first word, *he*, a pronoun, is the subject. Pronouns replace nouns (or other pronouns) and function in sentences in the same ways nouns function. While the number of nouns in the language is virtually limitless, there is a limited number of pronouns. In other words, listing every pronoun in the language in this text is possible. To list all words used as nouns in the language, though, would strain the memory of a large main-frame computer because nouns are continually being added to the language and because other parts of speech can function as nouns.

You have probably used words as nouns that no one else has ever used. For instance, a certain six-year-old boy calls a U-turn corridor under an expressway a "hookie-under." Have you ever said that? This child recently explained to his father: "Dad, to get to that MacDonald's, you have to go on the hookie-under." Probably the father invented the noun because he had no convenient word for such a place. His son heard it and used it. Will you now call this traffic corridor a "hookie-under"? Regardless what you call a "hookie-under," a limited number of pronouns can replace "hookie-under" in a sentence.

EXERCISE 7

Circle all pronouns in this list (*they*, *each*, *those*, *that*, *one*, *these*, *some*, *many*) that can replace "hookie-unders" in the following sentence.

Hookie-unders get you there faster.

EXERCISE 8

In the following sentence, a pronoun will replace both "hookie-under" and the modifiers of "hookie-under"—*the convenient*. Circle the pronouns from the list (*they*, *each*, *those*, *that*, *one*, *these*, *some*, *many*, *it*, *one*, *none*, *any*, *neither*) that can replace the complete subject of the sentence.

The convenient "hookie-under" gets you there faster. Did you find any pronouns

that would not sensibly replace the complete subject? If so, list them. _____

_____

_____

In addition to serving the same functions in sentences that nouns serve, a pronoun can replace a noun and its modifiers (more than one word) and is therefore econom-

Copyright © 1985 by Harcourt Brace Jovanovich, Inc. All rights reserved.

Pronouns					
Personal Pronouns		Relative Pronouns		Indefinite Pronouns	
Singular	Plural	Singular	Plural	Singular	Plural

I
you
he, she,
   it
	we
	you
	they
		who
		that
		which
			who
			that
			which
				one
				none
				anyone
				anybody
				either/
				   neither
				each
				everyone
				everybody
				somebody
				someone
					some
					all
					most

ical. When using pronouns, you must be careful to ensure that the reader has enough specific information so that the words a pronoun replaces are always clear. For example, to write *It is packed with them* does not tell enough to understand what the writer means. Is he writing about a can of sardines, a package of cigarettes, a crystal vase packed with plastic pellets, underwear in a suitcase, or a dimly lit theater packed with people? The pronoun *it* replaces the complete subject *the dimly lit theater*, and the pronoun *them* replaces *people* in the original sentence "The dimly lit theater is packed with people." Refer to the pronoun chart for a list of pronouns that can be used as subjects.

EXERCISE 9

From the chart of pronouns that can be used as subjects, choose a pronoun to replace each group of *italicized* words and write it in the blank. (*Hint:* Sometimes more than one pronoun can replace the italicized words.)

Example   _____ *they* _____   *Horror movies* are a tremendous catharsis.

1. _____ And *horror movies,* like roller coasters, have always been the province of the young.

2. _____ After all, by the time one turns 40 or 50, *one's appetite for double-twists or 360-degree loops* may be considerably depleted.

Copyright © 1985 by Harcourt Brace Jovanovich, Inc. All rights reserved.

3. _____ *Other young subjects* of scare include Regan in <u>The Exorcist</u> and Damien in <u>The Omen</u>.

4. _____ Even *Walt Disney* has ventured into the fright field with the film <u>The Watcher in the Woods.</u>

5. _____ *Society* demands that we suppress these emotions even when they're justifiable.

6. _____ You see, *the horror film* deliberately appeals to what's worst in us.

7. _____ *A fairly well-adjusted young person* can constructively reduce his anger and rage through a horror film.

8. _____ "I don't dwell on what I've seen because it's only make-believe," *17-year-old Jenny* adds.

9. _____ *Movies that overflow with death and destruction* allow us to deal with death without ever really being a part of it.

10. _____ *Stephen King* contends that horror movies "don't love death, as some have suggested."

Replacing a complete subject with a single pronoun in the above exercise has the advantage of brevity and economy. The disadvantage you notice is that details and specifics in the original sentences are lost. When you write, you should choose to use pronouns in contexts that will allow your reader to know precisely and exactly what you have in mind so that you will convey the full meaning of your thoughts to your reader. When you replace a noun with a pronoun, take care to choose a pronoun that has the same number (singular/plural) and gender (sex) that the noun has. This logic is called *agreement*.

EXERCISE 10

Choose the appropriate word from the pronoun chart to complete the blank.

1. _____'re daring yourself to do something, yet _____

know (or at least hope) that _____'ll come out the winner.

2. Or might _____ find being scared out of our seat a positive release?

Copyright © 1985 by Harcourt Brace Jovanovich, Inc. All rights reserved.

3. You see, the horror film, deliberately appeals to what's worst in us. _____ _____ puts us in touch with our negative emotions.

4. They say the very thing _____'re afraid to say and force us to confront emotions that society says we should keep hidden.

5. On top is the "gross out" level _____ stands for our surface reaction to what is taking place.

6. _____'s how the films affect us visibly.

7. However, the adolescent _____ has a tendency toward violence anyway may be triggered to exhibit his or her emotions after seeing violent behavior.

8. Then there are those of us _____ don't go to see horror movies simply because we don't enjoy them.

9. "_____ go to see scary movies because they're exciting and fun to watch," says 17-year-old Jenny.

10. "_____ don't dwell on what _____'ve seen because it's only make-believe," she adds.

11. "Horror creates excitement for teens," stated Dr. Shepherd-Look. "Often it's not the horror itself, but the suspense and excitement beforehand that _____ crave."

12. And when all is said and done _____ realize that no matter what your problems they're not now and probably never will be this bad.

13. After all, isn't it comforting to know that no matter how mad your dad may sometimes get at you, _____'s an absolute angel compared to the madman Jack Nicholson portrays in *The Shining*.

14. "Our culture has a tremendous fear of death," says Dr. Shepherd-Look. . . .

Copyright © 1985 by Harcourt Brace Jovanovich, Inc. All rights reserved.

''Movies that overflow with death and destruction allow us to deal with death without ever really being a part of it,'' _____ continues.

15. This is particularly important to teens since _____'re developmentally at a stage where _____'re beginning to confront death and are trying to understand it.

EXERCISE 11

Replace the *italicized* pronouns with a complete subject. (*Hint*: You can look in the reading section to find a context for the italicized pronoun.)

Example   *Some* are a tremendous catharsis.
                Horror movies _____

1. *It*'s like riding the big roller coaster at an amusement park. _____

2. *Some* are even gross enough to turn us off to popcorn permanently. _____

      _____

3. *They* say the very things we're afraid to say and force us to control emotions

      that society says we should keep hidden. _____

4. *It* delves into our souls and touches on the feelings and emotions that no one

      else knows. _____

5. *They* make us uncomfortable, tense and afraid. _____

6. *It*'s a way of coping with what scares them without experiencing these things

      firsthand. _____

7. And when all is said and done, you realize that no matter what your problems,

      they're not now and probably never will be this bad. _____

8. But by dwelling on deformity, *they* sing of health and energy. _____

      _____

Copyright © 1985 by Harcourt Brace Jovanovich, Inc. All rights reserved.

9. *Some* are still visibly shaken, but *most* are talking excitedly about what they've just witnessed. _____

10. *They*'ve sat through scenes that would scare the pants off their parents, teachers and even their 6'3", 235-pound uncle. _____

EXERCISE 12

A pronoun can always replace the extended or complete subject. Circle the complete subject in the following sentences. Then rewrite the sentences replacing the complete subjects with correct pronouns. (*Hint*: The complete subject contains all the words that belong to a subject.)

Example   (This year's selections of horror movies) are a catharsis.
   They are a catharsis.

1. The roller coaster twists through a complete 360-degree turn.

   _____

   _____

2. A fairly well-adjusted young person reduces anger and rage through a horror film.

   _____

   _____

3. Dee Shepherd-Look, a professor of psychology at California State University, Northridge, says horror movies serve different purposes.

   _____

   _____

4. Jack Nicholson portrays a madman in *The Shining*.

   _____

   _____

5. Our culture fears death tremendously.

   _____

Copyright © 1985 by Harcourt Brace Jovanovich, Inc. All rights reserved.

6. Steven King contends horror movies ''don't love death, as some have suggested.''

_____

_____

7. Seventeen-year-old Jenny from Houston, Texas, says, ''I go to see scary movies because they're exciting and fun to watch.''

_____

_____

8. Nature thrillers and earth invaders still draw big at the box office.

_____

_____

9. These terrifying tales provide us with a means for channeling our fears and anxieties.

_____

_____

10. Movies that overflow with death and destruction allow us to deal with death without ever really being a part of it.

_____

_____

EXERCISE 13

Underline the complete subject of each sentence. Then, select a pronoun to replace the complete subject and write it in the blank space. Finally, write the sentence using the pronoun you have selected.

Example   _**They**_   This year's selections of horror movies are a catharsis.
                              **They are a catharsis.**

1. _____ The dimly lit theater is packed with people.

Copyright © 1985 by Harcourt Brace Jovanovich, Inc. All rights reserved.

_____

_____

2. _____ This feeling is a common one.

_____

_____

3. _____ Horror movies, like roller coasters, have always been the province of the young.

_____

_____

4. _____ Other young subjects of scare include Regan in *The Exorcist* and Damien in *The Omen*.

_____

_____

5. _____ Horror movies are a tremendous catharsis for rage, anger, and other destructive feelings.

_____

_____

6. _____ The adolescent who has a tendency toward violence anyway may be triggered to exhibit his or her emotions after seeing violent behavior.

_____

_____

7. _____ Seeing old television reruns of *The Blob* and *Frankenstein* is enough to keep you awake at night.

_____

_____

Copyright © 1985 by Harcourt Brace Jovanovich, Inc. All rights reserved.

8. _____ The mass murderer is the latest fright figure to burst upon the screen.

_____

_____

9. _____ Each young viewer has learned another lesson in terror and has lived to tell about it.

_____

_____

10. _____ The undisputed master of the horror story, Stephen King, says, "In the final sense, the horror movie is the celebration of those who feel they can examine death because it doesn't yet live in their own hearts."

_____

_____

Copyright © 1985 by Harcourt Brace Jovanovich, Inc. All rights reserved.

ADJECTIVES

Adjectives are another of the eight parts of speech. They are words that describe features or characteristics of nouns (**young** viewers). They are also numbers (**one** film, **two** monsters) and colors (**black** sky, **red** blood), but they can denote other qualities as well (**scary** movie). Through this kind of description, the adjective lets you know that you are to understand the noun in a particular way. *Film* is a noun referring to many different kinds of movies or to the material used in various kinds of photography. The adjective **scary** adds detail about the word *film* and lets you know that the writer or speaker means a particular kind of movie, one which is frightening. *Scary* tells you also that *film* does not mean *photographic material*. When you use adjectives in your writing, you will add details and specifics which help your reader develop a mental picture of what you mean.

In working with pronouns, you learned that sometimes a pronoun replaces a complete subject. Complete subjects are simple subjects and other words attached to them which provide details or refine or restrict understanding of the subject. This refinement and restriction is called **modification**, and the words that modify nouns are adjectives, determiners, and pronominal adjectives. All three classes of words function in precisely the same ways that adjectives function. Once you understand the functions of adjectives, it will be easy for you to use determiners, pronominal adjectives, or adjectives in your writing.

Another way to understand adjectives is to understand their function. To do so, omit the second word of the first sentence in the reading selection.

The _____ poster reads: "The nightmare isn't over yet."

If you look back at the reading, you will see that the slot is filled with the word **movie** which gives specific information about the poster. In this sentence, **movie** is an adjective. As a matter of fact, any word you can place in this blank sensibly will be an adjective. **Movie** is only an adjective in this particular sentence because it fills an adjective slot. Try filling the blank with each of the following words—**giant, iridescent, crazy, brightly, colorful, sits, to, purple, small, funny**. Do you agree that three words from the list do not function in this slot? If you do, you understand the requirements for a word to be an adjective. List the three words which do *not* fill

the slot: _____, _____, _____. Adjectives are words that fill the slot and in this case, modify (or make more specific the meaning of) a noun.

Sometimes adjectives fill other slots. They can, for instance, be part of the complete predicate:

Scary movies are very frightening.

Try to substitute the following words for **frightening**: *expensive, massacres, ridiculous, old-fashioned, films, nightmares, entertaining, suspenseful, constructive, satis-*

Copyright © 1985 by Harcourt Brace Jovanovich, Inc. All rights reserved.

fying. As the sentence is stated, certain of the words will not function in the **frightening** slot. List the words which will not function in the **frightening** slot:

_____

_____

_____

Try these three words to see if they will function if *very* is omitted from the sentence.

Scary movies are _____ .

The words that fill the slot when *very* is removed but which will not follow *very* are not adjectives; indeed, here they are all nouns. The words which fill the slot following *very* are adjectives. One test, then, for adjectives is to insert mentally the word *very* before another word to see if the combination of the two words makes sense. If it does, you probably have an adjective. If not, you have another part of speech. The reason *very* works this way is that it is usually an adverb, and one function of adverbs is to modify adjectives.

DETERMINERS AND PRONOMINAL ADJECTIVES

Determiners and pronominal adjectives are special words that, like adjectives, signal the approach of a noun. Adjectives, however, can and often do occur between determiners and pronominal adjectives and the noun that will follow. Refer to the chart for a list of determiners and pronominal adjectives.

Both determiners and pronominal adjectives are words that mark or point towards nouns. They also, like adjectives, restrict the noun. Can you see any difference between **a** *movie* and **the** *movie*? **A** movie has an entirely different meaning from **the** movie. Some determiners, special kinds of pronouns such as **my**, **their**, **your**, **his**, **her**, **its**, **our** are also called pronominal adjectives or possessive pronouns. It is more important to understand how these words work in the language than to learn their names. Nonetheless, the name *pronominal adjective* may help you understand that

Determiners	Pronominal Adjectives
a, an	my
the	our
this	their
that	your
those	his
these	her
	its

Copyright © 1985 by Harcourt Brace Jovanovich, Inc. All rights reserved.

determiners and adjectives and pronominal adjectives (possessive pronouns) modify nouns and that they indicate that a noun will follow. These words can help you recognize nouns. (*Hint*: Recall the rule-of-thumb that states a noun to be a word you can use *the* in front of.)

EXERCISE 14

Circle the determiners and the pronominal adjectives. Put a check (√) over other adjectives. (*Hint*: Determiners are usually short words—**a, an, the**.) Remember that determiners and pronominal adjectives work just like adjectives: they mark nouns and add details about them.

Example   (This) year's selection of horror movies arouses (our) interest.

1. It's like riding the big roller coaster at an amusement park.

2. A really good horror movie may surprise a scream out of us at some point, the way we scream when the roller coaster twists through a complete 360-degree turn or plows through a lake at the bottom of the drop.

3. Other young subjects of scare include Regan in *The Exorcist* and Damien in *The Omen*.

4. Horror movies serve different purposes for different kinds of people.

5. Frightening films allow us to let those feelings out without actually doing anything.

6. No longer is the action confined to faraway Transylvania.

7. There's a fright film to play upon fear, a picture that'll allow you to experience what you dread most within the safe confines of a movie theater, a film able to stretch familiar subjects to almost ridiculous proportions.

8. But at the same time, horror movies touch on the one topic which evokes fear in almost everyone.

9. By showing us the miseries of the damned, they help us to rediscover the smaller joys of our own lives.

10. In the final sense, the horror movie is the celebration of those who feel they can examine death because it doesn't yet live in their own hearts.

Copyright © 1985 by Harcourt Brace Jovanovich, Inc. All rights reserved.

ADVERBS

Adverbs, another part of speech, do for verbs what adjectives do for nouns. They modify or limit the meaning of the verb.

> Carrie's mysterious powers annoy and **eventually destroy** almost everyone around her.

In the preceding sentence, the adverb **eventually** modifies the verb **destroy**.

Adverbs also modify adjectives or other adverbs. Take, for instance, *The dimly lit theater is packed with people.* Here, **dimly** is an adverb that modifies the adjective **lit**. In the following sentence is an example of an adverb modifying another adverb: *Some are **still visibly** shaken.* Here, **still** modifies the adverb **visibly**.

Many adverbs deal with time, such as **now**, **soon**; others show a negative quality such as **no**, **not**, **never**. Frequently, time-words such as the test words for finding verbs, ''now, yesterday, tomorrow'' are adverbs. Other words frequently used as adverbs are **still**, **too**, **how**, **when**, and **where**. If you are in doubt about the function of a word in something you have written, you can check to see if the word tells when, where, or how about the word it modifies. If a word lets you know one of those, it likely functions as an adverb. (Remember, before you can be certain what part of speech a word is, you must first determine the function and meaning of that word.)

Adverbs also modify verbs as in the following sentence:

> Horror films **deliberately** appeal to what's worst in us.

Try to substitute each of the following words in the slot occupied by **deliberately**: **absolutely**, **never**, **usually**, **always**, **frequently**, **fortunately**, **often**, **similarly**, **very**, **lovely**. Notice that the last two of the above words do not make sense in the **deliberately** slot. Sometimes they are adverbs, but their meanings are such that they do not work sensibly with the verb *appeal* in this sentence. So, you cannot rely on slot-filling alone to select adverbs. You must be aware of logic and meaning, too, to construct good sentences.

An adverb may also modify an entire sentence. In the following instance, **apparently**, an adverb, modifies the entire sentence rather than a particular word: **Apparently,** *there's a horror film for almost everyone.*

Something else you may have noticed about adverbs is that they frequently end in *-ly*. This feature is often helpful in deciding if a word you have used is an adverb. If used alone, though, this feature is not a reliable guide to know if you have written an adverb since words that are not adverbs can also end in *-ly*. For example, **rely** is not an adverb, and neither is **sly** in the sentence, **Sly** *burglars* **rely** *on the victim's carelessness.*

To be able to distinguish between adjectives and adverbs is important because college writing does not allow use of an adjective when an adverb is needed. For example, ''Horror movies are real scary'' is incorrect because the adverb *really* is

Copyright © 1985 by Harcourt Brace Jovanovich, Inc. All rights reserved.

necessary to modify the adjective *scary*. **Real** is an adjective. A second example, "In *Friday the 13th* several lovely girls are murdered," contains one adverb, *several*. **Lovely**, although it ends in *-ly*, is an adjective modifying *girls*.

EXERCISE 15

Circle the adverbs. Place a check (√) over the adjectives.

Example   Horror movies (always) scare me.

1. The films affect us visibly.

2. The feeling is common.

3. Horror movies are a tremendous catharsis for rage, anger, and other destructive feelings.

4. It's difficult to feel comfortable with something we can't fully understand.

5. Movies allow us to deal with death without ever really being a part of it.

6. This is particularly important to teens since they are developmentally at a stage where they are trying to understand death.

7. Our culture has a tremendous fear of death.

8. What is a fairly well-adjusted young person?

9. These terrifying tales provide us with emotional release.

10. The mass murderer is the latest fright figure to burst upon the screen.

EXERCISE 16

Circle all adverbs in this exercise. Draw an arrow from the adverb to the word that the adverb modifies unless the adverb modifies the entire sentence.

Example   Horror movies (always) scare me.

1. And each one is anxiously anticipating two hours of terror, suspense, ghosts, ghouls and gore.

2. Suddenly the lights are lowered, the curtains open and as promised, the nightmare begins.

3. You see, the horror film deliberately appeals to what's worst in us.

4. Actually, they affect us on two levels.

5. It's how the film affects us visibly.

Copyright © 1985 by Harcourt Brace Jovanovich, Inc. All rights reserved.

6. It's difficult to feel comfortable with something we can't fully understand.

7. No matter what your problem, they're not now and probably never will be . . . that bad.

8. This is particularly important to teens since they're developmentally at a stage where they're beginning to confront death and are trying to understand it.

9. They aren't merely vehicles for exhibiting pain, terror, violence and tragic deaths.

10. The mood is almost euphoric.

Copyright © 1985 by Harcourt Brace Jovanovich, Inc. All rights reserved.

Notes

SENTENCE COMBINING

To gain practice in using adjectives and adverbs, combine each of these four groups of sentences into a single sentence.

1. a. The theater is packed.
    b. The theater is lit.
    c. The lighting is dim.
    d. The theater is packed with people.
    e. The audience is under twenty-five years of age.
    f. Over half are under 25 years of age.

    _____

    _____

2. a. Dee Shepherd-Look is a professor.
    b. Dee Shepherd-Look teaches psychology.
    c. The teaching is at a university.
    d. The university is California State at Northridge.
    e. Dee Shepherd-Look is a psychologist.
    f. Dee Shepherd-Look is licensed.

    _____

    _____

3. a. Horror movies make us uncomfortable.
    b. Horror movies make us tense.
    c. Horror movies make us afraid.

    _____

    _____

4. a. The credits roll.
    b. The lights go on.
    c. The audience files out.
    d. They leave the theater.
    e. The audience is young.

    _____

    _____

Copyright © 1985 by Harcourt Brace Jovanovich, Inc. All rights reserved.

Notes

2.10 PROOFREADING POWER

Proofreading is an acquired skill that all competent writers must learn and use. As a writer, you proofread to make sure that your product—your final version—is ready to present to your reader.

Proofreading is not writing; nor is it revising. Proofreading occurs after writing. When you proofread, you stop writing and revising, and you begin to inspect your writing for any errors in spelling or faulty punctuation or mechanics. Other proofreading activities include checking to be sure you have used the right paper, that your writing is legible or your typed copy is clear enough to read, and that you have met any special format requirements. The guiding question to ask yourself is ''How does my audience expect me to deliver my writing?'' During proofreading you constantly make sure that your writing meets the standards your audience requires. Proofreading is a bit like making sure your hair is combed and your buttons all buttoned properly before you present yourself for an important interview. While proofreading you may spot a clumsy sentence or poorly chosen word which clouds your meaning. If so, you will need to do further revision. When that occurs, you stop proofreading and return to writing and revising. After you solve the writing problem, you can return to proofreading and continue until you stop again to revise or until you reach the end of your writing.

Another point to learn about proofreading is that it does not all have to be done at the same time. Although it is essential that you proofread your entire composition before submitting it to your reader, you may stop writing and begin to proofread your writing at any time during the writing process. In other words, you will proofread your draft before a peer editor sees it just as you will also proofread your final version before your teacher sees that, as a novelist proofreads the final manuscript before presenting it to a publisher. Sometimes interrupting your writing process to proofread when you are stuck for something else to say can help to get your thoughts flowing again. While you must proofread before you are through, you do not have to wait until after you have finished writing.

EXERCISE 1

Read this passage and identify the following kinds of errors. First, circle all verbs which do not agree with their subjects. Next, box all pronouns that do not agree with the noun or pronoun they replace or refer to. Finally, correct the capitalization of nouns. As you find errors, write your correction above each error. At first you may want to read the passage several times to check for each specific error. As you gain skill in proofreading, you will learn to spot several kinds of errors during one reading.

Copyright © 1985 by Harcourt Brace Jovanovich, Inc. All rights reserved.

The horror film deliberately appeal to what's worst in us. It puts you in touch with our negative emotions. It frightens you, makes you uncomfortable, and some are even gross enough to turn us off to Popcorn permanently. ''A fairly well-adjusted young person can constructively reduce their anger and rage through a horror film,'' she explain. ''However, the Adolescent which have a tendency toward violence anyway may be triggered to exhibit their emotions after seeing violent behavior. And this hold true not only for horror films but for violence on television and in books.'' Then there is those of us which don't go to see Horror Movies simply because we don't enjoy them. They makes us uncomfortable, tense, and afraid. So, if seeing old television reruns of ''The blob'' and ''frankenstein' are enough to keep you awake, it's safe to assume they should stay away from chillers like ''ghost story'' or ''friday the 13th.''

Copyright © 1985 by Harcourt Brace Jovanovich, Inc. All rights reserved.

2.11 DICTATION

Your instructor will choose a passage of approximately 100 words and read it aloud as you write what you hear. As you listen to each sentence, concentrate and maintain silence. Do not ask your teacher to repeat because any sound other than the instructor's voice reading will break not only your concentration but that of others. Your instructor may repeat key words and phrases during the dictation, will allow sufficient time for you to write what has been read, and will reread the entire passage a second time at a faster rate so that you can check what you have written and fill in any gap you may have.

You will want to write on every other line so that you will have space to correct your dictation upon the final reading in case you have made a mistake. Your instructor will show you the dictated passage and ask you to compare your version, or perhaps a classmate's version, to the original. Be especially alert when you check the dictation because this exercise will help you develop your sentence sense by translating spoken into written language.

2.12 WORD POWER

SUFFIXES

You have already learned to identify prefixes that were attached to base words and to combine prefixes with base words. One thing that you discovered about prefixes is that they sometimes alter their spellings when attached to base words.

In this section you are to study suffixes. A suffix is a syllable or a group of syllables that is added to a base word or to another suffix.

Example   hope (base word)
hope + less (suffix) = hopeless
hope + less (suffix) + ly (suffix) = hopelessly

One feature of suffixes that you will notice is that they rarely have multiple meanings. This feature makes determining the meaning of a word if you already know the meaning of the base easy. A few suffixes do change their spelling when attached to a base word.

EXERCISE 1

First, find words in "Why Fear Is Fun" (Section 2.2) which contain the suffixes listed below and draw a box around each suffix. Then, list the words containing these suffixes in the blanks provided. Each suffix appears in the selection at least once, but it may not appear six times. Some suffixes appear many more times than six. Once you

Copyright © 1985 by Harcourt Brace Jovanovich, Inc. All rights reserved.

have located six words with any one suffix, go to the next suffix. (*Hint*: Use your
pencil to mark the suffixes as your read rapidly.)

1. **-able**, **-ible**   means "capable of being"

    Example   manage⟨able⟩

    _____   _____

    _____   _____

    _____   _____

2. **-al**, **-eal**, **-ial**   means "relation to" or "that which"

    Example   typic⟨al⟩

    _____   _____

    _____   _____

    _____   _____

3. **-er**, **-or**   means "a person who"

    Example   audit⟨or⟩

    _____   _____

    _____   _____

    _____   _____

4. **-ful**   means "full of"

    Example   play⟨ful⟩

    _____   _____

    _____   _____

    _____   _____

5. **-ion**, **-tion**   means "action of" or "act of"

    Example   transporta⟨tion⟩

    _____   _____

    _____   _____

Copyright © 1985 by Harcourt Brace Jovanovich, Inc. All rights reserved.

_____   _____

6. **-ist**   means "a person who does, makes, or is something"
    Example   femin⊐ist⊏

    _____   _____

    _____   _____

    _____   _____

7. **-ity, -ty, -y**   means "like or characteristic of something"
    Example   acid⊐ity⊏

    _____   _____

    _____   _____

    _____   _____

8. **-ive**   means "relating to"
    Example   rest⊐ive⊏

    _____   _____

    _____   _____

    _____   _____

9. **-ize**   means "to cause to be" or "to become something"
    Example   hospital⊐ize⊏

    _____   _____

    _____   _____

    _____   _____

10. **-ly**   means "like in appearance" or "taking place regularly"
    Example   playful⊐ly⊏

    _____   _____

    _____   _____

    _____   _____

Copyright © 1985 by Harcourt Brace Jovanovich, Inc. All rights reserved.

11. **-ment** means "result of" or "act of"

   Example place⸢ment⸣

   _____   _____

   _____   _____

   _____   _____

12. **-ous** means "full of"

   Example monstr⸢ous⸣

   _____   _____

   _____   _____

   _____   _____

EXERCISE 2

Select a word from each suffix group in the preceding exercise and write a sentence using that word. Draw a box around the word in your sentence. If possible, select a word that you have not written in a sentence before. Always strive to build your word power.

Example *Horror movies make fear* ⸢*manageable*⸣.

1. _____

   _____

   _____

2. _____

   _____

   _____

3. _____

   _____

   _____

Copyright © 1985 by Harcourt Brace Jovanovich, Inc. All rights reserved.

4. _____

_____

_____

5. _____

_____

_____

6. _____

_____

_____

7. _____

_____

_____

8. _____

_____

_____

9. _____

_____

_____

10. _____

_____

_____

11. _____

_____

Copyright © 1985 by Harcourt Brace Jovanovich, Inc. All rights reserved.

_____

12. _____

_____

_____

EXERCISE 3

The suffixes which follow make adjectives or nouns of base words. All are common and appear often. Write words that have each of the following suffixes. You may use your dictionary or look in a magazine or book to locate a word with these suffixes.

1. **-ance**, **-ence** means "the name of an action"

    Example occurrence _____

2. **-ary** means "connected with"

    Example functionary _____

3. **-hood** means "like or characteristic of"

    Example brotherhood _____

4. **-ic** means "made of"

    Example syllabic _____

5. **-less** means "without"

    Example hopeless _____

6. **-like** means "like or characteristic of"

    Example ghostlike _____

7. **-ness** means "like or characteristic of"

    Example happiness, childishness _____

8. **-ship** means "like or characteristic of"

    Example statesmanship _____

9. **-some** means "tending to be" or "a specific number"

    Example handsome, threesome _____

10. **-ward** means "turning to" or "turning in the direction of"

    Example backward, frontward _____

Copyright © 1985 by Harcourt Brace Jovanovich, Inc. All rights reserved.

SPELLING

Some suffixes in English are difficult to spell because the vowels in them are all pronounced the same way, as "uh." These are the suffix pairs -**able** and -**ible**, -**ary** and
-**ery**, -**ance** and -**ence**. Although there are no reliable rules about how to spell these
suffixes, some rules of thumb—which have *many* exceptions—can help you. You will
be correct more often than not if you use them, but if you are uncertain about the
spelling of any word, look the word up in your dictionary.

1. Consider the noun that is related to the -**able** or -**ible** word. Nouns spelled with
    -**ation** will generally show you should use -**able** in forming the adjective, whereas
    nouns spelled with only -**ion** will indicate you should use -**ible**.

    Example   admir**ation** indicates admir**able**
                    but collect**ion** indicates collect**ible**

2. If the base is a complete word, use -**able**.

    Example   use + -able = useable

    Words which do not have a complete word as a base generally add -**ible**.

    Example   permiss + -ible = permissible

    These suffixes, -**able** and -**ible**, are usually added to nouns and to verbs to make
adjectives. The meaning of the suffix changes depending on whether it is added to a
noun or to a verb. When added to a noun, -**able** or -**ible** means "liable to" or "tending to." When added to a verb, -**able** or -**ible** means "capable of" or "worthy of."

EXERCISE 4

Test your understanding of the rules of thumb by adding -**able** or -**ible** to the following words. After you have written the words in the blanks, check the spelling in your
dictionary.

1. accept_____   6. defense_____

2. commend_____   7. excuse_____

3. write_____   8. justify_____

4. enjoy_____   9   play_____

5. pity_____   10. terror_____

The -**ance** and -**ence** words and the -**ant** and -**ent** words do have a rule of thumb,
but it is very complicated and involves knowing where the stress of the word falls.

Copyright © 1985 by Harcourt Brace Jovanovich, Inc. All rights reserved.

Therefore, look in your dictionary for words ending in these suffixes unless you have memorized them.

The -**ary** and -**ery** forms are much easier to handle, but first you must identify their function to know their part of speech. The lessons in this chapter will help you do that. Knowing the part of speech gives you a guide because -**ary** usually forms adjectives while -**ery** usually forms nouns.

Example   inflation (noun)   +   -ary   =   inflationary (adjective)

confection (noun)   +   -ery   =   confectionery (noun)

This rule of thumb will be most helpful in deciding when to use the demons **stationary** and **stationery**. Whenever you are talking about a thing, such as something one uses to write letters on, you use the -**ery** form since you need a noun. When you are describing a quality of something, use the -**ary** form since you need an adjective. (*Hint*: Station**ery** has **e**nvelopes.)

EXERCISE 5

Supply the correct forms of the suffix for the following words. (*Hint*: Some bases change.) Check the spelling in your dictionary when you have finished the exercise.

1. abund_____nt
2. adapt_____ble
3. appreci_____ble
4. complim_____nt
5. concur_____nt
6. cream_____ry
7. defer_____nce
8. desir_____ble
9. effici_____nt
10. emin_____nt
11. heredit_____ry
12. obedi_____nce
13. rectify_____ble
14. repress_____ble
15. extravag_____nt

EXERCISE 6

Studying the following list of words will probably convince you that you must look each -**able**, -**ible**, -**ance**, -**ence**, -**ary** and -**ery** word up in your dictionary unless you are absolutely certain of the spelling of any word that adds these suffixes. Learn to spell the words in this list which you cannot now spell correctly.

1. admissible
2. auxiliary
3. bribery
4. changeable
5. consequence
6. correctible
7. credible
8. disciplinary
9. excusable
10. existence
11. inference
12. occurrence
13. preference
14. prevalent
15. prominent
16. receivable
17. saleable
18. sanitary
19. sensible
20. useable

Copyright © 1985 by Harcourt Brace Jovanovich, Inc. All rights reserved.

UNIT THREE

WRITING
RECONSIDERED

3.1 GETTING STARTED BY READING

In previous lessons you have tried reading with and without a pencil in your hand. You know which technique works best for you. As with writing, the purpose for reading determines the reader's approach. As a reader, your purpose controls the ways you read in the same way purpose controls the ways you write. Successful, skilled readers vary the speeds at which they read; the reading speed depends upon the reader's purpose, the nature of the material read, and the reader's ability. Skilled, successful readers gauge their reading speeds within five broad categories. These categories reflect the specific purpose a reader has for reading anything.

As a reader, you can refine your reading skills by developing at least five different speeds for five identifiable purposes. The actual speeds at which you read for any purpose are relative to your particular reading skills. Your goal is to increase your speed in each category because research shows that *the faster you read, the more information you will retain.*

The five different identifiable reading speeds, listed from the fastest to the slowest speeds, are these: (1) skimming, (2) locating or searching for particular facts, (3) reading for pleasure/recreation, (4) reading for information and ideas, and (5) reading for study. In this lesson, use your skimming speed. Each of the other speeds will receive attention in later chapters.

Category	Skimming
Rate	As fast as you possibly can
Purpose	To plan
	To organize
	To evaluate
	To get a general impression
Typical uses	Thumbing through a book or magazine to decide if you want to buy or read it
	Paging through a story that an acquaintance wrote for a literary contest that you do not really want to read
	Flipping through a class assignment to estimate the amount of time you need to complete it
	Glancing or thumbing through a newspaper or magazine until something of interest catches your attention

As you skim ''Take This Fish and Look at It,'' try to notice answers to the following questions, but do not slow down or stop as you spot them.

1. Who describes this experience? How old is he? Where does the experience take place?
2. When does this experience happen? How much time has passed between the experience and this description of the experience?
3. Why does the man recall his student experience?

3.2 DESCRIPTION

Samuel H. Scudder   *''TAKE THIS FISH AND LOOK AT IT''*

It was more than fifteen years ago that I entered the laboratory of Professor Agassiz, and told him I had enrolled my name in the Scientific School as a student of natural history. He asked me a few questions about my object in coming, my antecedents generally, the mode in which I afterwards proposed to use the knowledge I might acquire, and, finally, whether I wished to study any special branch. To the latter I replied that, while I wished to be well grounded in all departments of zoology, I purposed to devote myself specially to insects.

''When do you wish to begin?'' he asked.

Copyright © 1985 by Harcourt Brace Jovanovich, Inc. All rights reserved.

"Now," I replied.

This seemed to please him, and with an energetic "Very well!" he reached from a shelf a huge jar of specimens in yellow alcohol. "Take this fish," he said, "and look at it; we call it a haemulon; by and by I will ask what you have seen."

With that he left me, but in a moment returned with explicit instructions as to the care of the object entrusted to me.

"No man is fit to be a naturalist," said he, "who does not know how to take care of specimens."

I was to keep the fish before me in a tin tray, and occasionally moisten the surface with alcohol from the jar, always taking care to replace the stopper tightly. Those were not the days of ground-glass stoppers and elegantly shaped exhibition jars; all the old students will recall the huge neckless glass bottles with their leaky, wax-besmeared corks, half eaten by insects, and begrimed with cellar dust. Entomology was a cleaner science than ichthyology, but the example of the Professor, who had unhesitatingly plunged to the bottom of the jar to produce the fish, was infectious; and though this alcohol had a "very ancient and fishlike smell," I really dared not show any aversion within these sacred precincts, and treated the alcohol as though it were pure water. Still I was conscious of a passing feeling of disappointment, for gazing at a fish did not command itself to an ardent entomologist. My friends at home, too, were annoyed when they discovered that no amount of eau-de-Cologne would drown the perfume which haunted me like a shadow.

In ten minutes I had seen all that could be seen in that fish, and started in search of the Professor—who had, however, left the Museum; and when I returned, after lingering over some of the odd animals stored in the upper apartment, my specimen was dry all over. I dashed the fluid over the fish as if to resuscitate the beast from a fainting fit, and looked with anxiety for a return of the normal sloppy appearance. This little excitement over, nothing was to be done but to return to a steadfast gaze at my mute companion. Half an hour passed—an hour—another hour; the fish began to look loathsome. I turned it over and around; looked it in the face—ghastly; from behind, beneath, above, sideways, at a three-quarters' view—just as ghastly. I was

Copyright © 1985 by Harcourt Brace Jovanovich, Inc. All rights reserved.

in despair; at an early hour I concluded that lunch was necessary; so, with infinite relief, the fish was carefully replaced in the jar, and for an hour I was free.

On my return, I learned that Professor Agassiz had been at the Museum, but had gone, and would not return for several hours. My fellow-students were too busy to be disturbed by continued conversation. Slowly I drew forth that hideous fish, and with a feeling of desperation again looked at it. I might not use a magnifying-glass; instruments of all kinds were interdicted. My two hands, my two eyes, and the fish: it seemed a most limited field. I pushed my finger down its throat to feel how sharp the teeth were. I began to count the scales in the different rows, until I was convinced that was nonsense. At last a happy thought struck me—I would draw the fish; and now with surprise I began to discover new features in the creature. Just then the Professor returned.

"That is right," said he; "a pencil is one of the best of eyes. I am glad to notice, too, that you keep your specimen wet, and your bottle corked."

With these encouraging words, he added:

"Well, what is it like?"

He listened attentively to my brief rehearsal of the structure of parts whose names were still unknown to me; the fringed gill-arches and movable operculum; the pores of the head, fleshy lips and lidless eyes; the lateral line, the spinous fins and forked tail; the compressed and arched body. When I finished, he waited as if expecting more, and then, with an air of disappointment:

"You have not looked very carefully; why," he continued more earnestly, "you haven't even seen one of the most conspicuous features of the animal, which is plainly before your eyes as the fish itself; look again, look again!" and he left me to my misery.

I was piqued; I was mortified. Still more of that wretched fish! But now I set myself to my task with a will, and discovered one new thing after another, until I saw how just the Professor's criticism had been. The afternoon passed quickly; and when, towards its close, the Professor inquired:

"Do you see it yet?"

Copyright © 1985 by Harcourt Brace Jovanovich, Inc. All rights reserved.

"No," I replied, "I am certain I do not, but I see how little I saw before."

"That is next best," said he, earnestly, "but I won't hear you now; put away your fish and go home; perhaps you will be ready with a better answer in the morning. I will examine you before you look at the fish."

This was disconcerting. Not only must I think of my fish all night, studying, without the object before me, what this unknown but most visible feature might be; but also, without reviewing my discoveries, I must give an exact account of them the next day. I had a bad memory; so I walked home by Charles River in a distracted state, with my two perplexities.

The cordial greeting from the Professor the next morning was reassuring; here was a man who seemed to be quite an anxious as I that I should see for myself what he saw.

"Do you perhaps mean," I asked, "that the fish has symmetrical sides with paired organs?"

His thoroughly pleased "Of course! Of course!" repaid the wakeful hours of the previous night. After he had discoursed most happily and enthusiastically—as he always did—upon the importance of this point, I ventured to ask what I should do next.

"Oh, look at your fish!" he said, and left me again to my own devices. In a little more than an hour he returned, and heard my new catalogue.

"That is good, that is good!" he repeated; "but that is not all; go on"; and so for three long days he placed that fish before my eyes, forbidding me to look at anything else, or to use any artificial aid. "Look, look, look," was his repeated injunction.

This was the best entomological lesson I ever had—a lesson whose influence has extended to the details of every subsequent study; a legacy the Professor had left to me, as he has left it to so many others, of inestimable value, which we could not buy, with which we cannot part.

A year afterward, some of us were amusing ourselves with chalking outlandish beasts on the Museum blackboard. We drew prancing starfishes; frogs in mortal combat; hydra-headed worms; stately crawfishes, standing on their tails, bearing aloft

Copyright © 1985 by Harcourt Brace Jovanovich, Inc. All rights reserved.

umbrellas; and grotesque fishes with gaping mouths and staring eyes. The Professor came in shortly after, and was as amused as any at our experiments. He looked at the fishes.

"Haemulons, every one of them," he said; "Mr. ——— drew them."

True; and to this day, if I attempt a fish, I can draw nothing but haemulons.

The fourth day, a second fish of the same group was placed beside the first, and I was bidden to point out the resemblances and differences between the two; another and another followed, until the entire family lay before me, and a whole legion of jars covered the table and surrounding shelves; the odor had become a pleasant perfume; and even now, the sight of an old, six-inch, worm-eaten cork brings fragrant memories.

The whole group of hacmulons was thus brought in review; and, whether engaged upon the dissection of the internal organs, the preparation and examination of the bony framework, or the description of the various parts, Agassiz's training in the method of observing facts and their orderly arrangement was ever accompanied by the urgent exhortation not to be content with them.

"Facts are stupid things," he would say, "until brought into connection with some general law."

At the end of eight months, it was almost with reluctance that I left these friends and turned to insects; but what I had gained by this outside experience has been of greater value than years of later investigation in my favorite groups.

Copyright © 1985 by Harcourt Brace Jovanovich, Inc. All rights reserved.

3.3 UNDERSTANDING WHAT YOU READ

EXERCISE 1

Now that you have skimmed the selection, answer these questions to see how much you can learn from skimming an assignment.

1. How long do you think it will take you to reread the selection to find answers to

    the questions in Exercise 2? _____

    _____

2. What kind of experience did you notice that the narrator talks about? _____

    _____

3. What kinds of people, in your opinion, would most likely be interested in the

    story Scudder tells? _____

    _____

4. Will you use a pencil to underline and make notes as you seek answers to the

    questions in Exercise 2? _____

    _____

   Skimming saves a reader time in the long run. You will find that having skimmed the selection will make rereading it for information faster and easier. A full discussion of how to read for information is in Unit Six. For now, read at a rate at which you can find answers to the following questions. Doing so will help you discover the reading rate most comfortable to you for finding information.

EXERCISE 2

1. Can you list three details about the narrator (the person the experience happened

    to) such as his age, his occupation, his location? _____

    _____

    _____

2. In your opinion, has the passing of time between the experience and the telling

Copyright © 1985 by Harcourt Brace Jovanovich, Inc. All rights reserved.

of it affected the narrator? How? _____

_____

_____

3. What do you think the narrator wants you to learn from his experience? In other words, can you imagine why he tells you this episode from his school days?

_____

_____

3.4 DISCOVERING IDEAS FOR WRITING

Fix in your mind a mental picture of a particular place, either a room or a building, where an event you remember occurred. Jot responses to the following questions to help you discover ideas and information to use in your essay (Section 3.6).

1. How old were you when this event took place? _____

_____

2. What were you wearing? _____

_____

3. Where did this event take place? What specific features of the place do you re-

call? _____

_____

4. Does this event evoke pleasant or unpleasant memories for you? _____

_____

5. How many people know about this event and what reaction did they have or do

you imagine they might have when they are told? _____

_____

6. In what ways has your understanding of the event changed since it occurred?

_____

Copyright © 1985 by Harcourt Brace Jovanovich, Inc. All rights reserved.

3.5 UNDERSTANDING WRITING

Getting started, most professional writers agree, is the most difficult part of writing. Because getting started is so difficult, writers develop personal habits that help them begin writing. If you have trouble getting started, you need to find some way to overcome your block. Even though you must eventually develop your own personal and unique routine for getting started, you may benefit from knowing how some professional writers have overcome their blocks.

A blank sheet of paper frightens most writers, and all writers have to discover a way to overcome this fear. To keep from having to face a blank page, Ernest Hemingway would interrupt himself in the middle of writing a paragraph so that he could return to a partially filled page the next time he sat down to write. That way he never had to start over again; he only had to continue. Other writers make lists of points they want to cover and write those lists on the strangest sorts of material, often chosen because they have some writing on them and are not blank. Typical materials used are gum wrappers, backs of old envelopes, and old cash register receipts. These writers never have to begin with a blank page since there is something already written on the materials they choose. Further, the size of the materials they choose limits how much they can write. An obvious advantage to getting started with a small piece of paper is that once that small piece of paper is filled, the writing can be transferred quickly to a blank page. Then the page is no longer blank.

Other habits experienced writers use to get started include making sure they have a clean desk and a supply of sharpened pencils. While they are clearing the desk and sharpening the pencils, they think about how they will start. These routines keep them from sitting at the desk staring at a blank sheet of paper while they are trying to begin writing. Still others overcome their writing block by writing letters to friends to "warm up." Writing thoughts and ideas in a journal provides yet another routine for getting started. Each of these routines eases you from non-writing towards writing and allows you to fuss with something connected with writing without meeting the writing task head on.

When you experience difficulty getting started, you may want to try one of these routines. If the one you have chosen works, fine; if not, try another. Because getting-started routines are entirely personal, you may find that none of these helps. If so, you will have to discover your own: you may have to put on a particular article of clothing, sit on a special chair, or have a certain color tablet of paper. Once you find a routine that helps you get started, use it every time you need to write. Do not hesitate to admit that you need the routine.

Modern technology has expanded the possible routines writers can use to get started. Those who compose while using a typewriter, cassette recorder, or word processor will get started in ways different from those who write with pencil or ballpoint. Regardless of your writing equipment, you must find a routine that will get you past your writing block and help you get started.

Copyright © 1985 by Harcourt Brace Jovanovich, Inc. All rights reserved.

3.6 WRITING—DESCRIPTION

Your responses to the questions in Section 3.3 have helped you understand the effect of time on an experience and what a person can learn from looking back on that experience. You gathered information about the narrator, his location, and people he worked with. Now remember the experience you explored in Section 3.4 that time has allowed you to view in a different way from the way you viewed it when it was happening. Think about details describing how old you were, what you were wearing, where you were, and how you felt at that time as well as your responses to the other questions in Section 3.4. All of these discovery activities are preliminary to drafting a description.

In a description, a writer presents details about people, places, objects, and feelings. As Scudder does in his, you can help to fix mental images in your reader's mind in your description by using specifics, particularly adjectives and concrete nouns.

In your description, you will focus on yourself, the other people, the place, and the feelings that were part of the event at the time it happened. Then you will describe the change(s) that has (have) occurred in your understanding of that event. In other words, you will tell your reader the effect time has had on understanding of the event.

WRITING ASSIGNMENT

Draft a 350- to 500-word description of the event that you remember. Your draft is your first version of your description and is an opportunity for you to rediscover the event for yourself and to explore what that event meant to you then and what it means to you now.

Reminder: For a full review of your responsibilities as a writer and of the composing process, return to Section 1.6. First, you discover ideas for writing, draft those ideas, revise your draft for your audience (your peer editor), revise after consideration of your peer editor's suggestions, proofread your paper to find any errors you overlooked. Finally, submit all versions of your writing and Editor's Evaluations to your instructor. Of course, you are really working on your final copy from the moment you begin to discover ideas, so don't think you will finish one writing activity before you begin another. You can always return to any writing activity at any time until you submit your essay. Remember that your instructor can answer questions and offer suggestions while you are writing. In this way, you can have immediate feedback without your instructor's having to read and mark your drafts. Your final version is likely to be far better if you seek your instructor's advice.

Copyright © 1985 by Harcourt Brace Jovanovich, Inc. All rights reserved.

3.7 *THE WRITING PROCESS*

During the drafting of a piece of writing you will pause from time to time to reread a passage you have written to see what you will write next. As you reread what you have written, you can also pay attention to your subjects and verbs. You can check for formal agreement between your subjects and verbs. At the same time you can test to see that there is a logical connection between them. Good writers make it easy for readers to connect subjects and verbs.

While rereading a passage you have written, it is not unusual to find mistakes in agreement. Even experienced writers make agreement errors in drafts, but they search them out and correct them before allowing anyone to read their writing. Questions 1 through 7 below will guide you through a process very similar to the one that experienced writers use and will help you identify any agreement errors you may have between your subjects and verbs. As you gain experience, you will automatically check your subjects and verbs whenever you reread something you have written. Until you do, use these questions to help you get your subjects and verbs to agree.

On occasion while checking over subject-verb agreement, experienced writers discover that they have buried the most important idea within the sentence. Because readers expect the subject of each sentence will usually carry the most important idea in that sentence, writers change those sentences to fulfill the reader's expectation. On other occasions they find that the logical subject is hidden by phrases such as "the fact is that," "the thing is," "it is my opinion that." At other times the logical subject is buried in other places such as in a prepositional phrase. For example, the following sentence contains the logical subject in a prepositional phrase.

Faulty   About dissecting the fish, it was difficult.
Improved   Dissecting the fish was difficult.

Questions 1 through 7 will guide you as you reconsider what you have written. Your responses to the questions will suggest ways for you to revise your writing before you give it to your reader so that each subject is always clearly expressed. Work through the first seven questions for each sentence before moving on to the next sentence. As you do so, be sure to use different colors as suggested because the colors will make it easier for you to spot where you need to revise. You should use these questions to guide your revisions for any essays you will write in the future until they become second nature.

1. Can you identify a verb in each of your sentences? (*Hint*: Using a colored pencil, put a box around the verb or verbs.)
2. Can you identify the complete subject in each of your sentences? (*Hint*: Using a pencil of a different color, underline the complete subject.)
3. Can you identify the simple subject in each of your sentences? (*Hint*: Circle the simple subject in the color you used to underline the complete subject.)

Copyright © 1985 by Harcourt Brace Jovanovich, Inc. All rights reserved.

4. Do the subjects and verbs of your sentences agree? (*Hint*: Connect the simple subject to the verb with a line. Then check to see if you need an "s" on your verb. Remember the rule of thumb: if a verb ends in an "s," the subject usually does not. If your subject and verb both end in "s," check the agreement again.)

5. How many of your subjects are words like "fact," "it," or "thing"? (*Hint*: Number them inside the circle you drew around your simple subject.)

6. Should you change any of the words you numbered to make your sentence exact and specific? (*Hint*: Do you have clauses such as "the fact is that . . . ," "the thing I like is . . . ," "it is my opinion . . ." which can be removed without changing your intended meaning?)

7. Is there some other part of the sentences identified in question 6 that states what you really intended to write about? (*Hint*: Sometimes a logical subject is buried in a prepositional phrase.)

8. How many sentences have you changed after considering the above questions?

9. Do you think that the changes will make your ideas clearer to your reader?

10. Do you feel a sense of satisfaction from having revised your writing?

3.8 PARAGRAPH POWER

The basic pattern you have learned for paragraph development, T-R-I-I, may take a variety of proven forms. Generally, a writer's choice of a particular form of development is determined by subject, audience, and purpose. That is, if you wish to write about an enormous tree you have observed in a redwood forest and you want to make someone who has never seen one visualize such a tree, you will most likely choose the descriptive form of development. Here you will learn to apply the T-R-I-I pattern to write a descriptive paragraph. Though a paragraph may contain several forms of development, often one dominates all others. In other words, when writing a descriptive paragraph, you may include narration though the major form of development is description. Such mixture of forms is the norm in good writing, and it is rare to find paragraphs with a single form. Nevertheless, learning the forms is useful because it will give you a variety of ways to develop or expand your ideas.

Description brings facts and details to bear upon a subject. These facts are concrete, sensory details which make your subject more immediate to your reader. For instance, if you are describing the tree, you may first note its most general features such as height, color, and the amount of space it occupies. Then you may move on to a description of the particular texture of the bark and color of the leaves; finally, you may note individual features that distinguish the tree you have in mind from others of its kind. Does your tree have a broken branch? a scar on the trunk? a peculiar forking pattern of the branches? This development of a descriptive paragraph goes from generalities to specific features. You could just as easily organize your para-

Copyright © 1985 by Harcourt Brace Jovanovich, Inc. All rights reserved.

graph in the reverse order, beginning with the specific features and moving to more general characteristics. Indeed, there are other options for organizing such a descriptive paragraph—to view the tree from top to bottom or from core outward, for example. For now, try to use the pattern of general to specific.

EXERCISE 1

Identify the topic, restriction, and illustrations in this paragraph from Scudder's "Take This Fish and Look at It." Underline the topic sentence, circle the restriction, and draw boxes around the illustrations.

I was to keep the fish before me in a tin tray, and occasionally moisten the surface with alcohol from the jar, always taking care to replace the stopper tightly. Those were not the days of ground-glass stoppers and elegantly shaped exhibition jars; all the old students will recall the huge neckless glass bottles with their leaky, wax-besmeared corks, half eaten by insects, and begrimed with cellar dust. Entomology was a cleaner science than ichthyology, but the example of the Professor, who had unhesitatingly plunged to the bottom of the jar to produce the fish, was infectious; and though this alcohol had a "very ancient and fishlike smell," I really dared not show any aversion within these sacred precincts, and treated the alcohol as though it were pure water. Still I was conscious of a passing feeling of disappointment, for gazing at a fish did not commend itself to an ardent entomologist. My friends at home, too, were annoyed when they discovered that no amount of eau-de-Cologne would drown the perfume which haunted me like a shadow.

EXERCISE 2

The paragraph in Exercise 1 contains many descriptive details. List descriptive words or phrases about bottles and stoppers.

_____   _____

_____   _____

_____   _____

_____   _____

Copyright © 1985 by Harcourt Brace Jovanovich, Inc. All rights reserved.

EXERCISE 3

The paragraph beginning "He listened attentively . . ." contains many details of the specific features of a particular kind of fish. List them below.

_____	_____
_____	_____

EXERCISE 4

Plan the development of your own descriptive paragraph using details from Section 3.4 and follow the suggested T-R-I-I pattern (topic, restriction, illustration, illustration). Review details from Section 3.4 and use them as you design your paragraph in the space provided. You may want to revise a paragraph from your draft, or you may want to write a new one to be added or to replace another paragraph in your next version of your description (Section 3.6).

In this paragraph, describe a building or a part of a building to a forty-year-old person who has never seen it. Include the features that make you react to the building or part of the building the way you do. Strive to use details in each of the boxes as you construct your descriptive paragraph. If you find you do not have enough details in Section 3.4 to complete the boxes, explore your memory again for additional details.

Copyright © 1985 by Harcourt Brace Jovanovich, Inc. All rights reserved.

Make a general statement about the place expressing a dominant image or impression.

T

Suggest why you have this impression.

R

Develop this impression by selecting the indicated kinds of details.

I	I	I
Activities in the building (real or imagined)	Construction materials	Architectural features

Copyright © 1985 by Harcourt Brace Jovanovich, Inc. All rights reserved.

Notes

3.9 *SENTENCE POWER*

CLAUSES

Once you grasp the concept of a sentence and can identify subjects and verbs, you are ready to work with clauses. Like sentences, clauses contain subjects and verbs. Some clauses can be sentences; however, not all clauses can stand as a sentence.

The English language has only two kinds of clauses. The first kind, a **main clause** or **independent clause**, has the same features as a sentence and sometimes is one.

> subj.   vb.
> He   asked   me a few questions.

It contains a subject and a verb, expresses an idea, and is perceived as a complete unit. With the proper punctuation, it can always stand as a sentence.

The second kind, a **subordinate clause** or **dependent clause**, also has a subject and a verb and expresses an idea, but a dependent clause is perceived as an **incomplete** unit because the first word of a dependent clause *links* or *relates* or *connects* it to an independent clause. For this reason, a dependent clause can never stand as a complete sentence.

> link   subj.   vb.
> When   he   asked   me a question

Responding to the questions about the following examples will help you grasp the idea of clauses and will help you understand the differences between an independent clause and a dependent clause. Study the examples by completing the blanks. Answers are furnished in the discussion following the questions.

A.   He asked me a few questions.

    1.   Find the verb: _____

    2.   Find the subject: _____

    3.   Does this sentence express an idea? _____

    4.   Do you perceive this sentence as a complete unit? _____

If you filled in *asked* in the first blank, *he* in the second, and *yes* in the third and fourth blanks, you see that the sentence fulfills the requirements for an independent clause. If you did not, study the example again.

B.   He asked me a few questions when I entered his office.

    1.   Find the verb of the independent clause: _____

    2.   Find the subject of the independent clause: _____

Copyright © 1985 by Harcourt Brace Jovanovich, Inc. All rights reserved.

3.   Find the verb of the dependent clause: _____

4.   Find the subject of the dependent clause: _____

5.   Find the first word of the dependent clause: _____
(*Hint*: This word links the dependent clause to the independent clause.)

If you filled the first blank with *asked*, the second with *he*, the third with *entered*, the fourth with *I*, and the fifth with *when*, you recognized that the dependent clause contains an idea that is related to the idea in the independent clause, and you recognized which idea was the more important of the two.

Good writers help their readers understand the relationships among their ideas by careful placement of them. Although many writers strive to place their most important idea in the independent clause, the most important idea may be placed in either a dependent clause or an independent clause. The first word in the dependent clause links the two ideas. These linking (connecting) words show the different kinds of relationships the ideas express. When you see that some of your ideas are more important than others and when you place your secondary ideas and your main ideas in their proper relationships, you will have made a major step toward improving your writing. Sentences that contain both an independent and a dependent clause are the sentences written most frequently by published writers. In fact, Edgar Allan Poe wrote this type of sentence (complex sentence) more than fifty percent of the time.

Refer to the chart that identifies five ways to link dependent clauses to independent clauses.

The chart of patterns for dependent clauses shows ways of linking dependent and independent clauses. Every linking word or phrase on the chart can attach a dependent clause to an independent clause. Dependent clauses can appear (a) before the independent clause begins, (b) after the independent clause ends or even (c) in the

---

Five Kinds of Links to Introduce Dependent Clauses

To link by
time   after, as long as, as soon as, before, once, since, till, until, when, whenever, while

place   where, wherever

reason   as, because, how, in order that, so that, since

condition   although, even though, even if, if, in case (that), once, though, unless, whether

additional information   that, which, who (whom), whose

Copyright © 1985 by Harcourt Brace Jovanovich, Inc. All rights reserved.

Dependent clauses appear in *italics.* Linking words appear in **boldface.**

a. At the beginning:

Time
After   }
As long as   }
As soon as   }
Before   }
Once   }
Since   }
Till   }
Until   }
When   }
Whenever   }
While   }
Place
Where   }
Wherever   }
Reason
As   }   *Dependent clause,* independent clause.
Because   }   **Example   When** *I entered the laboratory,* I was some-
In order that }   what nervous.
How   }
So that   }
Since   }
Condition
Although   }
Even though   }
Even if   }
If   }
In case (that) }
Once   }
Though   }
Unless   }
Whether   }
**Additional
information**
That   }
Which   }
Who   }
Whose   }

b. At the end: Independent clause **since** *dependent clause.*
                        Example   I was somewhat nervous **when** *I entered the*
                                      laboratory.

c. In the middle: Independent **after** *dependent clause* clause.
                        Example   I was, **when** *I entered the laboratory,* some-
                                      what nervous.

middle of the independent clause. Regardless of the position, the linking word or phrase, stated or understood, marks the beginning of a dependent clause.

PUNCTUATING DEPENDENT CLAUSES

Punctuating dependent clauses is not difficult when you keep in mind the three rules outlined here, with examples to compare to each other.

1. A comma **generally** follows introductory dependent clauses.

    Example   *When Mary broke her foot*, I went to see her.

2. When a dependent clause follows an independent clause, use a comma between them *only* when the dependent clause gives additional information about a noun that comes *immediately* before it. If a comma is used, the dependent clause must provide additional information about a noun.

    Example   I went to see Mary, *who broke her foot*.

    but

    Example   I dissected the fish *that Professor Agassiz kept in a jar*.

    When adverbial dependent clauses (those which show time, place, reason, or condition) come at the end of the sentence, they are rarely separated from the independent clause by a comma or any other mark of punctuation.

    Example   I went to see Mary *when she broke her foot*.

3. Sometimes commas separate dependent clauses occurring in the middle of the independent clause; sometimes they do not. If commas are used, they must be used in a pair.

    Example   I went, *when she broke her foot*, to see Mary.

EXERCISE 1

Underline each dependent clause in the following sentences; then draw a box around the linking word. Identify the kind of relationship shown between the two clauses by the linking word by writing *time*, *place*, *reason*, *condition*, or *additional information* on the blank provided.

Example   I was somewhat nervous [when] I entered the laboratory.

time _____

Copyright © 1985 by Harcourt Brace Jovanovich, Inc. All rights reserved.

1. I entered the laboratory where Professor Agassiz taught.

   _____

2. I hoped that I might acquire special knowledge about insects.

   _____

3. Professor Agassiz asked me whether I wished to study any special subject.

   _____

4. He showed me where I was to put the fish.

   _____

5. My friends were annoyed when they discovered my smell.

   _____

6. No amount of eau de cologne would drown the perfume which haunted me.

   _____

7. After I stared at the fish for ten minutes, I had seen all that could be seen in that fish.

   _____

8. I started to search for Professor Agassiz, who had left the museum, that afternoon.

   _____

9. When I returned, I dashed the fluid over the drying fish.

   _____

10. Because the fish began to look loathsome, I found myself getting nauseated.

    _____

11. I was in despair since no relief was in sight.

    _____

12. I drew forth that hideous fish which I had been staring at for hours.

    _____

Copyright © 1985 by Harcourt Brace Jovanovich, Inc. All rights reserved.

13. I counted the scales on the fish until I was tired.

   _____

14. My task, whether I liked it or not, was to discover something new about the fish.

   _____

15. The afternoon passed quickly until the professor arrived.

   _____

16. The professor examined me before I realized it.

   _____

17. The professor, who seemed to be quite anxious, wanted me to see all that he saw.

   _____

18. When he left me to my own devices, I amused myself by chalking outlandish beasts on the board.

   _____

19. Although I had been looking at the fish for hours, apparently, I had not yet seen everything.

   _____

20. Facts are stupid things until they are brought into connection with some general law.

   _____

Copyright © 1985 by Harcourt Brace Jovanovich, Inc. All rights reserved.

SENTENCE TYPES

Effective combination of clauses, independent and dependent, permits you to write all four structural sentence types. The number and kinds of clauses in a sentence are the keys to classifying any sentence into one of the four structural types: *simple*, *compound*, *complex*, and *compound-complex*.

Perhaps comparing the combinations of clauses that produce the four structural sentence types to the effects that can be achieved in dress will help make the concept of these four structural sentence types clear. Think of the independent (main) clause as a plain, well-tailored dress. A woman in this dress is fully clothed and can appear anywhere in public without embarrassment. A **simple sentence** *contains one independent clause*, and as this dress is basic to a woman's wardrobe, so the simple sentence is basic for a writer. The questions below will help you understand simple sentences.

EXAMPLES

A.   Professor Agassiz taught ichthyology.

    1.   Find the verb. _____

    2.   Find the subject. _____

    3.   How many independent clauses in this sentence? _____

    4.   What is the name of the structural sentence type? _____

B.   Sam and his friends hated the smell of the fish.

    1.   Find the verb. _____

    2.   Find the subject(s). _____

    3.   How many subjects in this sentence? _____

    4.   How many verbs in this sentence? _____

    5.   What word joins the subjects? _____
       (*Hint*: **And** is a coordinate conjunction and can join like elements.)

    6.   Do you agree that the subject is a compound subject? _____
       (*Hint*: When two like elements are joined by a coordinate conjunction, they are called **compound**.)

Copyright © 1985 by Harcourt Brace Jovanovich, Inc. All rights reserved.

7. What special kind of conjunction joins the two subjects? _____

8. How many clauses in this sentence? _____

9. What is the structural sentence type? _____

C. Professor Agassiz examined and evaluated Sam's work.

1. Find the verb(s). _____

2. Find the subject. _____

3. How many subjects in this sentence? _____

4. How many verbs in this sentence? _____

5. What word joins the verbs? _____

6. Do you agree that the verb is a compound verb? _____

7. What special kind of conjunction joins the two verbs? _____

8. How many clauses in this sentence? _____

9. What is the structural sentence type? _____

Answers

A. 1. taught;   2. Professor Agassiz;   3. one;   4. simple
B. 1. hated;   2. Sam, friends;   3. two;   4. one;   5. and;   6. yes;   7. coordinate;   8. one;   9. simple
C. 1. examined, evaluated;   2. Professor Agassiz;   3. one;   4. two;   5. and;   6. yes;   7. coordinate;   8. one;   9. simple

Compound sentences can also be explained by comparing them to dressing. In cold weather, a woman probably feels a need for a coat to keep her warm. If so, she may add a coat to her dress. The dress and the coat, two separate garments, could function independently of each other because each serves a different purpose. When the woman wears them at the same time, though, their effect is greater than the effect either could produce independently: they work together to keep her warm. Think of the second (or third or fourth) independent clause in a compound sentence as a coat.

Just as the woman would only wear a coat when it serves her purpose, independent clauses should only be joined (connected) to achieve a particular effect. When two independent clauses—the dress and the coat—are properly joined together, the result is a compound sentence. In fact, a woman *could* wear a dress, a long sweater-coat,

Copyright © 1985 by Harcourt Brace Jovanovich, Inc. All rights reserved.

an outer coat, and a raincoat, should the weather warrant. However, rather than wear three coats, most women would choose some other means of keeping warm. Just as wearing several coats is possible, connecting several independent clauses is possible. Regardless of the number of independent clauses in a sentence, the sentence type remains compound if every clause in the sentence is independent. In other words, a compound sentence cannot contain a dependent clause. The questions below will help you understand compound sentences.

EXAMPLES

D.   Professor Agassiz teaches ichthyology, and he evaluates students.

1.   Find the verb in the first independent clause. _____

2.   Find the subject in the first independent clause. _____

3.   Find the verb in the second independent clause. _____

4.   Find the subject in the second independent clause. _____

5.   What special kind of conjunction joins the two clauses? _____

6.   What, if anything, appears immediately before the word joining the two

clauses? _____

7.   How many clauses in this sentence? _____

8.   What is the structural sentence type? _____

E.   Sam hated the smell of fish; his friends did too.

1.   Find the verb in the first independent clause. _____

2.   Find the subject in the first independent clause. _____

3.   Find the verb in the second independent clause. _____

4.   Find the subject in the second independent clause. _____

5.   What special kind of punctuation joins the two clauses? _____

6.   How many clauses in this sentence? _____

7.   What is the structural sentence type? _____

Copyright © 1985 by Harcourt Brace Jovanovich, Inc. All rights reserved.

Answers

D. 1. teaches; 2. Professor Agassiz; 3. evaluates; 4. he; 5. coordinates; 6. comma;
    7. two; 8. compound
E. 1. hated; 2. Sam; 3. did; 4. friends; 5. ; (semicolon); 6. two; 7. compound

We can continue the comparison between sentence types and dressing to explain complex sentences. When wearing a simple dress, a woman often chooses to add an accessory—scarf, belt, jewelry—which will modify or change the appearance of the dress. Her choice of accessories should be appropriate for the kind of event she plans to attend. Her choice will be different if she plans to attend a funeral from her choice if she plans to attend a dance.

The accessories, when attached to a dress or a coat in any way, can represent **dependent clauses**. Worn by themselves, scarves, belts, or jewelry would be ludicrous and inappropriate at any time. Just as custom calls for linking accessories to a dress, usage demands that dependent clauses be linked to independent clauses. When you have linked a dependent clause to an independent clause, you have written a complex sentence. A **complex sentence consists of** *a single independent clause and at least one dependent clause* (**but possibly more**). Just as a woman uses judgment when choosing the kind and number of accessories to attach to her clothing, so a writer uses judgment when deciding the number of dependent clauses to link to a single independent clause. If a woman were wearing a diamond brooch, three strands of pearls, and a leather cowboy belt with a large rodeo buckle, most people would think she was wearing at least one too many accessories. The principle can guide you in writing complex sentences. Work through the following questions to gain understanding of complex sentences.

EXAMPLES

F. When Professor Agassiz taught ichthyology, Sam worked in his laboratory.

  1. What separates the two clauses? _____

  2. What is the first word of the independent clause? _____

      the last word? _____

  3. Find the verb of the independent clause. _____

  4. Find the subject of the independent clause. _____

  5. What is the first word of the dependent clause? _____

      the last word? _____

Copyright © 1985 by Harcourt Brace Jovanovich, Inc. All rights reserved.

6. Find the verb of the dependent clause. _____

7. Find the subject of the dependent clause. _____

8. What is the word that links or joins the dependent clause to the independent clause? _____

9. Which of the five kinds of relationships does the linking word show between the dependent and independent clauses? _____

10. What is the structural sentence type? _____

G. Professor Agassiz, who taught ichthyology, evaluated and examined the students.

1. What separates the two clauses? _____

2. What is the first word of the independent clause? _____

the last word? _____

3. Find the verb of the independent clause. _____

4. Find the subject of the independent clause. _____

5. What is the first word of the dependent clause? _____

the last word? _____

6. Find the verb of the dependent clause. _____

7. Find the subject of the dependent clause. _____

8. What is the word that links or joins the dependent clause to the independent clause? _____

9. Which of the five kinds of relationships does the linking word (conjunction) show between the dependent and independent clauses? _____

_____

10. What is the structural sentence type? _____

Copyright © 1985 by Harcourt Brace Jovanovich, Inc. All rights reserved.

H.   Sam disliked working in the laboratory because the fish smell lingered on him hours after he had left.

1.   Does any punctuation separate the clauses? _____

2.   What is the first word of the independent clause? _____

the last word? _____

3.   Find the verb of the independent clause. _____

4.   Find the subject of the independent clause. _____

5.   What is the word that links or joins the dependent clause immediately following the independent clause to it. _____

6.   What is the first word of this dependent clause? _____

the last word? _____

7.   Find the verb of this dependent clause. _____

8.   Find the subject of this dependent clause. _____

9.   Which of the five kinds of relationships does the linking word (conjunction) show between this dependent clause and the sentence? _____

10.   What is the word that links or joins the last dependent clause to the sentence? _____

11.   What is the first word of this dependent clause? _____

the last word? _____

12.   Find the verb of this dependent clause. _____

13.   Find the subject of this dependent clause. _____

14.   Which of the five kinds of relationships does the linking word (conjunction) show to the sentence? _____

15.   What is the structural sentence type? _____

Copyright © 1985 by Harcourt Brace Jovanovich, Inc. All rights reserved.

I. Although Sam enjoyed the study of ichthyology, he disliked working in the laboratory because the fish smell lingered on him hours after he had left.

   1. What is the first word of the independent clause? _____

      the last word? _____

   2. Find the verb of the independent clause. _____

   3. Find the subject of the independent clause. _____

   4. What is the first word of the introductory dependent clause? _____

      the last word? _____

   5. Find the verb of the introductory dependent clause. _____

   6. Find the subject of the introductory dependent clause. _____

   7. What is the word that links or joins the introductory dependent clause to the sentence? _____

   8. Which of the five kinds of relationships does the linking word (conjunction) show between the dependent clause and the sentence? _____

   9. What punctuation follows introductory dependent clauses immediately preceding an independent clause? _____

  10. What is the first word of the dependent clause which immediately follows the independent clause? _____the last word? _____

  11. Which of the five kinds of relationships does the linking word (conjunction) show to the sentence? _____

  12. What is the first word of the last dependent clause in the sentence? _____

      _____the last word? _____

  13. Which of the five kinds of relationships does the linking word (conjunction) show to the sentence? _____

  14. What is the structural sentence type? _____

Copyright © 1985 by Harcourt Brace Jovanovich, Inc. All rights reserved.

Answers

F. 1. comma;   2. Sam, laboratory;   3. worked;   4. Sam;   5. when, ichthyology;
    6. taught;   7. Professor Agassiz;   8. when;   9. time;   10. complex
G. 1. commas;   2. Professor Agassiz, student;   3. evaluated, examined;   4. Professor
    Agassiz;   5. who, ichthyology;   6. taught;   7. who;   8. who;   9. additional informa-
    tion;   10. complex
H. 1. no;   2. Sam, laboratory;   3. disliked;   4. Sam;   5. because;   6. because, ours;
    7. lingered;   8. smell;   9. reason;   10. after;   11. after, left;   12. had left;   13. he;
    14. time;   15. complex
I. 1. he, laboratory;   2. disliked;   3. he;   4. although, ichthyology;   5. enjoyed;
    6. Sam;   7. although;   8. condition;   9. comma;   10. because, hours;   11. reason;
    12. after, left;   13. time;   14. complex

(*Hint*: The subject and verb in the independent (main) clause are sometimes called the *main subject* and the *main verb* to distinguish them from the subjects and verbs of the dependent clauses.)

The final structural sentence type is the compound-complex sentence. By combining a simple sentence and a complex sentence you can create a compound-complex sentence. Think once more of the dress and the coat. Remember that both the coat and the dress represent independent clauses and that the addition of an accessory to either represents a dependent clause. A **compound-complex sentence must contain** *at least two independent clauses and at least one dependent clause*. Though it might be possible to combine as many dependent and independent clauses as you choose in a compound-complex sentence (so long as you have the minimum number—two independent, one dependent), the dress comparison may illustrate the silliness of overloading. While a dress and a coat with a scarf and perhaps even a pin may be appropriate, attaching numerous pieces of jewelry, belts, and so on may disguise the quality of the dress. When writing compound-complex sentences, you must not allow them to become so lengthy and burdensome that they obscure your ideas.

Understanding the structure of the compound-complex sentence allows you to analyze the sentence when you encounter it in your reading. In addition, if you write one, you can check to be sure the parts are all properly related and punctuated as well as check to be sure the logic and development of your ideas are accurate. The questions following the next sentence will guide you through the parts of a compound-complex sentence.

EXAMPLES

J. When he left the laboratory, Sam hated the smell of fish; his friends did too.

    1. What is the first word of the first independent clause? _____

        the last word? _____

Copyright © 1985 by Harcourt Brace Jovanovich, Inc. All rights reserved.

2. Find the verb of the first independent clause. _____

3. Find the subject of the first independent clause. _____

4. What is the first word of the second independent clause? _____

   the last word? _____

5. Find the verb of the second independent clause. _____

6. Find the subject of the second independent clause. _____

7. What is the first word of the introductory dependent clause? _____

   the last word? _____

8. Find the verb of the introductory dependent clause. _____

9. Find the subject of the introductory dependent clause. _____

10. What word links or joins the introductory dependent clause to the sentence?

    _____

11. Which of the five kinds of relationships does the linking word (conjunction)

    show between the dependent clause and the sentence? _____

12. What punctuation follows introductory dependent clauses immediately pre-

    ceding an independent clause? _____

13. What special kind of punctuation joins the two independent clauses? _____

14. What is the structural sentence type? _____

Answers

J. 1. Sam, fish; 2. hated; 3. Sam; 4. his, too; 5. did; 6. friends; 7. when, labora-tory; 8. left; 9. he; 10. when; 11. time; 12. comma; 13. semicolon; 14. com-pound-complex

Copyright © 1985 by Harcourt Brace Jovanovich, Inc. All rights reserved.

EXERCISE 2

Identify the following sentences as *simple*, *compound*, *complex*, or *compound-complex* by writing your answer in the blank.

_____ 1. It was more than fifteen years ago when I entered the laboratory of Professor Agassiz.

_____ 2. I had enrolled my name in the scientific school as a student of natural history.

_____ 3. He asked me a few questions about my object in coming and my antecedents.

_____ 4. Take this fish, and look at it.

_____ 5. With that, he left me, but in a moment he returned.

_____ 6. I was piqued; I was mortified.

_____ 7. I will examine you before you look at the fish, so I can evaluate where you need to begin.

_____ 8. The professor came in shortly and was amused at our experiments.

_____ 9. The sight of an old, six-inch, worm-eaten cork brings fragrant memories.

_____10. When I returned, I dashed the fluid over the fish as if I could bring it back to life.

EXERCISE 3

Combine the following groups of sentences to make one sentence of the structural type indicated. Punctuate each sentence correctly.

Example   *Complex*
I entered the laboratory.
I was somewhat nervous.
I was somewhat nervous when I entered the laboratory.

Copyright © 1985 by Harcourt Brace Jovanovich, Inc. All rights reserved.

1. *Simple*
   Sam studied fish.
   Sam got his hands smelly.

   _____

   _____

2. *Complex*
   Sam devoted himself to insects.
   Sam went to the university.

   _____

   _____

3. *Complex*
   The insects belonged to Professor Agassiz.
   Sam studied insects.

   _____

   _____

4. *Compound*
   Sam thought the fish looked loathsome.
   Sam felt like vomiting.

   _____

   _____

5. *Compound-Complex*
   The professor examined Sam about the fish.
   Sam could not answer the professor's questions.
   The professor left with an air of disappointment.

   _____

   _____

   _____

Copyright © 1985 by Harcourt Brace Jovanovich, Inc. All rights reserved.

6. *Simple*
   Sam walked home by the Charles River.
   Michael walked home with him.

   _____

   _____

7. *Compound*
   The professor hesitated to fail his students.
   The professor evaluated and examined his students.

   _____

   _____

8. *Compound-Complex*
   I studied ten minutes.
   I learned all I could about the fish.
   I left to search for the professor.
   The professor was in the museum.

   _____

   _____

   _____

9. *Complex*
   I must give an exact account of my day.
   I have a bad memory.

   _____

   _____

10. *Complex*
    I ventured to ask for my next assignment.
    The professor spoke happily and enthusiastically about my next assignment.

    _____

    _____

    _____

Copyright © 1985 by Harcourt Brace Jovanovich, Inc. All rights reserved.

FRAGMENTS

When you drop a glass on the floor, it breaks into pieces, or fragments. A fragment of the glass is not the whole glass and cannot serve the same purposes the whole glass was intended to serve. If you think of sentence fragments as pieces of broken glass, you will recognize the danger in using them. You cannot serve a Coke in a broken glass because it may not hold the Coke. The same principle is true for ideas in sentence fragments: a sentence fragment may hold your idea, just as it is possible to drink from a cracked or chipped glass. However, there is danger in drinking from one because you might cut your lip or Coke might leak onto your clothing. There is also danger in using fragments. A sentence fragment will not hold your ideas any better than a chipped or broken glass will hold a Coke. In college writing, you should present ideas in complete sentences, because sentence fragments do not serve as well. A sentence fragment is only a piece of a sentence.

SENTENCE FRAGMENTS COMMON TO COLLEGE WRITING

1. **Dependent clauses misused as sentences**. Dependent clauses have a subject and verb, yet they must be attached to a complete sentence. The first word (conjunction) in a dependent clause establishes the link or relationship between it and the complete sentence. To correct such fragments, link them to an independent clause.

   a. Sometimes the link is time.

      When I decided to study insects
      While I decided to study insects
      After I decided to study insects
      Since I decided to study insects
      Until I decided to study insects

   b. Sometimes the link is place.

      Where I decided to study insects

   c. Sometimes the link is a condition or reason.

      Because I decided to study insects
      If I decided to study insects

   All of the above dependent clauses are adverbial and can be joined to a complete sentence at its beginning, at its end, or close to its verb. Study the ways to change fragments into acceptable sentences.

   When *I decided to study insects,* I worked for Professor Agassiz.
   I worked, **when** *I decided to study insects,* for Professor Agassiz.
   I worked for Professor Agassiz *when I decided to study insects.*

Copyright © 1985 by Harcourt Brace Jovanovich, Inc. All rights reserved.

d. Sometimes the link between the dependent clause and the complete sentence is between the first word in the dependent clause (**who, whose, which, that**) and a specific noun in the complete sentence.

Who decided to study insects
Whose insects I decided to study
Which I decided to study
That I decided to study

(*Tip*: The linking words **who** (**whom**), **whose**, **which**, **that** used to give additional information are called *relative pronouns*.)

All of the above dependent clauses are fragments until they are linked to a complete sentence such as the one which follows.

Professor Agassiz teaches science at the university.

By positioning each of the four dependent clauses above immediately after the noun each clause refers to, the linking word (relative pronoun) attaches the dependent clause to the complete sentence.

Professor Agassiz, **who** decided to study insects, teaches science at the university.
Professor Agassiz, **whose** insects I decided to study, teaches science at the university.
Professor Agassiz teaches science, **which** I decided to study at the university.
Professor Agassiz teaches the science **that** I decided to study at the university.

(*Hint*: Notice *the* before *science*. When a dependent clause limits the word it refers to instead of giving additional information, do not use a comma between the linking word and the sentence.)

2. **No-verb fragments**. Sometimes a fragment has no verb.

We drew all kinds of creatures. *Starfish, frogs, and worms.*

Change the fragment to a complete sentence
a. *by attaching the fragment to another sentence*

Example   We drew all kinds of creatures—*such as starfish, frogs, and worms.*

or
b. *by making a new sentence.*

Example   *We particularly enjoyed drawing* starfish, frogs, and worms.

(*Hint:* You will probably have to add words.)

3. **No-subject fragments**. Some fragments lack a subject.

Copyright © 1985 by Harcourt Brace Jovanovich, Inc. All rights reserved.

At an early hour I concluded lunch was necessary. *Cleaned off my desk.*

Change the fragment to a complete sentence

a. *by attaching it to another sentence after supplying a subject,*

> **Example**   At an early hour I concluded lunch was necessary, *and I* cleaned off my desk.

or

b. *by supplying a subject to make a new sentence.*

> **Example**   At an early hour I concluded lunch was necessary. *I* cleaned off my desk.

4. **Verbal fragments**. Sometimes parts of verbs are used as complete verbs. A sentence must always contain a complete verb.

   a. *verb + -ing* form

   > The professor mused about his early years.
   > *Lingering over some of the odd animals stored in the upper apartment.*

   b. *to + verb* form

   > We studied under Professor Agassiz.
   > *To learn to do research in the laboratory.*

Change the sentence fragments to complete sentences

a. by attaching them to another sentence

> **Example**   1(a) Lingering over some of the odd animals stored in the upper apartment, the professor mused about his early years.

> **Example**   2(a) We studied under Professor Agassiz to learn to do research in the laboratory.

or

b. by changing the *-ing* or the *to* forms (verbals) to a complete verb and supplying a subject if necessary.

> **Example**   1(b) The professor lingers over some of the odd animals stored in the upper apartment.

> **Example**   2(b) We studied under Professor Agassiz, and we learned to do research in the laboratory.

(*Hint*: A rule of thumb to remember is that a word ending in *-ing* is not a complete verb if the *-ing* cannot be removed without losing all the meaning. For example, removing the *-ing* from *sing* leaves a meaningless letter, *s*; *-ing* from *singing*, though, leaves *sing*.)

Copyright © 1985 by Harcourt Brace Jovanovich, Inc. All rights reserved.

Theodore Lownik Library
Illinois Benedictine College
Lisle, Illinois 60532

EXERCISE 4

Write sentences following the patterns described below. Draw a box around the conjunction and underline the dependent clause in the sentences you write.

Example   Complex sentence with a medial dependent clause showing time
I was, [*when*] *I entered the laboratory, somewhat nervous*.

1. Complex sentence with an introductory dependent clause showing a time relationship

_____

_____

2. Complex sentence with a dependent clause in the middle (medial) that shows a time relationship

_____

_____

3. Complex sentence which ends in a dependent clause showing a time relationship

_____

_____

4. Complex sentence which ends in a dependent clause showing a place relationship

_____

_____

5. Complex sentence which begins with a dependent clause showing a reason relationship

_____

_____

6. Complex sentence which ends with a dependent clause showing a reason relationship

_____

Copyright © 1985 by Harcourt Brace Jovanovich, Inc. All rights reserved.

7. Complex sentence with an introductory dependent clause which shows the condition relationship

_____

_____

8. Complex sentence which ends with a dependent clause showing the condition relationship

_____

_____

9. Complex sentence with a medial dependent clause showing additional information

_____

_____

10. Complex sentence which ends in a dependent clause showing additional information

_____

_____

EXERCISE 5

Rewrite the pairs below by (a) attaching the fragment to the sentence and then by (b) changing the fragment into a new sentence. Use your sentence sense to create effective writing in both (a) and (b).

Example   I was somewhat nervous. About entering the laboratory.
    a. *I was somewhat nervous about entering the laboratory*.
    b. *I entered the laboratory.*

1. I enrolled in the Scientific School. Fifteen years ago as a student of natural history.

    a. _____

    _____

Copyright © 1985 by Harcourt Brace Jovanovich, Inc. All rights reserved.

b. _____

   _____

2. The professor questioned me. About my object in coming to the school to study zoology.

   a. _____

      _____

   b. _____

      _____

3. I dared not show my aversion to the laboratory. Distaste for the smells and the sights of it.

   a. _____

      _____

   b. _____

      _____

4. Each lesson had details of subsequent study. Charts, lists, questions, and diagrams of fish.

   a. _____

      _____

   b. _____

      _____

5. In a distracted state with my two perplexities. I walked home by the Charles River.

   a. _____

      _____

   b. _____

      _____

Copyright © 1985 by Harcourt Brace Jovanovich, Inc. All rights reserved.

EXERCISE 6

Rewrite the following pairs (a) by attaching the fragment to the sentence and (b) by changing the fragment into a new sentence. Use sentence sense effectively in both (a) and (b).

Example   I was somewhat nervous. Entered the laboratory.

  a. *I was somewhat nervous when I entered the laboratory.*

  b. *I entered the laboratory.*

1. Proposed to devote myself principally to insects. I wished to know all about zoology.

  a. _____

  _____

  b. _____

  _____

2. I was to keep the fish before me in a tin tray. Occasionally moisten the surface with alcohol and replace the stopper in the jar.

  a. _____

  _____

  b. _____

  _____

3. The professor plunged his hand to the bottom of the jar. Grabbed the fish and held it to my nose.

  a. _____

  _____

  b. _____

  _____

4. The scent of the fish haunted me like a shadow. Made me unbearable to myself and my friends.

  a. _____

Copyright © 1985 by Harcourt Brace Jovanovich, Inc. All rights reserved.

_____

b. _____

_____

5. Slowly I drew forth the hideous fish. With a feeling of desperation, again looked at it.

a. _____

_____

b. _____

_____

EXERCISE 7

Combine each of the following into a single sentence. Put a box around any word ending in *-ing* if it is part of a complete verb.

Example   Intending to be an ichthyologist. I enrolled in Professor Agassiz's class.
            Intending to be an ichthyologist, I enrolled in Professor Agassiz's

            class.

   or   *I was* ⬚*intending* *to be an ichthyologist when I enrolled*

            in Professor Agassiz's class.

1. Professor Agassiz listening attentively to my brief rehearsal of the structure of parts. Professor Agassiz smiled.

_____

_____

_____

2. Expecting more than I had given. He left the room.

_____

_____

3. In desperation wondering if I would ever learn about zoology. I sighed.

_____

Copyright © 1985 by Harcourt Brace Jovanovich, Inc. All rights reserved.

4. I searched for Professor Agassiz. To ask what I should do next.

5. For three days he placed that fish before my eyes. Forbidding me to look at anything else or to use any artificial aid.

Copyright © 1985 by Harcourt Brace Jovanovich, Inc. All rights reserved.

Notes

3.10 *PROOFREADING POWER*

Even though you revise your writing several times before proofreading the final copy, you sometimes discover fragments which you must revise before you can go on with proofreading. When you spot one, stop proofreading and revise it. Once you revise a fragment, you can return to proofreading and continue until you spot some other problem—or another fragment—that you must correct by revision.

If you have had to return to the revision process during proofreading, you will want to proofread your writing from start to finish to be sure that you have not overlooked some careless mistake such as a typo or omitted words or sentences during recopying. Make your final copy as correct as you possibly can because error-free writing reflects well on your image as a writer.

Proofread the paragraph below to discover any fragments it may contain and revise the passage correcting any errors you find.

In ten minutes I had seen all. That could be seen in that fish. Started in search of the Professor. Who had, however, left the Museum. When I returned, after lingering over some of the odd animals stored in the upper apartment. My specimen was dry all over. I dashed the fluid over the fish. As if to resuscitate the beast from a fainting fit. Looked with anxiety for a return of the normal sloppy appearance. This little excitement over. Nothing was to be done but to return to a steadfast gaze at my mute companion.

Copyright © 1985 by Harcourt Brace Jovanovich, Inc. All rights reserved.

Notes

3.11 *DICTATION*

Your instructor will choose a passage of approximately 100 words and read it aloud as you write what you hear. As you listen to each sentence read, concentrate and maintain silence. Do not ask your instructor to repeat because any sound other than the teacher's voice reading will break not only your concentration but that of others. Your instructor may repeat key words and phrases during the dictation, will allow sufficient time for you to write what you have heard, and will reread the entire passage a second time at a faster rate so that you can check what you have written and fill in any gap you may have.

You will want to write on every other line so you will have space to correct your dictation upon the final reading in case you have made a mistake. Your instructor will show you the dictated passage and ask you to compare your version, or perhaps a classmate's version, to the original. Be especially alert when you check the dictation because this exercise will help you develop your sentence sense by translating spoken into written language.

3.12 *WORD POWER*

VOCABULARY

Learning to attach prefixes and suffixes to base words you already know will increase your vocabulary rapidly. By selecting words from your expanded vocabulary, you can gain precision in your writing because you can find words to express your ideas exactly. Other advantages of your expanded vocabulary allow you to add variety and to shade meaning when you write.

Example   *happy* (base word)
un- (prefix)   +   *happy*   =   *unhappy*
happy   +   *-ly* (suffix)   =   *happily*
un-   +   *happy*   +   *-ly*   =   *unhappily*

The example illustrates how the combining of base words with prefixes and suffixes expands vocabulary. This combining creates three additional words from a single base word. In addition, by recognizing and knowing the meanings of prefixes, suffixes, and base words, you can frequently figure out the meanings of words you have never seen before. The following exercises will help you learn to combine base words with prefixes and suffixes.

EXERCISE 1

In this exercise are words you may know. Combine these base words with prefixes and suffixes you learned earlier. When you combine known prefixes, base words and/or

Copyright © 1985 by Harcourt Brace Jovanovich, Inc. All rights reserved.

suffixes, you acquire a new word. An example will get you started. *Agree* has the meaning "to be in harmony with." By addding the prefix *dis-,* you make a new word, *disagree,* which means "to be out of harmony with." The prefix *dis-* added its meaning "from or out of" to the meaning of the base word. The new word carries the meaning of both base word and prefix.

Combine each of the base words with the prefix given to form a new word. In the next column form another new word by combining one of the following suffixes with the word in column one: *-able, -ible; -al; -ation, -tion, -ion; -ful; -ly.*

Example	dis-	agree	*disagree*	*disagreeable*
1.	de-	nature		
		test		
2.	dis-	agree		
		close		
		color		
		prove		
		trust		
3.	im-, in-	consider		
		mature		
		perfect		
		prove		
4.	re-	consider		
		read		
		think		
		use		
5.	un-	change		
		collect		

Copyright © 1985 by Harcourt Brace Jovanovich, Inc. All rights reserved.

5. (*continued*)

un-   conscious   _____   _____

natural   _____   _____

print   _____   _____

profit   _____   _____

prove   _____   _____

treat   _____   _____

EXERCISE 2

The words in this exercise have been taken from the reading selection in the order in which they occur to make it easy for you to look at them in context. Each word contains a prefix, base word, and/or suffix studied in the previous exercise. Write your own sentence using the word to show that you know what the word means. (*Hint*: Make your sentences more than 12 words long.)

1. unhesitatingly _____

   _____

   _____

2. disappointment _____

   _____

   _____

3. companion _____

   _____

   _____

4. discover _____

   _____

   _____

Copyright © 1985 by Harcourt Brace Jovanovich, Inc. All rights reserved.

5. attentively _____

_____

_____

6. disconcerting _____

_____

_____

7. inestimable _____

_____

_____

8. preparation _____

_____

_____

9. reluctance _____

_____

_____

10. investigation _____

_____

_____

Copyright © 1985 by Harcourt Brace Jovanovich, Inc. All rights reserved.

EXERCISE 3

Create a new word by using the prefix or suffix shown in **boldface** type. You may change the word any way you choose as long as you retain the base word. Then, write a sentence using the new word. Notice that each of the words appeared in the previous exercise.

Example   agreeable (**dis-**) *disagreeably* _____

She spoke disagreeably during the meeting. _____

1. unhesitatingly (-**ion**) _____

   _____

   _____

2. disappointment (**re-**) _____

   _____

   _____

3. companion (-**ship**) _____

   _____

   _____

4. discover (**un-** and/or -**able**) _____

   _____

   _____

5. attentively (**in-**) _____

   _____

   _____

Copyright © 1985 by Harcourt Brace Jovanovich, Inc. All rights reserved.

Notes

SPELLING

Nouns ordinarily form plurals by adding -*s*.

Example   apple   +   -*s*   =   apples

Add -*es*, however, if

1. the noun ends in -*ch*, -*sh*, -*s*, or - *x*,

    Example   box   +   -*es*   =   boxes

2. the noun ends in a consonant + -*o*

    Example   echo   +   -*es*   =   echoes

3. the word ends in a consonant + -*y*, (after changing the -*y* to -*i*).

    Example   bod*y*   +   -*es*   =   bod*i*es

Sometimes words ending in -*f* or -*fe* change them to -*v* before adding -*s* or -*es*.

Example   kni*f*e   +   -*es*   =   kni*v*es
               lea*f*   +   -*es*   =   lea*v*es

Combined words spelled with a hyphen add -*s* to the base word.

Example   mother-in-law   +   -*s*   =   mother*s*-in-law

EXERCISE 4

Form plurals in this exercise by using the preceding rules and learn to spell the plurals of these 20 words.

1. aisle _____   8. muscle _____

2. course _____   9. nickel _____

3. environment _____   10. potato _____

4. hero _____   11. prejudice _____

5. meanness _____   12. process _____

6. medicine _____   13. quiz _____

7. minute _____   14. resource _____

Copyright © 1985 by Harcourt Brace Jovanovich, Inc. All rights reserved.

15. sister-in-law _____   18. strategy _____

16. speech _____   19. vengeance _____

17. statistic _____   20. wife _____

Copyright © 1985 by Harcourt Brace Jovanovich, Inc. All rights reserved.

UNIT FOUR

WRITING

CLARIFIED

4.1 GETTING STARTED BY READING

Skillful readers use the modified skimming speed to locate particular facts. Modified skimming allows you to skim until your eye locates the fact for which you are searching. You use modified skimming when you have a particular in mind that you will recognize as soon as you see it. The particular may be on a list, in an index, in a set of study questions, or even buried in a long passage of text. When you read at the modified skimming rate, your eye races past the beginning of the particular you are seeking. Then your eye jumps back to the start of the passage when your mind perceives that you have found what you are looking for. When you have found the beginning, you reduce speed to a rate slow enough to fix the particular in your mind. Once you have these particulars in mind, your reading rate increases to a skimming rate until you complete the selection or until you encounter something else you are interested in. If you intend to locate a single fact from a source, you would not continue to read once you have found it.

Category   Modified skimming
Rate   Skimming rate with interruptions

Purpose	To locate particulars
Typical	A name on the Vietnam Monument
uses	A certain fact in an encyclopedia
	Old love letters
	Computer screens
	Class notes
	Directions at an intersection
	Advertisements
	Titles of books or magazines in a library or bookstore
	Lists in telephone directories, in dictionaries, on computer screens, or on building locator directories
	Recipes (to decide if you have the necessary ingredients)
	A class reading assignment (to find specific answers to questions)
	Exam schedules
	Maps

You may have noticed as you skimmed the selection in Unit Three that you wanted very much to stop or slow down as you came across answers to the questions. You were instructed not to slow or stop at that time. You have, then, experienced the need to adjust your reading speed to modified skimming.

When reading to locate particulars, you will use modified skimming. At this speed your eye will move very quickly along the lines until you see the particular you are seeking. When your eye runs past the particular, you immediately reduce your reading speed and return to the particular. Once you locate the beginning of the passage, you read at a speed much slower than the skimming rate.

Read over the following questions and fix them in your mind before you read "Gumption." The answers to these questions are the particulars you will seek as you read. This set of questions is arranged in the order that the answers appear in "Gumption" although an orderly arrangement may not be appropriate when you use modified skimming at other times. If you like, mark the particulars in your book when you encounter an answer. Underline the answer, and note the number of the question in the margin.

1. What is the root meaning of "enthusiasm"?
2. What is the most important tool for repairing a motorcycle?
3. What two kinds of manuals are necessary for repairing a motorcycle?
4. What is a "gumption trap"?
5. How many kinds of "gumption traps" are there?
6. How do you get gumption?
7. What are two types of "gumption traps"?

Copyright © 1985 by Harcourt Brace Jovanovich, Inc. All rights reserved.

4.2 *DEFINITION*

Robert H. Pirsig   *"GUMPTION" from* ZEN AND THE ART OF MOTORCYCLE MAINTENANCE

I like the word "gumption" because it's so homely and so forlorn and so out of style it looks as if it needs a friend and isn't likely to reject anyone who comes along. It's an old Scottish word, once used a lot by pioneers, but which, like "kin," seems to have all but dropped out of use. I like it also because it describes exactly what happens to someone who connects with Quality. He gets filled with gumption.

The Greeks called it *enthousiasmos,* the root of "enthusiasm," which means literally "filled with *theos,*" or God, or Quality. See how that fits?

A person filled with gumption doesn't sit around dissipating and stewing about things. He's at the front of the train of his own awareness, watching to see what's up the track and meeting it when it comes. That's gumption.

The gumption-filling process occurs when one is quiet long enough to see and hear and feel the real universe, not just one's own stale opinions about it. But it's nothing exotic. That's why I like the word.

You see it often in people who return from long, quiet fishing trips. Often they're a little defensive about having put so much time to "no account" because there's no intellectual justification for what they've been doing. But the returned fisherman usually has a peculiar abundance of gumption, usually for the very same things he was sick to death of a few weeks before. He hasn't been wasting time. It's only our limited cultural viewpoint that makes it seem so.

If you're going to repair a motorcycle, an adequate supply of gumption is the first and most important tool. If you haven't got that you might as well gather up all the other tools and put them away, because they won't do you any good.

Gumption is the psychic gasoline that keeps the whole thing going. If you haven't got it there's no way the motorcycle can possibly be fixed. But if you *have* got it and know how to keep it there's absolutely no way in this whole world that motorcycle can *keep* from getting fixed. It's bound to happen. Therefore the thing that must be monitored at all times and preserved before anything else is the gumption.

Copyright © 1985 by Harcourt Brace Jovanovich, Inc. All rights reserved.

This paramount importance of gumption solves a problem of format of this Chautauqua. The problem has been how to get off the generalities. If the Chautauqua gets into the actual details of fixing one individual machine the chances are overwhelming that it won't be your make and model and the information will be not only useless but dangerous, since information that fixes one model can sometimes wreck another. For detailed information of an objective sort, a separate shop manual for the specific make and model of machine must be used. In addition, a general shop manual such as *Audel's Automotive Guide* fills in the gaps.

But there's another kind of detail that no shop manual goes into but that is common to all machines and can be given here. This is the detail of the Quality relationship, the gumption relationship, between the machine and the mechanic, which is just as intricate as the machine itself. Throughout the process of fixing the machine things always come up, low-quality things, from a dusted knuckle to an accidentally ruined "irreplaceable" assembly. These drain off gumption, destroy enthusiasm and leave you so discouraged you want to forget the whole business. I call these things "gumption traps."

There are hundreds of different kinds of gumption traps, maybe thousands, maybe millions. I have no way of knowing how many I don't know. I know it *seems* as though I've stumbled into every kind of gumption trap imaginable. What keeps me from thinking I've hit them all is that with every job I discover more. Motorcycle maintenance gets frustrating. Angering. Infuriating. That's what makes it interesting.

What I have in mind now is a catalog of "Gumption Traps I Have Known." I want to start a whole new academic field, gumptionology, in which these traps are sorted, classified, structured into hierarchies and interrelated for the edification of future generations and the benefit of all mankind.

Gumptionology 101—An examination of affective, cognitive and psychomotor blocks in the perception of Quality relationships—3 cr, VII, MWF. I'd like to see that in a college catalog somewhere.

In traditional maintenance gumption is considered something you're born with or have acquired as a result of good upbringing. It's a fixed commodity. From the lack

Copyright © 1985 by Harcourt Brace Jovanovich, Inc. All rights reserved.

of information about how one acquires this gumption one might assume that a person without any gumption is a hopeless case.

In nondualistic maintenance gumption isn't a fixed commodity. It's variable, a reservoir of good spirits that can be added to or subtracted from. Since it's a result of the perception of Quality, a gumption trap, consequently, can be defined as anything that causes one to lose sight of Quality, and thus lose one's enthusiasm for what one is doing. As one might guess from a definition as broad as this, the field is enormous and only a beginning sketch can be attempted here.

As far as I can see there are two main types of gumption traps. The first type are those in which you're thrown off the Quality track by conditions that arise from external circumstances, and I call these ''setbacks.'' The second type are traps in which you're thrown off the Quality track by conditions that are primarily within yourself. These I don't have any generic name for—''hang-ups,'' I suppose.

4.3 UNDERSTANDING WHAT YOU READ

1. List three or more activities that require ''gumption.'' _____

   _____

   _____

2. If these activities are performed without ''gumption,'' what are the likely results? _____

   _____

   _____

3. How do people refer to ''gumption'' if they don't know what it is? _____

   _____

   _____

Copyright © 1985 by Harcourt Brace Jovanovich, Inc. All rights reserved.

4.4 DISCOVERING IDEAS FOR WRITING

1. Make a list of three to five activities you have done or might do that in your opinion require "gumption." Beside each jot down why you think it requires

    "gumption." _____

    _____

    _____

    _____

    _____

2. In your opinion, how much gumption do you have? Where and when did you get it? Do you think you have sufficient gumption to perform the activities you

    listed in number one? Jot down why you think you do or do not. _____

    _____

    _____

    _____

    _____

3. Describe how you can use "gumption" to your advantage to complete an exact-

    ing task, job, or assignment successfully. _____

    _____

    _____

    _____

    _____

Copyright © 1985 by Harcourt Brace Jovanovich, Inc. All rights reserved.

4.5 UNDERSTANDING WRITING

Because experienced writers know the value of having material on hand when they have to write, they continuously collect it even though they have no immediate need for it. Though the particular way they gather material varies, successful writers have developed some way of collecting material. Sometimes it is organized, and sometimes it is not. Some writers clip from newspapers and magazines and file the clippings. If they are organized, they arrange them into categories; if not, they may stuff them into boxes or drawers or between pages of a book. Others jot notes in journals and diaries about things they have seen or read. Some record their impressions and thoughts in letters. All, though, observe carefully the world around them and are curious to understand themselves in relation to their world. They preserve their observations in some form of writing, either their own or someone else's.

Experience has taught writers that they can write no better than they can read. Because of its importance for writing, reading frequently from a variety of sources supplies writers with ideas. When writers encounter material that interests them during their reading, they may collect it for future use. Because of the range and variety of ideas encountered, writers store them in a unique system which they have developed. Their systems for collecting material are always personal; even so, their systems have two features in common. First, writers gather material even when not working on a project and when there is no definite purpose or planned use for the material. Second, writers keep the material where they can find it when they need it. The consistent gathering of material serves several purposes. First, when in a creative mood, writers can draw from the material. In different circumstances when not so creative, writers can discover a purpose for the material when sifting through it. Also, the store of material itself can help writers get over a writing block by reinforcing self-confidence.

During a writing block, minds go blank and writers can call up no ideas. At these times writers rely on the previously collected material. Experienced writers know that a writing block is temporary; and being temporary, it will pass. When you encounter your first writing block, you may feel that your ability to write will never return.

The experiences of other writers can help you past your writing block should one occur. You may want to try one of these suggestions, all of which have helped some writer at one time or another to get over a writing block. One way to get past a writing block is to read over what you have already written. If rereading does not help you over the writing block, then neatly copying a passage you have already written might. Rereading and recopying usually work well for most students who are writing in class. Sometimes exercising or going to a movie helps you get past a writing slump. At other times, you might read to divert yourself and to search for ideas. Perhaps thumbing through collected material helps you over a writing block most effectively.

As a neophyte writer, you need to recognize that there will be times that you cannot write because of a writing block. You cannot, however, use ''writing block'' as

Copyright © 1985 by Harcourt Brace Jovanovich, Inc. All rights reserved.

an excuse for not writing or for not submitting an assignment. Because writing blocks are temporary, and you can get over them, you must develop some routine to get you past one. Writing blocks last from a few minutes to hours or days and are usually in proportion to the size of the project you have undertaken. Writing blocks for class assignments rarely last more than a few minutes.

4.6 WRITING—DEFINITION

WRITING ASSIGNMENT

Your responses to the questions in Section 4.4 have helped you to understand ''gumption,'' situations in which you use it, and its benefits. Draft a 350- to 500-word essay in which you define both ''gumption'' and ''good grades'' and explain how gumption can help you get good grades.

A definition differs from description because definitions must follow a particular formula. You must include all three parts of a definition. When writing a definition, you first state the *term* you need to define; next, you put the term within a *class*; finally, you show any *differences* between the term you are defining and other similar things. In fact, few people write an entire essay in the form of a definition. You can, however, use the formula for a definition as your central design feature. In your draft, your definitions may not exactly fit the formula because you will probably use description and narration to illustrate what you are defining. Should you find that you did not formally define either *grades* or *gumption*, you can revise your draft to include exact definitions later. In fact, further explanation and practice of the definition formula can be found in Paragraph Power (Section 4.8).

Learning to use the definition formula is most helpful in college writing because you will be asked to write definitions on your college examinations, whether essay or objective. Unless you know the formula for definitions, you might omit one of its three requirements which your instructor expects you to include if you are to receive full credit for your answer.

Reminder: When you complete your draft, you are well into your writing process and have made considerable progress toward finishing the essay for this unit. It is important to recognize during writing that your goal is to create readable, error-free writing and that once you have a part of your writing that satisfies your purposes, you may keep that part through any additional rewriting that you do. That means that you can actually work on your final version from the moment you begin to discover ideas.

During revisions, look at your writing critically, but be prepared to recognize what is good in your writing and worth keeping even though you may have to revise other parts of your essay several times. Sometimes you will write things exactly the way

Copyright © 1985 by Harcourt Brace Jovanovich, Inc. All rights reserved.

you want them the first time. If you are not sure whether something you have written is worth keeping but think it may be, ask your instructor. This way, you can learn to recognize the good features of your writing as well as your faults. To know your strengths is as important as knowing your weaknesses.

For a detailed description of your responsibilities as a writer and of the composing process, review Section 1.6. A brief summary may be enough for you since you have reviewed them in each of the preceding units. First, you discover ideas for writing, draft those ideas, and revise your draft for your audience (your peer editor). Further revision comes after consideration of your peer editor's suggestions. Before you submit all versions of your writing to your instructor, you proofread your paper to correct any errors you may have missed. Your instructor, of course, will not read all your drafts and revisions but will respond to questions you have about writing problems.

If you are not satisfied with your writing, remember you can always return to any stage of the writing process whenever you want.

4.7 THE WRITING PROCESS

Language, written and spoken, takes on meaning in specific contexts. A word or a sentence in one context may have an entirely different meaning in another. Each time you use language you must make decisions and judgments about how your audience (readers, listeners) will understand what you intend. Everyone has a personal response to words. Sometimes those responses differ from the ones you intend. As you make choices about language, you will want to be guided by what your audience considers desirable and appropriate. Just as a bathing suit is appropriate dress for a beach party but not for a wedding, slang is appropriate in a letter to your friend but not in college writing.

All words have specific meanings called *denotation*. The denotations of words are the generally accepted, formal definitions found in a dictionary. But the formal definition that you find in a dictionary does not include all the personal meanings people attach to words. These personal meanings, called *connotations*, carry mental images and emotional responses. The connotation is everything that a word suggests and brings to mind.

In your writing you sometimes must choose among several words that will fit in any one slot in a sentence. Your final choice rests upon meaning, appropriateness, and the expectation of your audience. For example, you might write "He *walked* across the room." The verb, "walked," has the denotation "to move along on foot or by steps." But substituting any one of the following which has the same denotation as "walked" for "walked" will change your mental image (connotation). To experience the effects of connotation, fill in the blank with each of the following words: *ambled, paraded, padded, tiptoed, pranced, minced, prissed.*

Copyright © 1985 by Harcourt Brace Jovanovich, Inc. All rights reserved.

He _____ across the room.

As you consider the list, do you envision a person "moving along on foot or by steps"? How does your mental image change as you substitute different words for "walked"?

You can also make your nouns more precise. Insert "criminal," "robber," "thief," or "embezzler" in the following sentence.

The _____ was sentenced to a ten-year prison term.

Do you notice that your mental images become increasingly precise as you proceed through the list? Good writers strive to choose words that bring precise images to mind, but at all times good writers choose language appropriate for the purpose at hand.

The following questions will guide you in making decisions and judgments about the words you use in your writing. They will also assist you in selecting verbs with precise denotations and connotations. Controlling denotation and connotation will make your meaning clearer to your reader and give your writing a stronger impact.

1. Can you identify the verbs in your essay? (*Hint*: Circle all verbs in a color.)
2. Can you think of other words for some of the verbs circled? (*Hint*: If so, write one to five words above or below the verb circled.)
3. Do you think one of the verbs on your list would create a more specific mental image in your reader's mind than the one you originally used? (*Hint*: Draw a line through a verb as you eliminate it from your list.)
4. Do you need to rearrange some sentences to use a particularly effective verb? (*Hint*: The verbs *am*, *is*, *was*, and *were* sometimes require you to rearrange your sentence or even combine sentences when you replace them with other verbs.)
5. Can you identify the subjects in your essay? (*Hint*: Draw a box around the subjects in a color different from the one you used to circle verbs.)
6. Can you think of other nouns for some of the subjects you boxed? (*Hint*: If so, jot one to five words above or below the subject you boxed.)
7. Do you think one of the nouns on your list would create a more specific mental image in your reader's mind than the one you originally used? (*Hint*: Draw a line through a noun as you eliminate it from your list.)
8. Are there other nouns in your essay that could be made more precise? (*Hint*: Put a check over any noun you want to consider.)
9. Can you think of other nouns for some of those you checked? (*Hint*: If so, jot one to five nouns above or below the noun you checked.)
10. Do you think your reader will have a more precise idea of what you intended after your rewriting?

Copyright © 1985 by Harcourt Brace Jovanovich, Inc. All rights reserved.

4.8 PARAGRAPH POWER

The following one-sentence definition contains the three requirements of a formal definition.

        term   **class**   **difference**
A chair is a piece of furniture used for sitting.

Notice that the **term** being defined, *chair*, appears first. The definition next places a *chair* in its usual **class**, *piece of furniture*; then it distinguishes the kind of furniture a *chair* is from all other kinds by showing that it is *used for sitting*, **difference**. Complete formal definitions require all three parts.

THE THREE STEPS TO A FORMAL DEFINITION

1. Name what you intend to define
2. Place it in its usual class
3. Show the difference

A modification of the formal definition formula provides a useful plan for developing paragraphs when your purpose is to define. Even though such paragraphs develop more leisurely than formal definitions, they have all three features: term, class, differences. Furthermore, these three features, when expanded into a paragraph, produce a T-R-I-I paragraph. For instance, your topic sentence (T) can name the term you are defining. The next sentence might contain the identification of class (R). The remaining sentences of the paragraph could present the differences (I, I . . .). Such an approach is only one of many possibilities for writing definition paragraphs. Once you have control of this pattern, you can vary it to suit your particular purpose for writing.

In your reading, you will often find variations of definition paragraphs that contain elements of other modes such as description and narration. Since a paragraph expands an idea through sentences, writers of definition paragraphs have the opportunity to include a variety of details to interest an audience and explain a topic thoroughly. When you find evidence of other modes in paragraphs, do not be alarmed; rather, recognize that good writers mix modes and rearrange established patterns all the time. Understanding that good writers mix modes will reduce any anxiety you may feel about combining modes and altering patterns in your own writing.

Further, you may find that your definition requires more explanation than you can include in a single paragraph. That is all right, too. When your purpose for writing is to define, you should complete your definition by including all the elements whether in a single sentence, a paragraph, a series of related paragraphs, or an entire essay. Indeed, you can extend a definition to control a long piece of writing as Pirsig does

Copyright © 1985 by Harcourt Brace Jovanovich, Inc. All rights reserved.

in the passage from *Zen and the Art of Motorcycle Maintenance*. Nevertheless, the pattern to write a definition paragraph is particularly useful in college writing because examinations and class assignments frequently ask students to define.

EXERCISE 1

Identify the parts of a definition in the following sentence. Draw a box around the named term. Circle the part of the definition that puts the term into its class. Finally, draw a wavy line under that part of the sentence that distinguishes this item from others in its class.

Gumption is the psychic gasoline that keeps the whole thing going.

EXERCISE 2

Write five formal definitions in sentence form.

1. A dormitory _____

_____

2. Grades _____

_____

3. A motorcycle _____

_____

4. Gumptionology 101 _____

_____

5. A gumption trap _____

_____

EXERCISE 3A

Identify the topic, restriction, and illustrations in the following definition paragraph from Pirsig's *Zen and the Art of Motorcycle Maintenance*. (*Hint*: This paragraph contains two topic sentences. One is a restatement of the other.) Underline the topic sentence, circle the restriction, and draw boxes around the illustrations.

Copyright © 1985 by Harcourt Brace Jovanovich, Inc. All rights reserved.

But there's another kind of detail that no shop manual goes into but that is common to all machines and can be given here. This is the detail of the Quality relationship, the gumption relationship, between the machine and the mechanic, which is just as intricate as the machine itself. Throughout the process of fixing the machine things always come up, low-quality things, from a dusted knuckle to an accidentally ruined "irreplaceable" assembly. These drain off gumption, destroy enthusiasm and leave you so discouraged you want to forget the whole business. I call these things "gumption traps."

EXERCISE 3B

Examine the preceding paragraph and find the defined term, the class, and the differences. Write each in the space provided below.

Term _____

Class _____

Differences _____

EXERCISE 4

Plan a definition paragraph following the suggested T-R-I-I pattern of topic, restriction, illustration, illustration. Use your formal definition of *grades* from Exercise 1 as the subject of your paragraph. You may want to revise a paragraph from your draft (4.6) or write an entirely new one to insert into the next version of your definition essay.

Copyright © 1985 by Harcourt Brace Jovanovich, Inc. All rights reserved.

Notes

Make a general statement about what grades are.

T

Suggest why you have this impression.

R

Develop this impression by selecting the indicated kinds of details.

I	I	I
Activities required to earn grades	Objective vs Subjective grading standards	Reasons for grades

Copyright © 1985 by Harcourt Brace Jovanovich, Inc. All rights reserved.

Notes

4.9 ORGANIZING AN ESSAY

Essays vary in length from a few paragraphs to many pages. The form of an essay allows a writer to develop a topic in an organized way. Even though the ways to organize an essay are limitless, you can learn a basic organization for an essay if you use a well-constructed paragraph as a plan for your longer piece of writing. Like the paragraph, assigned essays frequently deal with a single topic.

One straightforward way to organize an essay is to use the paragraph you wrote in Exercise 4 as the plan or blueprint for an essay you intend to develop. Such a paragraph may be called a kernel paragraph. Even though the kernel paragraph you intend to develop hardly ever appears as such in a finished essay, you can transform each part of a T-R-I-I paragraph into paragraphs for an essay.

Just as an acorn changes form when it grows into an oak tree, a kernel paragraph changes form when it grows into an essay. A kernel paragraph is not an essay in miniature, just as a blueprint is not a building in miniature; both are designs or plans for a structure. A building is a structure and an essay is a structure.

Before you can transform your kernel paragraph into an organized essay, you will need guidance on how to proceed. Though you may not construct paragraphs for your essay in the precise order the kernel paragraph takes, you may transform each of the parts of your T-R-I-I paragraph into individual paragraphs which you may arrange into a proper sequence for an organized essay once you have written them. For instance, you can develop the topic and restriction into an introductory paragraph which contains your thesis sentence and the particular focus or limitation (R) you follow in your essay. (This paragraph may not be the first paragraph you write.) Each of the illustrations (evidence, proof, or support) will become at least a paragraph, but perhaps more than a single paragraph. A good way to develop a paragraph is to consider each of the illustrations as potential material. If, for example, you have three illustrations, you will have three paragraphs. If you have two illustrations, you will have two paragraphs. As you practice organization of your essays, you may even learn to expand a single illustration into more than one paragraph. For now, you can concentrate on developing a single paragraph in your essay for each of the illustrations in your kernel paragraph.

Because many professional writers produce chunks or blocks of writing in a rather disorganized way, you may too. You will likely complete your chunks in an order far different from the order your paragraphs will take in your final copy. In other words, very few writers compose in a straight line from the first word to the last. If you are like most writers, you will have to rearrange chunks of your writing before you can present a completed version to your reader. Many writers have to rearrange their material more than once, adding and deleting chunks as they work. Expect to do such rearrangement: It is normal. Without careful arrangement, your writing will appear disorganized and unplanned.

Once you have transformed each of your illustrations (evidence, proof, support) in

Copyright © 1985 by Harcourt Brace Jovanovich, Inc. All rights reserved.

the kernel paragraph into separate paragraphs, you will want to place them into the most appropriate arrangement for presenting your ideas to your reader. For over two thousand years successful writers have organized writing in a prescribed order. They have used this order because of its effect on an audience. While prescribed order is not the only way to organize an essay, it is an effective one. It will help you understand the principles of organization, and it can help you produce an organized essay. To do this, you follow your introductory paragraph with the one that contains your strongest or most important evidence (illustration, proof, support). Your next strongest evidence should come in the paragraph immediately before your conclusion, if you have one. Any other evidence should come in the middle paragraphs, those that fill the space between your strongest evidence in the paragraph after the introduction and your next strongest evidence in the paragraph before the conclusion.

When you follow this plan, you will be well along in writing an organized essay. In the final arrangement your essay begins with an introductory paragraph which you have constructed by using the topic (T) and restriction (R) from your kernel paragraph. These both may need expansion before they become a suitable introductory paragraph.

Finally, if your essay is of sufficient length to require a conclusion, you may summarize or evaluate what you have written in a paragraph. Sometimes a conclusion is simply a restatement of the topic in a succinct manner. At other times essays may be so short or straight forward that they do not need a conclusion.

4.10 SENTENCE POWER

VERBS

This section examines progressively features of the verb which will help you understand how to shape this most flexible part of the sentence to its best effect. The verb is unique because it is the only required part of the sentence. You can have a "sentence" without a subject or an object or any other part of a sentence, but you must have a verb to have a sentence. That is why the verb is the most important part of any sentence. A sure hand in managing verbs allows you to shade meaning and to add precision to your writing.

VERB TENSE

The *tense* of a verb indicates when an action or condition *is*, *was*, or *will be* in effect. It also shows that something exists or is equal to something else. The examples below demonstrate how different forms of the same verb indicate precise time relationships. Observe that forming some tenses requires the use of more than one word. In these cases the verb is called a "verb phrase"; the words which precede the verb are

Copyright © 1985 by Harcourt Brace Jovanovich, Inc. All rights reserved.

auxiliary (helping) verbs. When you need to find the verb in a sentence, you must give the entire verb; in other words, if it is a verb phrase, you include any auxiliaries.

The six sentences below provide examples of the six different tenses that we traditionally learn.

1. Present Tense

    Today, I *ride* my motorcycle.

2. Past Tense

    Yesterday, I *rode* my motorcycle.

3. Future Tense

    Tomorrow, I *will ride* my motorcycle.

4. Present Perfect Tense

    For two years, *I have ridden* my motorcycle.

5. Past Perfect Tense

    Before my wreck, I *had ridden* my motorcycle for two years.

6. Future Perfect Tense

    When I graduate from college, I *will have ridden* my motorcycle for six years.

As you study the six tenses, observe their patterns or forms. Each of the six tenses has the basic and the progressive forms; the present and the past tenses also have the emphatic form. Once you have mastered those patterns or forms, you can figure out tenses for any verb you wish. The principle for forming verb tenses is consistent for regular verbs and for irregular verbs.

Forms of Verb Tenses for Irregular Verbs			
Tense	Basic	Progressive	Emphatic
present	ride(s)	am (are, is) riding	do (does) ride
past	rode	was (were) riding	did ride
future	will ride	will be riding	
present perfect	have (has) ridden	have (has) been riding	
past perfect	had ridden	had been riding	
future perfect	will have ridden	will have been riding	

Copyright © 1985 by Harcourt Brace Jovanovich, Inc. All rights reserved.

Forms of Verb Tenses for Regular Verbs			
Tense	Basic	Progressive	Emphatic
present	walk	am (are, is) walking	do (does) walk
past	walked	was (were) walking	did walk
future	will walk	will be walking	
present perfect	have (has) walked	have (has) been walking	
past perfect	had walked	had been walking	
future perfect	will have walked	will have been walking	

All six of the verb tenses—present, past, future and present perfect, past perfect, future perfect—have more than one form. All six have a progressive form, and the present and past tenses have an emphatic form. Simply add *progressive* or *emphatic* to express the name of the other forms of the tenses. For example, *is riding* is called the "present progressive"; *do ride*, "present emphatic." By choosing one form of a tense instead of another, you can gain precision and clarity in your writing.

EXERCISE 1

Write the name of the tense in the blank after each verb. If a verb has one or more auxiliaries (helping verbs), write the auxiliary or auxiliaries in the blank labeled "auxiliary."

Auxiliary

1.   will talk _____*future*_____   _____*will*_____

2.   talked _____   _____

3.   talks _____   _____

4.   had talked _____   _____

5.   are talking _____   _____

6.   will have talked _____   _____

7.   did talk _____   _____

Copyright © 1985 by Harcourt Brace Jovanovich, Inc. All rights reserved.

8. writes _____   _____

9. wrote _____   _____

10. will write _____   _____

11. had written _____   _____

12. will have written _____   _____

13. are writing _____   _____

14. does write _____   _____

15. will be writing _____   _____

16. will have been writing _____   _____

17. did write _____   _____

18. has been writing _____   _____

19. were writing _____   _____

20. write _____   _____

Copyright © 1985 by Harcourt Brace Jovanovich, Inc. All rights reserved.

Notes

PRINCIPAL PARTS

Verbs in English, whether regular or irregular, have five principal parts. Each of the principal parts is used in forming the six verb tenses which follow the same system whether the verb is regular or irregular. The principal parts of regular verbs follow a predictable pattern. Irregular verbs have patterns, too; because irregular verbs occur so frequently, you can memorize them more easily than you can learn their rather complex patterns.

Principal Parts of Regular Verbs				
Base (Infinitive)	Present Participle	Present	Past	Past Participle
(to) walk	walking	walk she walks	walked	walked
(to) heat	heating	heat it heats	heated	heated
(to) clean	cleaning	clean he cleans	cleaned	cleaned

Principal Parts of Irregular Verbs				
Base (Infinitive)	Present Participle	Present	Past	Past Participle
Present, Past, and Past Participle Identical				
(to) beat	beating	beat(s)	beat	beat(-en)
(to) bid	bidding	bid(s)	bid	bid
(to) burst	bursting	burst(s)	burst	burst
(to) cost	costing	cost(s)	cost	cost
(to) cut	cutting	cut(s)	cut	cut
(to) hit	hitting	hit(s)	hit	hit
(to) hurt	hurting	hurt(s)	hurt	hurt
(to) let	letting	let(s)	let	let
(to) put	putting	put(s)	put	put
(to) read	reading	read(s)	read*	read*
(to) set	setting	set(s)	set	set
(to) shut	shutting	shut(s)	shut	shut
(to) split	splitting	split(s)	split	split
(to) spread	spreading	spread(s)	spread	spread
(to) thrust	thrusting	thrust(s)	thrust	thrust
(to) wet	wetting	wet(s)	wet(-ted)	wet(-ted)

*Notice sound change.

Copyright © 1985 by Harcourt Brace Jovanovich, Inc. All rights reserved.

Principal Parts of Irregular Verbs

Base (Infinitive)	Present Participle	Present	Past	Past Participle
		Past Tense and Past Participle Identical		
(to) bend	bending	bend(s)	bent	bent
(to) bind	binding	bind(s)	bound	bound
(to) bite	biting	bite(s)	bit	bit(-ten)
(to) bring	bringing	bring(s)	brought	brought
(to) build	building	build(s)	built	built
(to) buy	buying	buy(s)	bought	bought
(to) catch	catching	catch(es)	caught	caught
(to) cling	clinging	cling(s)	clung	clung
(to) creep	creeping	creep(s)	crept	crept
(to) fight	fighting	fight(s)	fought	fought
(to) find	finding	find(s)	found	found
(to) fling	flinging	fling(s)	flung	flung
(to) get	getting	get(s)	got	got(-ten)
(to) grind	grinding	grind(s)	ground	ground
(to) hang	hanging	hang(s)	hung	hung
(to) hold	holding	hold(s)	held	held
(to) keep	keeping	keep(s)	kept	kept
(to) lay	laying	lay(s)	laid	laid
(to) lead	leading	lead(s)	led	led
(to) leave	leaving	leave(s)	left	left
(to) lose	losing	lose(s)	lost	lost
(to) pay	paying	pay(s)	paid	paid
(to) say	saying	say(s)*	said	said
(to) seek	seeking	seek(s)	sought	sought
(to) send	sending	send(s)	sent	sent
(to) shine	shining	shine(s)	shined, shone	shined, shone
(to) show	showing	show(s)	showed	showed, shown
(to) sit	sitting	sit(s)	sat	sat
(to) sleep	sleeping	sleep(s)	slept	slept
(to) spend	spending	spend(s)	spent	spent
(to) spin	spinning	spin(s)	spun	spun
(to) stand	standing	stand(s)	stood	stood
(to) stick	sticking	stick(s)	stuck	stuck
(to) sting	stinging	sting(s)	stung	stung
(to) strike	striking	strike(s)	struck	struck
(to) swing	swinging	swing(s)	swung	swung
(to) teach	teaching	teach(es)	taught	taught
(to) win	winning	win(s)	won	won
(to) wind	winding	wind(s)	wound	wound
(to) wring	wringing	wring(s)	wrung	wrung

*Notice sounds change.

Copyright © 1985 by Harcourt Brace Jovanovich, Inc. All rights reserved.

Principal Parts of Irregular Verbs				
Base (Infinitive)	Present Participle	Present	Past	Past Participle
Past Tense and Past Participle Different				
(to) be	being	am, is, are	was, were	been
(to) begin	beginning	begin(s)	began	begun
(to) blow	blowing	blow(s)	blew	blown
(to) break	breaking	break(s)	broke	broken
(to) come	coming	come(s)	came	come
(to) dive	diving	dive(s)	dove, dived	dived
(to) do	doing	do(es)	did	done
(to) draw	drawing	draw(s)	drew	drawn
(to) drink	drinking	drink(s)	drank	drunk
(to) drive	driving	drive(s)	drove	driven
(to) eat	eating	eat(s)	ate	eaten
(to) fall	falling	fall(s)	fell	fallen
(to) fly	flying	fly(flies)	flew	flown
(to) freeze	freezing	freeze(s)	froze	frozen
(to) give	giving	give(s)	gave	given

All regular verbs form their principal parts by adding a suffix to the base. Observe the pattern in the regular verbs *walk*, *heat*, and *clean*.

Answer the following questions:

1. What suffix is added to the base to form the present participle? _____

2. What difference is there between the base and the present tense? _____

3. When do you use the ''s'' form in the present tense? _____

4. When do you use the form without the ''s'' in the present tense? _____

5. What suffix is added to the base to form the past tense? _____

6. What suffix is added to the base to form the past participle? _____

7. What is another name for the base of a verb? _____

8. What principal part of the verb appears in boldface in this statement? **To run** makes me feel good. _____

Copyright © 1985 by Harcourt Brace Jovanovich, Inc. All rights reserved.

9.   What principal part of the verb appears in boldface in this statement? **Waving**

to the crowd, Kris Kristofferson entered the hotel. _____

10.   What principal part of the verb appears in boldface in this statement? The **sealed**

documents were strewn across the floor. _____

Answers

1. -ing;   2. -s and/or none;   3. in the present tense (3rd singular);   4. unless the subject is "he, she, it, Jack, mouse," etc. (unless subject is 3rd singular);   5. -ed;   6. -ed;   7. infinitive;   8. infinitive (base);   9. present participle;   10. past participle.

EXERCISE 2

Supply the past tense for the following verbs.

1.   When he (buy) _____ his motorcycle, his registra-

tion (cost) _____ him less than he (pay) _____
for his helmet.

2.   As he (ride) _____ down the freeway, he (fling)

_____ the apple core into the brush beside the road.

3.   The rider (seek) _____ gumption during the jour-

ney he (make) _____ across the country.

4.   After his motorcycle (break) _____ in Montana, he

(tear) _____ it apart before he (throw) _____

_____ the cracked piston into the ravine.

5.   Throughout his westward journey the cyclist (strive) _____

to understand each day before he (sleep) _____ .

Supply the present perfect tense for the following verbs.

1.   The cyclist (beat) _____ his record many times, yet

Copyright © 1985 by Harcourt Brace Jovanovich, Inc. All rights reserved.

he (lose) _____ all desire to compete in cross-country biking events.

2. The cyclist's study of the classics (bring) _____ him

   joy and understanding which (keep) _____ him from abandoning his journey.

3. The cyclist and his son (build) _____ close relationship during their trip from Chicago to San Francisco.

4. The father and son (spend) _____ three weeks traveling west on their motorcycle.

5. One day the father said to his son, "We (fall) _____

   into a bad habit and (begin) _____ to substitute snacks for meals."

Supply the past perfect tense for the following verbs.

1. The sun (shine) _____ seven days before the rain began.

2. The man and boy (creep) _____ through the mountains because they loved the sparkling streams and tall redwoods.

3. They lost their way several times because they (forget) _____ to include a roadmap in their gear.

4. Since they (strike) _____out without preparation, they had

   to spend time and much needed money for things they (leave) _____ behind.

5. Although they (spread) _____ a tarpaulin over themselves before going to sleep, they found the next morning that they (get)

   _____ wet anyway.

Copyright © 1985 by Harcourt Brace Jovanovich, Inc. All rights reserved.

Notes

CONJUGATING VERBS

Learning to conjugate a verb is a useful way to fix the system of verb tenses in your mind. A conjugation is the orderly arrangement of a verb in its several persons (I, you, he [she, it], we, you, they), numbers (singular or plural), and tenses. To conjugate a verb, simply combine the pronouns *I, you, he (she, it), we, you, and they* with the appropriate form of the verb. The conjugation of the verb *ride* is presented on these pages.

Answer each study question to help you notice details about conjugating verbs. The terminology used here is only to help you observe the function and changes in verbs.

1. How many principal parts does a verb have? _____

2. What change do you observe between the third person singular, simple present tense and all other forms of the simple present tense? _____

3. What changes do you observe between the third person singular, present emphatic tense and all other forms of the present emphatic tense? _____

4. What is the infinitive of the verb that is used as an auxiliary to form the progressive tenses? _____

5. What is the first person singular, present tense of the auxiliary used to form the present progressive tense? _____

6. What is the second person (singular or plural) of the auxiliary used to form the present progressive tense? _____

7. What is the third person singular of the auxiliary used to form the present progressive tense? _____

8. What is the infinitive of the auxiliary used to form the present and past emphatic tenses? _____

9. What is the infinitive of the auxiliary used to form the present perfect? _____

10. What is the infinitive of the auxiliary used to form the past perfect tense? _____

11. What is the auxiliary used to form the future tense? _____

Copyright © 1985 by Harcourt Brace Jovanovich, Inc. All rights reserved.

Complete Conjugation of a Verb				
Principal Parts				
Infinitive	Present Participle	Present	Past	Past Participle
(to) ride	riding	ride(s)	rode	ridden

Singular	Plural

———————————— Present tense ————————————

	Singular	Plural
1st	I ride	We ride
2nd	You ride	You ride
3rd	He, (she, it) rides	They ride

Present tense (progressive form)

	Singular	Plural
1st	I am riding	We are riding
2nd	You are riding	You are riding
3rd	He (she, it) is riding	They are riding

Present tense (emphatic form)

	Singular	Plural
1st	I do ride	We do ride
2nd	You do ride	You do ride
3rd	He (she, it) does ride	They do ride

———————————— Past tense ————————————

	Singular	Plural
1st	I rode	We rode
2nd	You rode	You rode
3rd	He (she, it) rode	They rode

Past tense (progressive form)

	Singular	Plural
1st	I was riding	We were riding
2nd	You were riding	You were riding
3rd	he (she, it) was riding	They were riding

Past tense (emphatic form)

	Singular	Plural
1st	I did ride	We did ride
2nd	You did ride	You did ride
3rd	He (she, it) did ride	They did ride

———————————— Future tense ————————————

	Singular	Plural
1st	I will ride	We will ride
2nd	You will ride	You will ride
3rd	He (she, it) will ride	They will ride

Future tense (progressive form)

	Singular	Plural
1st	I will be riding	We will be riding
2nd	You will be riding	You will be riding
3rd	He (she, it) will be riding	They will be riding

Copyright © 1985 by Harcourt Brace Jovanovich, Inc. All rights reserved.

Complete Conjugation of a Verb				
Principal Parts				
Infinitive	Present Participle	Present	Past	Past Participle
(to) ride	riding	ride(s)	rode	ridden

Singular	Plural

——————————— Present perfect tense ———————————

	Singular	Plural
1st	I have ridden	We have ridden
2nd	You have ridden	You have ridden
3rd	He (she, it) has ridden	They have ridden

Present perfect tense (progressive form)

	Singular	Plural
1st	I have been riding	We have been riding
2nd	You have been riding	You have been riding
3rd	He (she, it) has been riding	They have been riding

——————————— Past perfect tense ———————————

	Singular	Plural
1st	I had ridden	We had ridden
2nd	You had ridden	You had ridden
3rd	He (she, it) had ridden	They had ridden

Past perfect tense (progressive form)

	Singular	Plural
1st	I had been riding	We had been riding
2nd	You had been riding	You had been riding
3rd	He (she, it) had been riding	They had been riding

——————————— Future perfect tense ———————————

	Singular	Plural
1st	I will have ridden	We will have ridden
2nd	You will have ridden	You will have ridden
3rd	He (she, it) will have ridden	They will have ridden

Future perfect tense (progressive form)

	Singular	Plural
1st	I will have been riding	We will have been riding
2nd	You will have been riding	You will have been riding
3rd	He (she, it) will have been riding	They will have been riding

12. What difference do you observe between the present perfect tense and the future perfect tense? _____

13. What principal part of the verb is used to form the progressive tenses? _____

_____

Copyright © 1985 by Harcourt Brace Jovanovich, Inc. All rights reserved.

14. Do you notice any change in the verb in any of the plural forms of any of the

    tenses? _____

15. Do you realize that by knowing the principal parts of any verb and following the system demonstrated above, you could form any verb in the lan-

    guage? _____

Answers

1. five; 2. -s; 3. *does* instead of *do*; 4. be; 5. am; 6. are; 7. is; 8. do; 9. have; 10. have; 11. will; 12. will; 13. present participle; 14. no; 15. If not, study and ask your teacher.

EXERCISE 3

Write the third person singular form for each of the tenses indicated.

Example _____ *it will have rung* _____

1. future perfect of *ring* _____

2. future of *grow* _____

3. future perfect progressive of *smell* _____

4. present emphatic of *steal* _____

5. present perfect progressive of *run* _____

6. past of *grin* _____

7. present of *clean* _____

8. present perfect of *burst* _____

9. present emphatic of *sit* _____

10. past progressive of *feed* _____

11. future progressive of *awake* _____

12. present of *wash* _____

13. past perfect of *fix* _____

Copyright © 1985 by Harcourt Brace Jovanovich, Inc. All rights reserved.

14. present progressive of *leave* _____

15. past emphatic of *buy* _____

16. present perfect of *let* _____

17. past perfect progressive of *find* _____

18. past of *swim* _____

19. present of *sing* _____

20. past perfect of *thrown* _____

TENSE SEQUENCE

In English, the verb tenses help establish logical relationships among experiences. Every experience logically happens at this moment (present), before this moment (past), or after this moment (future). Careful writers choose among the various forms of the tenses to express time relationships exactly. By observing the sequence of tenses in the verb charts, you can learn to express those relationships exactly and to subordinate one idea to another in your writing. As you develop skill in choosing the precise tense for your main verb which governs your choice of tense in your subordinate verb, you can control the precise time relationships you have in mind.

Rule of Thumb. If the main verb is in a progressive form, the verb in a subordinate clause will ordinarily be in the present or past tense. Similarly, if the main verb is in one of the perfect tenses, the verb in a subordinate clause will be present or past.

To increase your familiarity with tense sequences, answer these questions by studying the chart that outlines the sequences of verb tenses.

1. If a main verb is in the present tense, how many different tense forms can follow

   in the subordinate clause? _____

2. Are there verb tense forms that cannot follow a main verb in the present tense?

   _____

3. If a main verb is in the past tense, how many different tense forms can follow

   in the subordinate clause? _____

4. To what tense do all the verb tense forms that follow a main verb in the past

   tense belong? _____

Copyright © 1985 by Harcourt Brace Jovanovich, Inc. All rights reserved.

Sequence of Verb Tenses		
Main Verb	Subordinate Verb	Relationship
Main Verb in Present Tense		
I see that you	**present** *draw* now **pres. emph.** *do draw* now **pres. prog.** *are drawing* now	*Seeing* and *drawing* happen at the same time (present).
I see that you	**past** *drew* yesterday **past emph.** *did draw* yesterday **past prog.** *were drawing* yesterday **pres. perf.** *have drawn* recently **pres. perf. prog.** *have been drawing* recently	The *drawing* happens before the *seeing*.
I see that you	**past perf.** *had drawn* yesterday **past** and *finished* **past perf. prog.** *had been drawing* yesterday **past** and *finished*	The *drawing* happens before the *finishing*— both of which happen before the *seeing*.
I see that you	**future** *will draw* tomorrow **future perf. prog.** *will be drawing* tomorrow	The *seeing* happens before the *drawing*.
I see that you	**fut. perf.** *will have drawn* **pres.** before I *return* **fut. perf. prog.** *will have been drawing* **pres.** before I *return*	The *seeing* happens before the *drawing*— both of which happen *before the returning*.

Copyright © 1985 by Harcourt Brace Jovanovich, Inc. All rights reserved.

Sequence of Verb Tenses		
Main Verb	Subordinate Verb	Relationship
Main Verb in Past Tense		
I saw that you	**past** *drew* yesterday **past emph.** *did draw* yesterday **past prog.** *were drawing* yesterday	All events happen before now (present).
I saw that you	**past perf.** *had drawn* yesterday **past perf. prog.** *had been drawing* **past** when I *arrived*	The *drawing* happens before the *seeing* and the *arriving*; the *seeing* and the *arriving* happen at the same time.

5. When is the auxiliary "will" repeated in a subordinate clause if the main verb

is in the future tense? _____

(*Hint*: The future tense uses the auxiliary "will.")

Answers

1. 14 (all of them);   2. no, all forms may;   3. 5 (only forms of past tense);   4. any form of the past tense;   5. never (Ordinarily do not use the same form of an auxiliary in both the main and the subordinate clauses.)

    When checking your tense sequence in your writing, compare the time relationship that you have in mind with the tense forms and sequences used in the chart to express those relationships. If you use tense forms and sequences differently from those on the chart, your problem will probably not be one of logic. Rather, it is more likely that you are using the tense sequences of one of the many dialects that enrich the English language. Since tense sequences in dialects are predictable and regular, it will be easy for you to equate any sequence pattern you may be using to the sequence pattern of Standard Written English, the dialect required for college writing. Successful college students have more than one dialect, and they learn to use them at the appropriate times.

Copyright © 1985 by Harcourt Brace Jovanovich, Inc. All rights reserved.

Sequence of Verb Tenses		
Main Verb	Subordinate Verb	Relationship
Main Verb in Future Tense		
I will see if you	**pres.** *draw* tomorrow **pres. emph.** *do draw* tomorrow **pres. prog.** *are drawing* tomorrow	Both the *seeing* and the *drawing* will happen in the future—at the same time.
I will see if you	**past** *drew* yesterday **past emph.** *did draw* yesterday **past prog.** *were drawing* yesterday **pres. perf.** *have drawn* recently **pres. perf. prog.** *have been drawing* recently	The *drawing* happens before the *seeing*.

PASSIVE VOICE

Another feature of the verb is its *voice*, of which there are only two: *active* and *passive*. All of the verbs in the conjugations are in the active voice. A conjugation of the passive voice has no emphatic forms and only two progressive forms: present and past. Otherwise, it has the same forms as a conjugation in the active voice. In the passive voice, a form of (*to*) *be* combined with the past participle of a verb controls the tense.

Answer each of the following study questions by referring to the chart on page 211. Your answers will help you think through the details of the passive voice.

1. What is the last word in every passive verb phrase above? _____

Copyright © 1985 by Harcourt Brace Jovanovich, Inc. All rights reserved.

Common Tenses of the Passive Voice (Third Person Singular Only)			
present progressive	it is ridden it is being ridden	present perfect	it has been ridden
past progressive	it was ridden it was being ridden	past perfect	it had been ridden
future	it will be ridden	future perfect	it will have been ridden

2. What is the name of the principal part of the verb that occupies the final position in a passive verb phrase? _____

3. Which tenses have more than one form of the passive voice? _____

4. What part of the verb phrase is the clue to what the tense is in the passive voice?

   _____

5. How do you form the present progressive passive if the subject of the verb phrase is *I*? I _____

6. How do you form the past perfect passive if the subject of the verb phrase is *we*? We _____

7. How do you form the present passive if the subject of the verb phrase is *they*? They _____

8. How do you form the future passive if the subject of the verb phrase is *she*? She _____

9. How do you form the past passive if the subject of the verb phrase is *you*? You _____

10. How do you form the present perfect passive if the subject of the verb phrase is *Frank*. Frank _____

Copyright © 1985 by Harcourt Brace Jovanovich, Inc. All rights reserved.

Answers

1. ridden;   2. past participle;   3. present and past;   4. auxiliary (a form of *to be*);   5. I am being ridden;   6. we had been ridden;   7. they are ridden;   8. she will be ridden;   9. you were ridden;   10. Frank has been ridden

(*Tip*: Being able to name the tenses of the passive voice is not the purpose of these questions. What is important is to be able to construct passive verbs when you need them.)

In college writing, use the active voice in preference to the passive voice because the active voice emphasizes the actor whereas the passive voice emphasizes the action. When you choose the passive voice, be sure it serves a particular purpose and it helps you achieve the effect you intend in your writing. The passive voice provides an option that allows you to express an action and its effect without having to be concerned about who performed the action. Writers use the passive voice most frequently to report information when they do not know who performed an action or when they want to withhold who performed the action they are reporting.

A word of caution about the use of the passive voice: Even though the sequence of tenses for the passive voice is the same as for the active voice (see chart "Sequence of Verb Tenses"), problems may occur if you use the passive voice in both the main clause and the subordinate clause. Specifically, your reader may think you are trying to be evasive or to displace responsibility for an action if you use the passive voice in both clauses. Consider the following sentence:

Example   It is said that the motorcycle was ridden.

In this example, the reader is in doubt about who made the statement and who did the riding if riding happened at all. Of course, if your purpose is to deemphasize the rider, then the passive voice in both clauses serves you well. If you have a different intention, the active voice may serve your purpose in at least one of the clauses. Compare the following examples with the preceding one.

Example   Glenda said that Frank rode the motorcycle.
　　　　　　　　　active　　　　　　active

　　　　　　　　　passive　　　　active
　　　　　　　It was said that Frank rode the motorcycle.

　　　　　　　　　active　　　　　　　　　passive
　　　　　　　Glenda said that the motorcycle was ridden.

In English, the expected sentence order is subject first, verb next, and direct object last.

Example 1   The professor rides the motorcycle.
　　　　　　　　　　　S　　　V　　　DO

Copyright © 1985 by Harcourt Brace Jovanovich, Inc. All rights reserved.

The passive voice provides an alternative to this expected sentence pattern:

	S	V	O Preposition
Example 2	The motorcycle is ridden by the professor.		

Compare the two examples and answer the questions which follow.

1. In example 1, what is the subject of the sentence? _____

2. In example 2, what is the object of the preposition *by*? _____

3. In example 2, what is the subject of the sentence? _____

4. In example 1, what is the direct object? _____

5. In example 1, what is the verb? _____

6. In example 1, what is the tense of the verb? _____

7. In example 2, what is the verb? _____

8. In example 2, what is the tense of the verb? _____

9. What part of the sentence does the subject in example 1 move to in example 2?

    _____

10. What part of the sentence does the direct object in example 1 move to in ex-

    ample 2? _____

11. In addition to the form of the verb *to be*, what word has to be added to change

    example 1 to example 2? _____

12. When would you choose example 2 (the one with the verb in the passive voice)

    rather than example 1 (the one with the verb in the active voice)? _____

Answers

1. professor; 2. professor; 3. motorcycle; 4. motorcycle; 5. rides; 6. present; 7. is ridden; 8. present passive; 9. object of preposition; 10. subject; 11 by; 12. when you want to emphasize **motorcycle** rather than **professor**

Copyright © 1985 by Harcourt Brace Jovanovich, Inc. All rights reserved.

EXERCISE 4

Rewrite these sentences, using the active voice to focus on the actor or to emphasize responsibility for the action.

Example   The boat was blown by the wind.
           The wind blew the boat.

1. Cars and motorcycles are made of steel.

     _____

2. Bob's motorcycle was stolen by my best friend Bill.

     _____

3. Special skills are needed to cook meat over an open campfire.

     _____

4. Many lessons about the woods and nature are learned by an observant biker during a trip.

     _____

5. The grocery store was cheated out of a pound of coffee by my mother.

     _____

6. Farmer Brown's haystack was destroyed last week when my new motorcycle was ridden cross country.

     _____

7. While supper is being cooked by a friend, a biker can be occupied by repair.

     _____

8. The other racers were outsmarted by the biker when the creek was cut through by her.

     _____

9. Maintenance gumption is considered something you are born with.

     _____

10. Gumption was used by pioneers when they settled America.

     _____

Copyright © 1985 by Harcourt Brace Jovanovich, Inc. All rights reserved.

4.11 *PROOFREADING POWER*

Even though you revise your writing several times before your final copy, you sometimes discover a faulty tense sequence or an incorrectly formed tense during proofreading. If you discover one, you should revise it before continuing to proofread. As a test of your skill in spotting problems with verb tenses, proofread the following selection and change any errors you detect in the verbs. Ordinarily, you will not find as many errors when proofreading your own writing as you will find in the following exercise because you will have already revised several times.

(**3**) *Zen and the Art of Motorcycle Maintenance*, a popular book by Robert Pirsig, tell the tale of a father and son that all college students should be reading at least once. (**2**) It has been narrated by the father, who either did repair his motorcycle or else was talking about philosophical things like ''gumption.'' (**3**) Because the father and his son had gave up all the comforts of home during their trip, they will have to be resourceful to find a place to camp where they have been finding bath facilities. (**4**) During the trip, both begun to appreciate each other and to understanding that everybody have to have his say in things. (**5**) This lesson will be a valuable lesson for them to learn when they will get home. (**6**) It also be one that everyone would have knowed if they had read the book. (**7**) If you like stories about fathers and sons, you will enjoy Pirsig's narrative, and you will learn a lot from it.

4.12 *DICTATION*

Your teacher will choose a passage of approximately 100 words and read it aloud as you write what you hear. As you listen to each sentence, concentrate and maintain silence. Do not ask your instructor to repeat because any sound other than the instructor's voice reading will break not only your concentration but that of others. Your instructor may repeat key words and phrases during the dictation, will allow sufficient time for you to write what you have heard, and will reread the entire passage a second time at a faster rate so that you can check what you have written and fill in any gap you may have.

You will want to write on every other line so that you will have space to correct your dictation in case you have made a mistake. Your instructor will show you the dictated passage and ask you to compare your version, or perhaps a classmate's version, to the original. Be especially alert when you check the dictation because this exercise will help you develop your sentence sense by translating spoken into written language.

Copyright © 1985 by Harcourt Brace Jovanovich, Inc. All rights reserved.

4.13 WORD POWER

WRITE IT RIGHT

In the haste of writing a draft, it is easy to use a word that sounds like the word you had in mind but is spelled differently. Correct word usage and spelling provide yard-sticks for readers to judge your competency and thus your ideas. Good writers are careful to use the right word and to spell it correctly. In fact, correct spelling remains the mark of an educated person. When you reread your writing you can notice if you have made an error in spelling if you are aware that words which have the same or similar sounds and forms are spelled differently and have entirely different meanings and uses.

EXERCISE 1

To increase your awareness of words that have the same or similar sounds and forms, match column 2 to column 1 in the following exercise. The words in column 1 appear in the reading selection in the order presented below. Those in column 2 have similar sounds, but they could never substitute for their sound-alikes. The words in column 2 appear in column 1 in later exercises. (*Hint:* If you discover words that you confuse with any of the words on this list, learn the differences between them to keep from confusing your reader when you write. A good way to do this is to *skim* the selection until you encounter one of the sound-alike words; then, notice how the author has used the word in the passage you have been skimming. Modified skimming used in this way helps you learn meanings of words in context.)

____ 1.	I	a.	sense
____ 2.	to	b.	buy
____ 3.	own	c.	on
____ 4.	hear	d.	eye
____ 5.	no	e.	too
____ 6.	you're	f.	your
____ 7.	sit	g.	set
____ 8.	since	h.	here
____ 9.	there	i.	know
____ 10.	by	j.	their

Copyright © 1985 by Harcourt Brace Jovanovich, Inc. All rights reserved.

The English language contains a number of words which sound alike or look alike because they have the same or similar sounds or forms. Even experienced writers can make slips in diction with these troublesome words. You may have experienced the same difficulty. Study the italicized words in each sentence to learn their meanings and usage from context (the surroundings a word appears in). The use of a word (whether it is a noun, verb, preposition, and so forth) is often the key to separating it from its sound-alike or look-alike. Sometimes a memory aid or explanation is provided to help you distinguish among them.

1. a. The amount of time Mai Tsai *needs* to study keeps her from watching soap operas on television.
   b. Mai Tsai had learned to *knead* dough while she reviews her notes.
2. a. Aaron hollered loudly from the yard so his mother could *hear* him.
   b. His mother responded, "Come *here*, Aaron and help me carry in the groceries!"
3. a. Smokey, a furry Persian cat, rubbed *its* ears on Bill's leg as he sat at the desk.
   b. *It's* comforting to have a furry cat around when you study late at night. (*Hint:* The apostrophe in *it's* **always** stands for the "i" in *is*. *It's* is a contraction of **two** words, *it is*.)
4. a. Herman Melville told of his experiences at *sea* in *White Jacket*.
   b. You can *see* Melville's grave at one New York cemetery.
5. a. *Since* graduating from high school, Anthony has wrecked two pickups and his sister's Trans Am. (*Hint: Since* is a conjunction which shows a time relationship between actions.)
   b. Angela replaced her car with the insurance money, but she refuses to let Anthony drive it because she says he doesn't have any *sense*.
6. a. Members of student government contributed *their* services as ushers for the Rolling Stones concert. (*Hint: Their* refers to *members* and shows that the *services* belong to them.)
   b. The trophy stood *there* near the president's office until vandals destroyed it. (*Hint: There* indicates specific location.)
   c. *They're* organizing a committee to raise funds to replace the trophy. (*Hint: They're* is a contraction for *they are*.)
7. a. The victorious Seattle Seahawks retired *to* the locker room. (*Hint:* If you pronounce *to* as "tuh," it is usually a preposition.)
   b. The Seattle Seahawks were *too* tired to celebrate. (*Hint:* Notice the difference in sound between the adverb *too* and the preposition *to*. If you keep this rule of thumb in mind, you will never confuse the two.)
   c. The Washington Redskins have won *two* superbowls. (*Hint: Two* is the number 2, and you can replace it with the number as a test.)
8. a. The *whole* glee club sang in concert during the commencement exercises.
   b. As the glee club sang, water dripped on them through a *hole* in the roof.

Copyright © 1985 by Harcourt Brace Jovanovich, Inc. All rights reserved.

9.   If *you're* observant, you can improve *your* writing by avoiding the pitfalls of sound-alike words. (*Hint: You're* is a contraction for *you are*. The apostrophe replaces the ''a'' in ''are.'' *Your* is the possessive of *you* and shows the relationship between *you* and the *writing* you do: your writing.)

10. a.   Every choice you make sets you on *one* road or another.
    b.   When your school has *won* a championship, every student can take pride in the victory.

11. a.   Fishermen are *quiet* so as not to frighten the fish away.
    b.   Sitting silently to fish can be *quite* a difficult task.

12. a.   A *week* of isolation on a motorcycle trip can help you acquire ''gumption.''
    b.   The enthusiasm and energy necessary to acquire ''gumption'' is not for the *weak*.

13. a.   The world can *seem* disorganized and confused if you lack ''gumption.''
    b.   When you've got ''gumption,'' you feel as if you're bursting at the *seams*.

14. a.   Your *mind* operates in a different way when you have ''gumption.''
    b.   I hope that ''gumption'' is a quality of yours and *mine*.

15. a.   A person filled with ''gumption'' looks at life in a *new* way.
    b.   If a person *knew* how to acquire ''gumption,'' why would he live without it?

16. a.   Because having ''gumption'' changes the way you do things, it is an *affective* force for good in your life.
    b.   To understand basic truths about your world is an *effective* way to acquire ''gumption.''

17. a.   The *sight* of landscape from a speeding motorcycle blends one image into another.
    b.   Pirsig *cites* a definition of ''enthusiasm.''
    c.   A camp *site* situated on a mountain top lets you have a panoramic view of the surrounding countryside.

18. a.   Once you acquire ''gumption,'' you never want to *lose* it.
    b.   A *loose* motorcycle chain will damage the drive shaft.

19. a.   To be *thrown* from a speeding motorcycle usually results in serious injury.
    b.   Riding a motorcycle can make you feel as if you were sitting on the *throne* of kings.

20. a.   Keeping your tools in a *bin* will keep them from getting mixed up with the usual clutter in a garage.
    b.   Most who have *been* touring on a motorcycle enjoyed it.

EXERCISE 2

Write your own sentences to show your mastery of the sound-alikes studied in the previous sentences. Strive to write sentences that will interest your reader and that have variety.

Copyright © 1985 by Harcourt Brace Jovanovich, Inc. All rights reserved.

1. quiet _____
   _____

2. quite _____
   _____

3. mine _____
   _____

4. bin _____
   _____

5. weak _____
   _____

6. a lot _____
   _____

7. thrown _____
   _____

8. seam _____
   _____

9. its _____
   _____

10. loose _____
    _____

11. since _____
    _____

12. their _____

Copyright © 1985 by Harcourt Brace Jovanovich, Inc. All rights reserved.

_____

13. too _____

_____

14. whole _____

_____

15. site _____

_____

EXERCISE 3

Supply the proper look-alike or sound-alike word to complete the meaning of the following sentences.

1. It's/its _____ important too/two/to _____ understand the subtleties of language.

2. Mothers insist that they're/there/their _____ daughters stay here/hear

   _____ .

3. The Redskin line opens a whole/hole _____ for the fullback to/too/two

   _____ charge through.

4. The affect/effect _____ of conscientious practice can reinforce the

   fundamentals introduced during the weak/week _____ .

5. You're/your _____ attention to/too/two _____ details can

   help you lose/loose _____ bad habits.

6. The site/sight/cite _____ of natural beauty adds a whole/hole

   _____ new/knew _____ effective/affective _____

   dimension to/too/two _____ your/you're _____ search for
   gumption.

Copyright © 1985 by Harcourt Brace Jovanovich, Inc. All rights reserved.

7. To no/know _____ who is to sit/set _____ on the

throne/thrown _____ can help you see/sea _____ how
history works itself out.

8. Sense/since _____ your/you're _____ here/hear _____ ,

your/you're _____ required to be quite/quiet _____ .

9. Won/one _____ week/weak _____ is allot/a lot _____

to be thrown/throne _____ away.

10. New/knew _____ cites/sites/sights _____ help develop

your/you're _____ mind/mine _____ .

Copyright © 1985 by Harcourt Brace Jovanovich, Inc. All rights reserved.

Notes

SPELLING

Because you must be concerned about so many different things when you write, you may occasionally write a sound-alike word for the word you need—*who's* for *whose* or *canvass* for *canvas*. Even published writers make such slips from time to time, but they find and correct them during proofreading. When you make such a slip, correct the error as soon as you spot it. By learning the meanings and spellings of the sound-alike words, you are more likely to spot errors in using them when you proofread.

Even with study the chances of overlooking an error are greater when you incorrectly use a sound-alike word that is also a look-alike word. These words look alike because they are approximately the same length and contain many of the same letters. When you read over them during proofreading, you may miss the error because the word may be spelled correctly but used incorrectly. Whenever you encounter one of these words, then, you should be alert to notice whether you have used the word you need or its look-alike. Study the list and learn any of the words on the list that you are not sure of. For any words you are not sure of, look in your dictionary.

bath	council	lightning
bathe	counsel	lightening
breath	desert	prophecy
breathe	dessert	prophesy
canvas	later	though
canvass	latter	thorough
conscience	liable	
conscious	libel	

EXERCISE 4

Write the correct word in the blank.

1. Whenever I take a bath/bathe _____ , I am careful to bath/bathe

   _____ behind my ears.

2. Every time I breath/breathe _____ , I wonder if it will be my last

   breath/breath _____ .

3. When I cross the desert/dessert) _____ , I enjoy having icecream for

   desert/dessert _____ .

Copyright © 1985 by Harcourt Brace Jovanovich, Inc. All rights reserved.

4. By lightning/lightening _____ my load, I was able to climb to the cave before the lightning/lightening _____ storm.

5. Though/thorough _____ I had done a though/thorough _____ investigation through my thoughts and research, I wondered if I were through.

6. I was conscience/conscious _____ of my conscience/conscious _____ telling me to be careful.

7. I will discuss the later/latter _____ of the two problems later/latter _____ .

8. The student council/counsel _____ arranges for employers to council/counsel _____ students on career day.

9. If you make false statements in print about someone, you are libel/liable _____ to be accused of libel/liable _____ .

10. People who claim to be clairvoyant prophesy/prophecy _____ that their most recent prophesy/prophecy _____ will come true.

11. The church rented a number of canvas/canvass _____ chairs for the census takers who were to canvas/canvass _____ the community.

Copyright © 1985 by Harcourt Brace Jovanovich, Inc. All rights reserved.

UNIT FIVE
WRITING
TAILORED

5.1 GETTING STARTED BY READING

Every day many people take time for light reading because it eases the pressures and soothes the hassles of a busy life. Since light reading does not require the attention serious reading demands, it can help you rest and relax or pass time pleasurably. Sometimes when reading for pleasure or recreation, you will remind yourself of things you already know; at other times, you may chase outlaws in the old west, live the life of an international spy, or explore galaxies as yet undiscovered. The books, magazines, or newspapers you choose for light reading will reflect your interests and will afford ways to pass time, satisfy curiosity, and get ideas for interesting conversation.

During light reading, move along as fast as you can comfortably to still catch the ideas. When you read at this speed, you do not intend to recall exact details or even fix ideas in your mind though an impression will likely stay with you which you might mention in conversation.

Category	Light reading
Rate	Slower than skimming
Purposes	To pass time
	To remind yourself of something you already know
	To satisfy curiosity

	To get ideas for interesting conversation
	To participate in imaginary worlds
Typical	Mysteries
light	Westerns
reading	Travel stories
	Adventure novels
	Science fiction
	Weekly news magazines
	Fashion magazines
	Hobby magazines
	Sunday newspaper supplements
	Reviews of movies or other cultural events
	The sports page
	Vacation brochures
	Collections of trivia

Read ''How to Make a Terrarium'' as fast as you can and enjoy discovering what may become a new interest. As you read, try to form honest responses to these questions.

1. Would I prefer reading this to staring into space while waiting for an appointment? If your answer is no, what kind of reading on the preceding list would you prefer?
2. Is making a terrarium something I would like to do sometime?
3. Would anyone I know be interested in making a terrarium?

5.2 PROCESS

Nancy Bubel   *''HOW TO MAKE A TERRARIUM''*

If you need an excuse for a walk in the woods, make a terrarium. Gathering terrarium ingredients sharpens one's appreciation of the rich variety of life at boot level. Terrarium makers see the world in fine. No detail escapes their attention. A confirmed devotee could probably wander in a redwood grove with gaze fixed on the ground— looking for moss of just the right texture, tiny seedling trees, interesting bark chips. After I made my first terrarium, I found myself gathering tiny plants, lichens, and pebbles on every walk—and mentally collecting when I was not walking our own land.

Woodland plants are perfect for the terrarium. Most things that grow on the forest

Copyright © 1985 by Harcourt Brace Jovanovich, Inc. All rights reserved.

floor thrive in cool, moist, partly shady situations, which are easy to provide under glass. Many house plants adapt equally well to life in a terrarium. You can even grow exotics like the Venus flytrap, which requires warmth and moisture and gets along on soil nutrients when no flies happen by.

Whether you gather the makings of your miniature landscape on the trail, in a greenhouse, or from among your houseplants, the procedure for assembling the terrarium is the same. First, you need a container. Any kind of transparent, waterproof, easily covered container may be used to house a terrarium. Some of the more popular enclosures for these self-contained gardens include brandy snifters, apothecary jars, fish bowls, rectangular aquarium cases, and large glass carboys. Wine jugs, large test tubes, butter jars, mason jars, gallon mayonnaise jars (from restaurants), and even baby-food jars may also be used. Jean Hersey, the authority on wildflowers, once constructed a terrarium in the globe of a 150-watt light bulb with the threaded end broken off.

Wide-mouthed containers are easiest to plant by hand; those with narrow necks are tricky but by no means impossible. You need a few tools—a planter made of a length of wire coat hanger straightened out, with a loop on one end to hold the plant; a tamper, which could be a dowel stuck into a cork, or whatever you can improvise from materials at hand; a digger, a long-handled spoon, or any kind of long, thin poker capable of making a hole in loose soil. A long-handled tweezers is also useful. Use a rolled-up newspaper as a funnel to direct the soil to the bottom of the jug.

Begin by putting down a base composed of several layers, as follows, remembering that each layer serves a purpose. First, put down a mat of moss to absorb moisture and form an attractive lining. Then pour a layer of sand or fine gravel over the moss to promote drainage and prevent waterlogging. Next scatter a handful of charcoal pieces over the gravel to prevent souring of the soil.

Now add the final layer—soil. Bagged sterilized soil is fine, but if you want to mix your own, aim for the following proportions:

2 parts topsoil
1 part sand
1 part leafmold or compost

Copyright © 1985 by Harcourt Brace Jovanovich, Inc. All rights reserved.

Put in a thin layer, just covering the charcoal. Then set the plants in place and firm the remainder of the soil around their roots. Much of this soil will later settle lower around the roots.

Arranging the topography of the terrarium is a matter of taste. You might keep in mind that a variety of leaf textures is usually pleasing, and that plants of different heights and shapes—pyramidal, tall and spiky, short and shrubby, trailing—make the scenery interesting. If your container is large enough you can even make a small hill or a path within its bounded wildness. Color may be provided by including partridge berries, mushrooms, lichens, and stones. No well-made terrarium needs a plastic deer or a china bird, but the woods are full of props that can add local color to your small scene: mossy twigs, weathered pieces of wood, scraps of textured bark, squirrel-gnawed nutshells. A weird craggy stone may be just the boulder you need for a classic gothic scene—a *romantische Landschaft* in miniature.

The pleasure of terrarium building, though, has more to do with the freedom to improvise, collect, seed, play with your materials, arrange a world as *you* would have it, than with conformity to a form. Do with it what you wish. Arrange and rearrange the plants until you are happy with the way they look.

When all the plants are in place, water the soil lightly, using less water than you think you'll need. You can always add more but you can't remove it. Overwatering encourages rot, mold, and fungus.

Covering the terrarium makes it a self-contained system, with its own weather: water vapor condenses on the walls and returns to the soil. Use the cover provided with the vessel or simply place a circle of glass over the top. (Plastic wrap is a more temporary but nonetheless practical cover.) Since each terrarium is a different ecosystem with its own water balance, it is impossible to formulate definite schedules for watering. Observation is the key. If the glass is misty, or if you notice mold anywhere within it, or water pooling on the bottom, the terrarium needs to be ventilated. Uncover it for about a day. Some people ventilate their terrariums rountinely once a week.

When should you add water? Seldom, if at all. If the terrarium is too dry, the soil

Copyright © 1985 by Harcourt Brace Jovanovich, Inc. All rights reserved.

will be lighter in color and the whole thing will feel lighter than normal when you pick it up. Use an eye dropper to add water—you'll be less likely to overwater.

Terrarium plants need some light, but direct sun will cook them. Indirect light on a table or light from a north window should suit most plant populations. If leaves turn brown, the terrarium is probably too hot. Try putting it in a cooler place.

Those of us accustomed to fertilizing houseplants may tend to include the terrarium in that routine, but it is best to keep terrarium soil on the lean side, lest the plants outgrow the container. Choice of plants influences the length of their stay too, of course. Our first house—a mid-nineteenth-century Philadelphia weaver's cottage—is now guarded by a pine that spent its first two years in a terrarium. When its top hit the cover we planted it in front of the loom shed. Now, twenty years later, it towers over the house. The loom shed is gone, but pine needles fall around its foundation. Everything lasts, we think as we drive by—just in a different form, sometimes.

5.3 UNDERSTANDING WHAT YOU READ

After completing your reading of "How to Make a Terrarium," answer the following questions to discover your reaction to what you have read and to record your impressions about learning to enjoy new activities.

1. a. Can you think of an activity that requires the same kind of abilities that making a terrarium does? What is it?

    _____

    b. What are the abilities terrarium making requires?

    _____

2. What are three steps that need to be included by a veteran when showing someone how to do the activity chosen in number one? Show the steps in logical order. (Are there additional steps that need to be included to ensure that the newcomer does not fail when performing the activity?)

    _____

    _____

Copyright © 1985 by Harcourt Brace Jovanovich, Inc. All rights reserved.

3. How are your activity and making a terrarium similar?

_____

_____

5.4 DISCOVERING IDEAS FOR WRITING

1. Make a list of three to five chores that you would do if you lived alone. _____

_____

_____

2. Which of these chores do you need to learn how to do? _____

_____

_____

3. Which of these chores can you teach someone else to do? _____

_____

_____

4. How could you improve the way you do these chores? _____

_____

_____

5. Are there any similarities between the way chores are performed when you do them alone and when you do them with someone else? With a group? With a crowd? What are they? _____

_____

_____

Copyright © 1985 by Harcourt Brace Jovanovich, Inc. All rights reserved.

5.5 UNDERSTANDING WRITING

Experienced writers regularly use some organizational principle to unify their writing and to provide a sense of order for their readers. Organization and unity result from planning.

The amount of planning each writer does before beginning to write differs from writer to writer and from project to project. Some writers think through an entire project before putting words in paragraphs, yet others plunge ahead with a sketch of the direction they intend to follow. Both may change or modify their plans to account for new thoughts, ideas, or directions which occur to them as they write.

As a developing writer, you can benefit from understanding the value of planning before beginning a draft and from recognizing that plans are usually altered during writing. There is no one ''right'' way to plan; all plans are ''right'' if they work for you. The only wrong plan is the one that you slavishly follow without being willing to change it when new insights come to you.

As a result of planning, writers often make informal outlines, list major points, or write a paragraph that summarizes the ideas to be included. Outlines, lists, and summaries help writers remember their plans. You have learned the discipline of a seasoned writer when you plan the organization of a piece of writing. At the same time, you should acquire the flexibility which gives you the freedom to change or modify that plan with new insights.

5.6 WRITING—PROCESS ANALYSIS

Your responses to the questions in 5.4 helped you analyze the process you use for managing your weekly chores. Explaining a process requires that you guide your reader step by step through an activity or set of activities. A set of instructions on how to do something and an account of how something happens explain processes. For example, a recipe explains a process; directions on a washing machine do too; instructions in a do-it-yourself manual may lead you through a number of processes. An explanation of a process is more than a list; it anticipates possible wrong moves, blind alleys, or even dangers that might be encountered in performing the activity. It also gives enough information so a reader can complete the process without having to get additional help.

WRITING ASSIGNMENT

Write a 350- to 500-word draft in which you explain your processes for organizing weekly chores to a roommate or mate who has never lived away from home before. **Reminder:** In your draft you will likely use the modes you have already learned—

Copyright © 1985 by Harcourt Brace Jovanovich, Inc. All rights reserved.

narration, analysis, description, definition—to explain your process. When you explain a process that is familiar to you, it is easy to leave out steps you do almost automatically. Your peer editor can help you spot such omissions by trying to follow the process. When you have completed your draft, ask your peer editor to examine it to see if the process can be followed step by step. If your process appears to break down, the editor can explain what does not work. When you understand what has gone wrong, you can add steps if some have been omitted or rearrange those that have been presented out of order. Sometimes you might have included unnecessary steps or repeated steps unnecessarily. You may find that you have processes within your process. For example, if you are going to make egg salad, you might have to explain how to prepare the eggs so they will be completely cooked, cooled, and peeled before you continue with the recipe for the salad. During revision you may discover you have omitted such processes and will need to add them.

When you write a process analysis, it is particularly important to work through your paper several times to get it properly organized. These revisions are the responsibility of the writer, and you should not expect that your instructor will review and reorder the steps in your process for you. If you settle those matters yourself or with the aid of your peer editor, your instructor will be freed from the necessity of marking early drafts and can comment on your best version instead of your early attempts. Of course, you can ask your instructor specific questions about your process or about your writing throughout the time you are working on drafting and revising.

Before you submit your process analysis to your instructor, you should have asked your peer editor to read it at least a second time so that you can have a check on the accuracy of your revisions. When you finally submit your essay along with all your drafts and your Editor's Evaluation forms, be certain that you have not omitted any steps in your process and that you present all steps in the proper order. If your reader can follow your process easily, your instructor can suggest ways to improve your writing instead of trying to sort out what steps are out of order, omitted, or unnecessary.

When you write, you first discover ideas for writing, draft those ideas, revise your draft for your audience (your peer editor), revise after consideration of your peer editor's suggestions, proofread your paper to bring it to the required form, and finally submit all versions of your writing to your instructor. Of course, you are really working on your final copy from the moment you begin to discover ideas, so don't think you must finish one writing activity before you can begin another. You can always return to any activity at any time until you hand your essay to your instructor.

5.7 THE WRITING PROCESS

These sections on the writing process introduce you to a variety of writing strategies that can help you evolve your own. Until you develop your own strategies, you can

Copyright © 1985 by Harcourt Brace Jovanovich, Inc. All rights reserved.

adapt these suggestions and strategies to your own use. Because the writing process differs in details for every writer, you can tailor the successful solutions you imitate to your own needs.

As you adapt the writing process, you are learning an essential principle of writing: Writing must be tailored to fit specific needs—those of the writer and those of the audience. As a writer you have to determine exactly what the character of your audience is so that you can adjust your writing to its expectations. The earlier you know your audience, the better. The questions below will guide you as you analyze and assess the common interests of your audience. Once you have a specific audience in mind, and before you have finished with any piece of writing, you should adjust your writing to fulfill whatever expectations your audience may have.

1. What kinds of experiences has your audience had (occupational, recreational, educational, and others)?
2. Is your audience exclusively male or female, or does it include both men and women?
3. What is the approximate age of your audience?
4. What are the particular ethnic or religious values of your audience?
5. Where does your audience live? How long have they lived there?
6. What social values are most important to your audience (love and friendship, money and power, or physical fitness and sports, or others)?
7. What adjustments must you make after answering the questions to tailor your essay to your audience?
   a. Have you used vocabulary (diction) appropriate for your subject and your audience (connotations, denotations, slang, and so on)?
   b. Is the topic of your essay suitable for your audience?
8. How much does your audience know about your subject?
9. How willing will your audience be to accept your ideas (for example, does your essay challenge their commonly held opinions)?
10. How will the physical appearance of your essay affect your audience?
    a. Will your audience approve of the paper you have used?
    b. Should your essay be typed or handwritten?
    c. Have you indented paragraphs?
    d. Does your audience expect blue or black ink or is pencil or colored ink acceptable?

5.8 PARAGRAPH POWER

PROCESS ANALYSIS

When you tell somebody how to do something, you are explaining a process. An explanation of a process should be complete enough to guide somebody through it

Copyright © 1985 by Harcourt Brace Jovanovich, Inc. All rights reserved.

successfully. Writers use the process mode for many kinds of explanations including those in recipes, instruction booklets, textbooks, and research reports.

The first step in explaining a process is to identify it exactly. For example, you may explain how to make a terrarium or how to prepare clothes for laundering. If your purpose is to direct, as in ''How to Make a Terrarium,'' you first state the principles which control the process and define any special terms required. Then, list all materials or tools needed to complete the process. Finally, lead the reader through the necessary steps to achieve the desired result.

Always present the necessary steps in strict chronological order so that the process will work as you intend. You cannot assume the reader will read the entire set of instructions before beginning to follow them. For example, if you were to explain how to launder clothes, you would not instruct the reader to wash all the clothes in hot water before giving the instruction to separate the white clothes from those that may fade. If you did, the reader would probably dye the white clothes pink or gray because you presented the steps of the process out of sequence. Keep in mind that any explanation of a process should be logical and move step by step from beginning to end.

Two additional ways can help you make sure that the process is clear to the reader. Many times an example or illustration of a step in the process is helpful. If the process you are explaining contains a step which has several parts, you will find that you likely have a process within a process. For instance, if you are explaining how to change a tire, you will have to explain the process of placing the jack under the car before you can explain how to loosen the wheel and replace it with the spare. Sometimes alerting the reader about opportunities to use the process helps to make the process clearer because the reader can imagine doing it.

The process mode described above adapts easily to the T-R-I-I paragraph pattern. The statement of the kind of operation you will perform will most likely appear as the topic sentence (T) of your paragraph. Your list of tools and/or materials or your statement of principles and definition of terms are the restriction element (R) of the paragraph. Your explanation of the steps to be followed are the illustrations (I, I . . .). Being clear, being complete, and being logical are the most important qualities of a process whether it is explained in a paragraph or in a longer piece of writing.

Copyright © 1985 by Harcourt Brace Jovanovich, Inc. All rights reserved.

EXERCISE 1

Analyze the brief process in the following paragraph from "How to Make a Terrarium." Your analysis will be useful in helping you see how process paragraphs are constructed. Draw a box around the topic. Circle the restriction. Then draw a wavy line under each illustration.

Arranging the topography of the terrarium is a matter of taste. You might keep in mind that a variety of leaf textures is usually pleasing and that plants of different heights and shapes—pyramidal, tall and spiky, short and shrubby, trailing—make the scenery interesting. If your container is large enough you can even make a small hill or a path within its bounded wildness. Color may be provided by including partridge berries, mushrooms, lichens, and stones. No well-made terrarium needs a plastic deer or a china bird, but the woods are full of props that can add local color to your small scene: mossy twigs, weathered pieces of wood, scraps of textured bark, squirrel-gnawed nutshells. A weird craggy stone may be just the boulder you need for a classic gothic scene—a *romantische Landschaft* in miniature.

EXERCISE 2

Using the T-R-I-I pattern (topic, restriction, illustration, illustration) plan and write a process paragraph of your own on sorting clothes for laundering. For the topic, state the kind of operation you will perform. Then, for the restriction, list the tools and materials, or the principle you will follow. Finally, explain or illustrate briefly the steps you will follow in doing the process. You may want to revise a paragraph from your draft (Section 5.6) or you may want to write an entirely new one to insert into the next version of your process assignment.

Copyright © 1985 by Harcourt Brace Jovanovich, Inc. All rights reserved.

Notes

Make a general statement about how to sort laundry.

T

List the principles you will follow. (For example, no laundry should fade.)

R

Detail the steps used to sort laundry.

I	I	I
Colors	Fabrics	Degree of soil

Copyright © 1985 by Harcourt Brace Jovanovich, Inc. All rights reserved.

Notes

INTRODUCTORY PARAGRAPHS

A specialized variety of paragraph, the introductory paragraph, functions to interest and encourage your reader to continue. Good introductory paragraphs help to make your writing more interesting and better organized. Look at the introductory paragraph in ''How to Make a Terrarium.''

In some ways, an introductory paragraph is similar to the entrance of a building. If a building is well-designed, its entrance will be inviting and will lead those who go into the building to find their way easily and pleasantly. You may have had the experience of entering a building which has doors that are difficult to manage and that lead to a blank wall or to a long corridor rather than to a pleasant and functional lobby. A successful introductory paragraph will function much as a pleasant lobby of a building functions by leading the reader into the body of the essay rather than to a blank wall or to a long corridor. It shows the reader exactly where the writer is taking him and as it points the direction, it arouses the reader's interest and encourages him to continue reading.

In addition to creating interest for the reader, introductory paragraphs set the tone of a piece of writing and define its form. In other words, the level of written expression and the length of your introduction must be appropriate for your essay. You can learn to make appropriate judgments about language and length from reading skilled writers. With experience and observation, you can become adept at selecting words and expressions appropriate to your particular purpose. You will learn to choose vocabulary and construct sentences suitable for an informal essay when your purpose is to write an informal essay. Just as the level of expression should be appropriate for your purpose, the length of your introductory paragraph should be in proportion to the body of your essay. For essays that you write in this course, it is likely that you will only need one paragraph as an introduction. Later, if you write a book, your introduction may be a complete chapter of fifty pages with many paragraphs.

As you consider the proportion of the essay, you may find the number five plus two $(5+2)$ or minus two $(5-2)$ useful. Psychologists tell us that people remember more easily if they perceive a whole in parts that do not exceed seven. In fact as the parts approach seven the difficulty in keeping the parts in mind increases. Writers can make use of this ''rule of seven'' whenever they organize their material. If your essay is 500 words long, and if you have seven paragraphs (one introductory paragraph, five paragraphs of explanation, and one concluding paragraph), you could divide the total number of words by seven to determine the approximate length of your introductory paragraph. The rule of seven is a guide that helps you adjust proportions among the parts of your essay.

Copyright © 1985 by Harcourt Brace Jovanovich, Inc. All rights reserved.

EXERCISE 3

Write or revise an introductory paragraph of the appropriate length and using the appropriate language for your essay on organizing chores. How long will your paragraph be? Consider also your responses to the questions in Section 5.7 to help you adjust your language to your audience.

5.9 *SENTENCE POWER*

RUN-ON SENTENCES AND COMMA SPLICES

A run-on sentence, sometimes called a run-together or fused sentence, is two or more complete sentences that are punctuated as if they were one sentence. To find if you have written run-on sentences, you need to examine the clauses in your sentences to see if you have joined them in unacceptable ways. To correct run-ons, (1) break them into shorter sentences, (2) separate independent clauses with the appropriate coordinate conjunction, (3) separate independent clauses with a semicolon only, or (4) separate independent clauses with a semicolon followed by a conjuctive adverb. Even though any one of five ways will "fix" the run-on, as a writer you will choose to correct your run-on in a way that will make your writing effective for your reader.

Like fragments, your run-ons can be the result of carelessness and haste. Other times, when you discover a run-on in your writing, you find that the faulty sentence structure parallels a partially formed idea. In such instances, (5) rewrite the passage and sharpen the focus of your idea to rid your writing of a run-on.

FIVE WAYS TO CORRECT RUN-ONS

1. Break run-ons into shorter sentences.

Run-on	The sudden crash startled me the tent collapsed in a heap.
Revision	The sudden crash startled me. The tent collapsed in a heap.

    Observe that the run-on has been divided into two shorter sentences by placing a period at the close of the first clause and beginning the second clause with a capital letter. Because of the suggestion of harsh, sharp sounds and disorder from the crash, short sentences provide an effective way to suit the sentence length to the sentence sense.

2. Separate independent clauses in run-ons with coordinate conjunctions (*and*, *but*, *for*, *nor*, *or*, *yet*, *so*) preceded by a comma.

Run-on	He hiked west with his backpack he reached the ridge before dark.
Revision	He hiked west with his backpack, and he reached the ridge before dark.

Copyright © 1985 by Harcourt Brace Jovanovich, Inc. All rights reserved.

Punctuation Guide for Compound Sentences		
Independent clause ,	and but for nor or yet so	independent clause.

Usage of Coordinate Conjunctions		
Conj.	Use	Example
and or nor	Use to show an **addition** or **restatement** of your idea	Planning solves problems, **and** it makes you self-reliant.
but yet	Use to **contrast** your ideas	Planning solves problems, **yet** it requires time and foresight.
for	Use to show a/the **cause** of your ideas	Planning solves problems, **for** it lets you connect with quality.
so	Use to show a/the **result** of your idea	Planning solves problems, **so** campers need it.

Here, the ideas in the two clauses have equal grammatical importance. When that is the case, you will want to show the coordination of the ideas by using a coordinate conjunction to separate the two clauses. Place a comma before a coordinate conjunction which separates independent clauses. A comma splice occurs when independent clauses are joined by a comma alone instead of being linked by a coordinate conjunction preceded by a comma.

3. Separate independent clauses in a run-on with a semicolon.

Run-on   Accident-free camping requires common sense and planning it means thinking ahead.

Revision 1a   Accident-free camping requires common sense and planning; it means thinking ahead.

''Accident-free camping'' is the logical subject of both of these clauses. Using a semicolon to join them emphasizes the close relationship between ''it'' (the subject of the second clause) and ''camping,'' (the word it restates). To place a

Copyright © 1985 by Harcourt Brace Jovanovich, Inc. All rights reserved.

period after "planning" and to begin the next clause with "It" would have a completely different effect. The clauses would then appear to be unrelated, and the effect would be choppy and disjointed. Furthermore, without the semicolon, the reader could read the sentence with a totally different meaning.

> **Revision 1b**   Accident-free camping requires common sense, and planning it means thinking ahead.

Be careful when punctuating independent clauses. A comma can only separate them when a coordinate conjunction stands between them. Otherwise, a comma between two independent clauses produces a comma splice. (*Hint:* If you count all the subject-verb pairs in a sentence, and then count all the conjunctions in that sentence, you should have one—and only one—more subject-verb pair than you have conjunctions. For the purpose of this hint, semicolons are counted as conjunctions, and conjunctive adverbs are not counted at all.)

4. Separate independent clauses in a run-on with a semicolon and a conjunctive adverb.

> **Revision 2a**   Accident-free camping requires common sense and planning; therefore, it means thinking ahead.

In revision 2a, a conjunctive adverb, *therefore*, follows the semicolon, and binds the two independent clauses together by stressing a cause-effect relationship between them. This revision shows a much different attitude toward "planning" than revision 1 does.

When conjunctive adverbs stand between two independent clauses, they are always preceded by a semicolon and may be followed by a comma. Conjunctive adverbs indicate relationships between clauses that are similar to those indicated by coordinate conjunctions, but they are not the same as coordinate conjunctions. Coordinate conjunctions always stand between the two clauses. Conjunctive adverbs may stand between clauses, or they may occupy another position in one of the independent clauses. When they do, they are often preceded and followed by commas. Consider this version of revision 2:

> **Revision 2b**   Accident-free camping requires common sense and planning; it, therefore, means thinking ahead.

Instead of using a conjunctive adverb to separate two independent clauses, consider revising your sentence to make one of the clauses subordinate to the other.

When writing, choose conjunctive adverbs carefully to clarify logical connections between clauses. Your choice can indicate addition, contrast, or cause and effect and can help your reader understand the specific relationship you intend among ideas.

Copyright © 1985 by Harcourt Brace Jovanovich, Inc. All rights reserved.

Punctuation Guide for Compound Sentences
Independent clause ; independent clause. Independent clause ;{conjunctive adverb} (,) independent clause.

List of Common Conjunctive Adverbs		
Conjunctive Adverb	Use	Example
also finally furthermore incidentally indeed likewise moreover next then	addition	Winds increased during the night; **furthermore,** rain began about dawn.
besides however instead meanwhile nevertheless nonetheless still	contrast	Winds increased during the night; **however,** rain began about dawn.
consequently hence therefore thus	cause/effect	Winds increased during the night; **consequently,** rain began about dawn.

5. Rewrite the run-on.

Run-on Your companions are not planning a shore lunch a good idea would be to limit your refills on coffee at breakfast.

Revision If your companions are not planning a shore lunch, a good idea would be to limit your refills on coffee at breakfast.

Using a dependent clause beginning with "if" shows clearly that one idea is subordinate to the other; that is, the first clause makes more sense when it is

Copyright © 1985 by Harcourt Brace Jovanovich, Inc. All rights reserved.

attached to the second clause as a condition. It sets up an expectation to which the reader can respond in the following clause. When correcting a run-on sentence, choose the most effective solution, not simply one which will make the sentence technically correct. You should be guided by the relationships you intend among your ideas, the expectations of your audience, and the purpose for your writing. The first solution that comes to mind when correcting a run-on may not provide the precision your purpose, audience, and ideas require. A good way to learn to judge which solution will be most effective is to notice how professional writers arrange their ideas. As always, reading helps your writing, and being an observant reader will help you learn to arrange your ideas within your clauses and to bind them in the most effective way.

EXERCISE 1

Rewrite the run-on sentences into (a) short sentences, (b) compound sentences using a coordinate conjunction, (c) compound sentences using a semicolon, (d) compound sentences using a conjunctive adverb, and (e) complex sentences using subordination. Place a check in front of the version you believe to be most effective and be prepared to explain your choice.

Example   Accident-free camping requires common sense and planning it means thinking ahead.

   a. *Accident-free camping requires common sense and planning.*

       It means thinking ahead.

   b. *Accident-free camping requires common sense and planning,*

       for it means thinking ahead.

   c. *Accident-free camping requires common sense and planning;*

       it means thinking ahead.

   d. *Accident-free camping requires common sense and planning;*

       therefore, it means thinking ahead.

   e. *Because accident free camping requires common sense and*

       planning, it means thinking ahead.

1. You see a newcomer in trouble he has fallen overboard.

   a. _____

Copyright © 1985 by Harcourt Brace Jovanovich, Inc. All rights reserved.

b. _____

c. _____

d. _____

e. _____

2. You have come on the trip you enjoy the sport and the environment.

a. _____

b. _____

c. _____

Copyright © 1985 by Harcourt Brace Jovanovich, Inc. All rights reserved.

d. _____

_____

_____

e. _____

_____

_____

3. Friends try to be generous with their own supplies someone is outfitted with the wrong equipment or runs low on essentials.

a. _____

_____

_____

b. _____

_____

_____

c. _____

_____

_____

d. _____

_____

_____

e. _____

_____

_____

4. I reluctantly described the mishap the senior angler on board calmly reported his experience everybody was interested.

Copyright © 1985 by Harcourt Brace Jovanovich, Inc. All rights reserved.

a. _____

_____

_____

b. _____

_____

_____

c. _____

_____

_____

d. _____

_____

_____

e. _____

_____

_____

5. He can't swim he has on hip-waders.

a. _____

_____

_____

b. _____

_____

_____

c. _____

_____

Copyright © 1985 by Harcourt Brace Jovanovich, Inc. All rights reserved.

d. _____

_____

_____

e. _____

_____

_____

EXERCISE 2

In the following exercises, expand the independent clause provided by attaching another with the precise coordinate conjunction that shows the relationship specified by the word in parentheses. (*Hint*: Be careful to change punctuation and capitalization if required.)

Example   *Independent clause*: The soil will be light in color.

(addition)   **The soil will be light in color**, and **the whole thing will feel lighter when you pick it up.**

1. *Independent clause*: Sometimes you lose all of your lures the first day of fishing.

   a. (addition) _____

_____

_____

   b. (restatement) _____

_____

_____

   c. (contrast) _____

_____

_____

   d. (cause) _____

Copyright © 1985 by Harcourt Brace Jovanovich, Inc. All rights reserved.

_____

_____

e. (results) _____

_____

_____

2. *Independent clause*: Try not to act on impulse.

a. (addition) _____

_____

_____

b. (restatement) _____

_____

_____

c. (contrast) _____

_____

_____

d. (cause) _____

_____

_____

e. (result) _____

_____

_____

EXERCISE 3

Change and expand each sentence below by adding at least one other independent clause related to the sentence by the precise conjunctive adverb indicated. Try not to

Copyright © 1985 by Harcourt Brace Jovanovich, Inc. All rights reserved.

repeat any conjunctive adverb. (*Hint*: Be careful to change punctuation and capitalization as required.)

Example   Put down a mat of moss to absorb moisture.

(addition)   *Put down a mat of moss to absorb moisture*; then, *pour a layer of sand or fine gravel over the moss.*

1. Teaching a friend to make a terrarium has its own rewards.

    a. (addition) _____

    _____

    _____

    b. (contrast) _____

    _____

    _____

    c. (cause/effect) _____

    _____

    _____

2. A veteran naturalist praises a newcomer for any triumphs.

    a. (addition) _____

    _____

    _____

    b. (contrast) _____

    _____

    _____

    c. (cause/effect) _____

    _____

Copyright © 1985 by Harcourt Brace Jovanovich, Inc. All rights reserved.

_____

3. Tempers may flare when the weather turns bad.

   a. (addition) _____

   _____

   _____

   b. (contrast) _____

   _____

   _____

   c. (cause/effect) _____

   _____

   _____

EXERCISE 4

Identify each of the following as a run-on, comma splice, or correctly punctuated sentence by writing "run-on," "comma splice," or "correct" in the blank. Rewrite correctly any sentence that contains an error.

1. _____ Heave ho and hard alee! The sailors chant on the boat it goes through the waves.

   _____

   _____

   _____

2. _____ Standing at attention, the boatswain piped the visitors aboard, they climbed the ladder to the deck.

   _____

   _____

   _____

Copyright © 1985 by Harcourt Brace Jovanovich, Inc. All rights reserved.

3. _____ The boatswain smiled cordially as his friends pretended to be officials from another country they enjoyed the fun of the mock military ceremony.

_____

_____

_____

4. _____ After the guests received their crewing assignments, they stood by to cast off lines.

_____

_____

_____

5. _____ The captain reversed the boat's engine, he backed it out of the slip and came about into the wind.

_____

_____

_____

6. _____ Turning off the engine, the captain gave the order to hoist the main sail.

_____

_____

_____

7. _____ A badly sunburned muscular man used all his strength to raise the heavy sail he wrapped the free end of the line around the cleat to secure it.

_____

_____

Copyright © 1985 by Harcourt Brace Jovanovich, Inc. All rights reserved.

8. _____ After they were under way, they all relaxed and enjoyed the quiet slicing of the boat through the water they appreciated the cooling effect of the breeze.

_____

_____

_____

9. _____ The sun and the breeze made everyone drowsy however when the captain offered cold drinks, they all accepted eagerly.

_____

_____

_____

10. _____ The day came to an end too quickly, nevertheless all the new sailors were tired.

_____

_____

_____

EXERCISE 5

Punctuate these sentences correctly. If a sentence is already correctly punctuated, put a check in the margin next to the number of the sentence.

1. Many are hunting with a camera and they find it as pleasurable as hunting with a rifle.
2. A real camera enthusiast will carry several cameras that way the right equipment is on hand for all photographic conditions.
3. Some will carry a telescopic lens and others will carry a wide-angle lens but all will have a 35mm camera.
4. Capturing a stag jumping a fallen log on film makes a better trophy for the new

Copyright © 1985 by Harcourt Brace Jovanovich, Inc. All rights reserved.

photographic hunter than a set of antlers but to understand this feeling you almost have to experience the thrill of the moment.

5. To spy a doe and a faun in a clearing and to stay still so as not to scare her away needs nerves of steel because the click of the shutter will shatter the scene and a second chance may never come.

6. The only legal way to hunt an eagle is with a camera for the eagle is an endangered species.

7. A movie camera allows the photographer to capture the eagle in flight yet it is bulky to carry.

8. Most hunters have never seen an eagle except on film however any hunter would prize close ups of an eagle perched atop a rock.

9. Bears make marvelous subjects for pictures but a photographer must never forget that bears are dangerous animals.

10. Mountain goats grazing in a high meadow must be filmed with a telescopic lens for they are very shy and scatter at the slightest noise.

Copyright © 1985 by Harcourt Brace Jovanovich, Inc. All rights reserved.

LINKING VERBS

Linking verbs connect the subject to a word or words that describe or rename the subject.

Example   The roses *grow* tall.
The water *turned* green.
The acorn *became* a tree.

Linking verbs may be regular or irregular, have five principal parts, and form their tenses like any other regular or irregular verb.

Some of the verbs in the chart may show actions. Sometimes linking verbs function as action verbs. To test if one of these verbs functions as an action verb instead of a linking verb, substitute the corresponding tense of *to be*. If the replacement makes sense, the original verb functions as a linking verb. If it does not make sense, the original verb functions as an action verb.

To be functions as a linking verb more often than any of the other linking verbs. Study the common forms of *to be* shown in the chart. *Note:* Like other verbs, *to be* may also combine with helping verbs: can, could, may, might, must, shall, should, will, would.

Principal Parts of Linking Verbs				
Base (Infinitive)	Present Participle	Present	Past	Past Participle
(to) appear	appearing	appear(s)	appeared	appeared
(to) be	being	am, are, is	was, were	been
(to) become	becoming	become(s)	became	become
(to) feel	feeling	feel(s)	felt	felt
(to) grow	growing	grow(s)	grew	grown
(to) look	looking	look(s)	looked	looked
(to) remain	remaining	remain(s)	remained	remained
(to) seem	seeming	seem(s)	seemed	seemed
(to) smell	smelling	smell(s)	smelled	smelled
(to) sound	sounding	sound(s)	sounded	sounded
(to) stay	staying	stay(s)	stayed	stayed
(to) taste	tasting	taste(s)	tasted	tasted
(to) turn	turning	turn(s)	turned	turned

Copyright © 1985 by Harcourt Brace Jovanovich, Inc. All rights reserved.

Common Forms of *To Be*	
Present	am, are, is
Present Progressive	am being, are being, is being
Past	was, were
Past Progressive	was being, were being
Future	will be
Present Perfect	has been, have been
Past Perfect	had been
Future Perfect	will have been

EXERCISE 6

Locate the verb in the following sentences. Write it in the blank and label it as an action verb or a linking verb. (*Hint*: Remember to test with a form of *to be*.)

Example　　The fish seem to be biting today.
　　　　　　　seem　(linking)

1.　The puppy smelled the dead fish at the edge of the lake.

2.　The lake seemed calm before we turned into the cove.

3.　The captain sounded angry, but he appeared as jolly as ever.

4.　Our lunch tasted like fish because it had remained in the cooler with our catch.

5.　The newcomer stayed in the cabin with the seasoned fishermen.

Copyright © 1985 by Harcourt Brace Jovanovich, Inc. All rights reserved.

6. The guide grew testy and looked as if he were about to shout.

_____

_____

_____

7. Flounder must be difficult to catch since they remain on the bottom.

_____

_____

8. Mary became intent upon her fishing and stayed three days longer at the coast than she had planned.

_____

_____

_____

9. My mother should have been introduced to fishing as a young woman because she feels squeamish at the thought of baiting a hook.

_____

_____

10. My father taught both his daughters to hunt and fish because he felt that women should become confident at those sports.

_____

_____

_____

Copyright © 1985 by Harcourt Brace Jovanovich, Inc. All rights reserved.

Notes

PREPOSITIONAL PHRASES

Prepositional phrases are introduced by prepositions, another of the eight parts of speech, and consist of a preposition and its object. Of course, there may be other words between a preposition and its object, but the two essential parts of a prepositional phrase are the preposition and its object.

To define prepositions is not very helpful in learning to recognize them, but an example will make them clear. To learn about prepositions take a pencil in your right hand and a book in your left. Then read the following sentence making the motion directed as you fill the blank with each of these prepositions in turn: *around, against, across, above, after, at, before, below, beneath, beside, by, down, from, in, inside, into, near, off, on, onto, outside, over, past, through, throughout, to, toward, under, up, upon, with, within, without.* Any word that will fill the blank will be a preposition.

> The pencil goes _____ the book.

The prepositions that fill this blank show space relationships (location) between the book and the pencil. Prepositions also show ownership and time relationships.

Ownership	the grades *of the students*
	the door *of the house*
	the children *of war*
Time	He stayed *after the game.*
	before
	during
	till
	until

The prepositional phrases in the preceding examples are italicized. Notice that the preposition is the first word in the phrase, and the object is the last word. All of the objects here are nouns, but pronouns can also function as objects.

> They want to learn *about me.*
> They want to keep it a secret *from him.*
> Give the book *to them.*

The prepositions in the following list express other kinds of relationships. (Sometimes prepositions function as conjunctions—such as *after, before, besides, since, till, until* when used to introduce dependent clauses or *for, but* when used to connect independent clauses.)

along	except	during
among	for	for
besides	like	regarding
but	out	since

Copyright © 1985 by Harcourt Brace Jovanovich, Inc. All rights reserved.

When you analyze sentences, you can usually omit prepositional phrases and leave a complete sentence. Although you will have removed information which may be important, a prepositional phrase is rarely essential to the basic structure of sentences. Sometimes, though, it may be the subject.

Example

                         subject
           Before breakfast is too early.

Prepositional phrases are very useful for providing essential details, but they can become awkward or even clumsy when too many of them occur together. If you have more than three in a row, you should revise your sentence.

Faulty   You might keep in mind that a variety of leaf textures in a terrarium by the light on your table in the living room is usually pleasing.

Revised   You might keep in mind that near a lighted table a terrarium with varied leaf textures gives your living room a pleasant touch.

A further advantage of understanding prepositional phrases comes when you are trying to identify subjects and verbs of long sentences. You can identify prepositional phrases by finding a preposition and then locating its object. (*Hint*: If a word often used as a preposition appears without an object, it functions in the sentence as an adverb and not as a preposition.) Once you have found the prepositional phrases, you can eliminate them from consideration when you look for the subject and verb (unless the prepositional phrase functions as the subject as in the example above). Infinitive phrases such as *to run*, *to strike*, *to ride* are not prepositional phrases even though they contain *to*.

EXERCISE 7

Put parentheses around each prepositional phrase in the passage from "How to Make a Terrarium." The passage contains at least 15 prepositional phrases and at least one infinitive phrase. Do not confuse the infinitive phrase with a prepositional phrase. Put a box around any infinitive phrases you find.

Those of us accustomed to fertilizing houseplants may tend to include the terrarium in that routine, but it is best to keep terrarium soil on the lean side, lest the plants outgrow the container. Choice of plants influences the length of their stay too, of course. Our first house—a mid-nineteenth-century Philadelphia weaver's cottage—is now guarded by a pine that spent its first two years in a terrarium. When its top hit the cover we planted it in front of the loom shed. Now, twenty years later, it towers

Copyright © 1985 by Harcourt Brace Jovanovich, Inc. All rights reserved.

over the house. The loom shed is gone, but pine needles fall around its foundation. Everything lasts, we think as we drive by the house—but in a different form, sometimes.

EXERCISE 8

Because prepositions relate one object or idea to another, they are an economical way to increase the amount of detail in your sentences. Combine the following short sentences into one longer one containing prepositional phrases.

1. Matt was fishing.
   The place was Lac La Croix.
   Matt dropped his lures.
   The lures were in the lake.
   Matt borrowed lures.
   The lures were Tom's.

   _____

   _____

   _____

2. Ron takes a trip.
   Ron brings the wrong equipment.
   Ron hated the black flies, blisters, and sunburn.
   Ron wanted a luxurious resort.

   _____

   _____

   _____

3. We worked out.
   We were sweaty.
   We took a shower.
   We saw a movie.
   We used four seats.

   _____

   _____

Copyright © 1985 by Harcourt Brace Jovanovich, Inc. All rights reserved.

4. Hunters like coffee.
   Mugs hold coffee.
   Hot coffee steams.
   The air is crisp.
   Crisp air makes coffee steam.
   Coffee has a pleasant aroma.

   _____

   _____

   _____

5. Sleeping outdoors gives me a backache.
   Sleeping outdoors is fun.
   Wild animals make sleeping outdoors dangerous.
   Sleeping outdoors makes me appreciate my comfortable bed.

   _____

   _____

   _____

Copyright © 1985 by Harcourt Brace Jovanovich, Inc. All rights reserved.

5.10 PROOFREADING POWER

As you proofread your paper, look for any error, mistake, or slip of the pen that you should correct or revise before you deliver it to your reader. When you identify a problem in your writing, fix it so that your reader will be able to concentrate on your ideas rather than having to wrestle with a writing problem. All writing problems, especially faulty grammar, create communication barriers between writer and reader. So that your reader will identify as closely as possible with your ideas, strive to present error-free writing—no easy task. Such writing requires that you be constantly aware of your reader throughout your writing, but especially during proofreading because that is your last opportunity to make any change that may help you remove barriers.

In actual writing, any writing problem may surface during proofreading. In this exercise, however, the writing problems are limited to run-ons, comma splices, and sound-alike words. Proofread the following passage and correct any error or mistake.

If you need an excuse for a walk in the woulds, make a terrarium. Gathering terrarium ingredients sharpens one's appreciation of the rich variety of life at boot level. Terrarium makers sea the world in fine no detail escapes their attention. A confirmed devotee could probably wander in a readwould grove with gaze fixed own the ground—looking for moss of just the write texture, tiny seedling trees, interesting bark chips. After I made my first terrarium; I found myself gathering tiny plants, lichens, and pebbles on every walk—and mentally collecting when I was knot walking hour own land.

5.11 DICTATION

Your instructor will choose a passage of approximately 100 words and read it aloud. You are to write what you hear. As you listen, concentrate and maintain silence. Do not ask your instructor to repeat because any sound other than the instructor's voice reading will break not only your concentration but that of others. Your instructor may repeat key words and phrases during the dictation, will allow sufficient time for you to write what you have heard, and will reread the entire passage a second time at a faster rate so that you can check what you have written and fill in any gap you may have.

Write on every other line so that you will have space to correct your dictation upon the final reading in case you have made a mistake. Your instructor will show you the dictated passage and ask you to compare your version, or perhaps a classmate's ver-

Copyright © 1985 by Harcourt Brace Jovanovich, Inc. All rights reserved.

sion, to the original. Be especially alert when you check the dictation because this exercise will help you develop your sentence sense by translating spoken into written language.

5.12 WORD POWER

HOMONYMS

Homonyms (sound-alike words, words that have different spellings and meanings) cause inexperienced writers a great many problems. If you find mistaken identities and confusion of words (misused homonyms) in your own writing, you can correct them and feel proud of yourself for catching your slip in diction. At the same time you may feel a little sheepish for having made the error in the first place. If, however, you do not catch your slip in diction, your readers will because they do not know what you intended to write, and they may think that you do not know any better. Of course, experience in reading from a variety of sources is one of the best ways to acquire accurate usage of sound-alike words because you become familiar with the way they appear in context. Because so many of these words occur commonly in writing and present so many problems to inexperienced writers, you will benefit from additional study of them.

EXERCISE 1

To increase your awareness of words that have the same or similar sounds or that look alike, match columns in the following exercise by writing the correct letter in each blank.

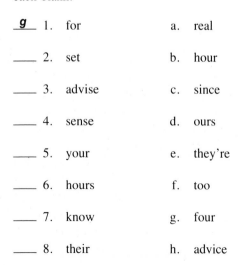

_g_	1. for	a.	real
___	2. set	b.	hour
___	3. advise	c.	since
___	4. sense	d.	ours
___	5. your	e.	they're
___	6. hours	f.	too
___	7. know	g.	four
___	8. their	h.	advice

Copyright © 1985 by Harcourt Brace Jovanovich, Inc. All rights reserved.

____ 9.	two	i.	maid
____10.	reel	j.	an
____11.	eye	k.	you're
____12.	our	l.	no
____13.	made	m.	own
____14.	and	n.	I
____15.	on	o.	sit

The English language contains a number of words which sound alike, look alike, or have similar sounds or forms. The troublesome words which follow can cause problems even for experienced writers. You may have had the same difficulty. Study the italicized words in each sentence to learn their meanings and usage from context (the surroundings a word appears in). The use of a word (whether it is a noun, verb, preposition, or other kind of word) is often the key to separating it from its sound-alike or look-alike.

1. a. When *asking* your buddies to head for the outdoors on the weekend, make sure you have lots of refreshments on hand.
   b. When *axing* limbs from trees to clear a camp site, use care to preserve the natural beauty of the forest.
2. a. A hiker's motto is "safety first" because a fall from a false step could *break* a bone.
   b. To walk out of a *brake* with a broken bone in a splint would be very painful and difficult because of the dense brushwood and briers in a *brake*.
   c. A hiker's routine includes checking the *brakes* on the vehicle to be driven over the trails to where the hike will begin.
3. a. Experienced campers choose a camp site *close* to a source of water.
   b. Experienced campers choose *clothes* that will protect their skin from scratches.
4. a. *Do* make a list of rules for children before setting out on a hike.
   b. Cover exposed equipment before turning in for the night to keep the *dew* off; otherwise, you'll wake up with damp socks.
   c. In the back woods, a hiker needs a compass that marks the direction of *due* north.
   d. A realistic camper recognizes that on the trail there are no special privileges *due*.
5. a. The majestic and *great* outdoors offer nature lovers another world on weekends and during vacations.

Copyright © 1985 by Harcourt Brace Jovanovich, Inc. All rights reserved.

    b.   When building a campfire, use a *grate* provided by the park rangers to keep from scarring the trails.

6. a.   A *loose* stone along a trail can cause a hiker to *lose* footing.

    b.   Hikers prefer to wear *loose* clothes instead of tight fitting ones on the trail.

    c.   On a hike there is neither a *loser* nor a winner because each hiker competes against the inner-self instead of other hikers.

7. a.   It would be nice to have a *maid* along on a hike to take care of some chores, but that kind of help would spoil the sense of self-reliance gained from hiking.

    b.   If self-reliance *made* no difference to a hiker, it is doubtful that anyone would go to the trouble to hike.

8. a.   The news of a *new* trail opened to hikers raises anticipation for a hiking enthusiast.

    b.   If city slickers *knew* the pleasure of hiking, they'd buy boots and jeans and tramp the trails on weekends.

9. a.   Every hiker learns an important *lesson* when a flying branch narrowly misses hitting between the eyes.

    b.   Every hiker can *lessen* the danger to those following by holding a branch until the next person has caught it.

10. a.   The weekend allows time to *meet* your buddies and head for the outdoors.

    b.   Special skills are needed to cook *meat* over an open campfire.

11. a.   Some hikers use a *pole* as a third leg on the trail, and the same *pole* holds the tent up at night.

    b.   If supplies run short while hiking, *poll* all members of the camping party and make a complete list of supplies left so a plan can be made on how to use them.

12. a.   If a hiker hopes to spy a deer or rabbit on the trail, *quiet* must be observed because noise scares animals.

    b.   If hikers do not talk and remain quiet, it is *quite* likely that they will spy animals along a trail.

13. a.   *Rough,* hilly trails offer a hiker a real challenge, but the energy required causes fatigue.

    b.   No hiker would wear a *ruff* around the neck because it would get caught in branches.

14. a.   When hiking it is a good idea to lessen the *weight* of your backpack if you become fatigued.

    b.   When hiking it is a good idea to *wait* until those who have fallen behind catch up.

15. a.   Usually hikers can find fallen tree branches and other pieces of dry *wood* to use for a campfire.

    b.   No nature lover *would* build a campfire if there were any danger of destroying the woods.

Copyright © 1985 by Harcourt Brace Jovanovich, Inc. All rights reserved.

EXERCISE 2

Write your own sentences to show your mastery of the troublesome words studied in the preceding sentences. Strive to write sentences that will interest your reader and that have variety.

1. asking _____

   _____

2. axing _____

   _____

3. brake _____

   _____

4. break _____

   _____

5. close _____

   _____

6. clothes _____

   _____

7. due _____

   _____

8. great _____

   _____

9. grate _____

   _____

10. knew _____

   _____

Copyright © 1985 by Harcourt Brace Jovanovich, Inc. All rights reserved.

11. new _____

   _____

12. lessen _____

   _____

13. lesson _____

   _____

14. loose _____

   _____

15. lose _____

   _____

16. loser _____

   _____

17. made _____

   _____

18. maid _____

   _____

19. meat _____

   _____

20. meet _____

   _____

21. pole _____

   _____

22. poll _____

   _____

Copyright © 1985 by Harcourt Brace Jovanovich, Inc. All rights reserved.

23. quiet _____

_____

24. quite _____

_____

25. ruff _____

_____

26. rough _____

_____

27. weight _____

_____

28. wait _____

_____

29. wood _____

_____

30. would _____

_____

EXERCISE 3

Supply the correct words from the pairs of troublesome words to complete the meaning of the following sentences.

1. When cooking meat/meet _____ over a great/grate

_____ use a poll/pole _____ to move

it to keep it from charring.

2. If an accident is due/dew/do _____ to the choice of

close/clothes _____ a hiker is wearing, axing/asking

Copyright © 1985 by Harcourt Brace Jovanovich, Inc. All rights reserved.

_____ for advice/advise _____ may

bring new/knew _____ways to reduce the wait/weight _____

a knew/new _____ hiker has to pack.

3. If hiking through rough/ruff _____ country, a ruff/rough

_____ would be silly and impractical.

4. Its/It's _____ important to poll/pole _____

your buddies to see/sea _____ if they have maid/made

_____ arrangements to meet/meat _____

on Friday to ax/ask _____ the trail for Sunday's hike.

5. A sturdy poll/pole _____ can help maintain footing along

a rough/ruff _____ path.

6. Where wood/would _____ a hiker build a campfire?

7. Looser/loser _____ clothes maid/made _____

for chopping wood/would _____ are sometimes quite/quiet

_____ expensive.

8. Whe hiking through a break/brake _____ hold branches so

they will not snap or brake/break _____ and fly into another hiker's face.

9. In hiking, nobody has to be a looser/loser _____ to make
another a winner.

10. If a hiker knew/new _____ all the trails where he might

lose/loose _____ the way, it might not make a grate/great

_____ difference whether a compass were packed or not.

Copyright © 1985 by Harcourt Brace Jovanovich, Inc. All rights reserved.

SPELLING

The old jingle is probably still the best way to remember when to use *ei* and when *ie*.

> *I* before *e*
> except after *c*,
> and when sounded as *a*
> as in *neighbor* or *weigh*.

EXERCISE 4

Fill in the blank space in each of the following words with either **-ei-** or **-ie-**. Remember the jingle.

1. rec_____ve	5. fr_____nd	9. r_____gn
2. ach_____ve	6. conc_____t	10. y_____ld
3. p_____ce	7. bel_____ve	
4. s_____ge	8. fr_____ght	

Most of the words having **-ie-** or **-ei-** combinations of letters follow the "rule" expressed in the jingle. A few do not. Those are the ones you really need to work on.

1. Words with the sound of **-ei-** in **seize** are exceptions: **either, leisure, neither, seize, seizure, weird.** For this to be helpful, you must pronounce these words with the same vowel sound. The best way to remember these is to memorize them.
2. You should also memorize the words **height** and **stein.**
3. Finally, a group of words such as for**ei**gn and counterf**ei**t use **-ei-**.

EXERCISE 5

Write the proper combination of letters in the blank provided.

1. sover_____gn	5. _____ght	9. surf_____t
2. forf_____t	6. l_____sure	10. n_____ther
3. h_____ght	7. s_____ze	
4. w_____rd	8. st_____n	

Copyright © 1985 by Harcourt Brace Jovanovich, Inc. All rights reserved.

EXERCISE 6

Complete the spelling of the words below by writing *-ie-* or *-ei-* in the blanks.

1. Most people bel_____ve that fresh air is good for them.

2. I wonder what the ch_____f outdoor recreational activity is.

3. A mountain climber I once knew said that a good climber had to have a lot of

    conc_____t.

4. If you've never been fishing, it is hard to conc_____ve of the thrill of catch-
    ing a big fish.

5. Nowadays many companies produce conven_____nt lightweight foods for
    backpacking.

6. Sometimes sailors are dec_____ved by how strong the wind really is.

7. Exper_____nce is really the best teacher of rock-climbing techniques.

8. An outdoorsman's best fr_____nd is his own self-reliance.

9. Sky divers parachute out of airplanes from a great h_____ght.

10. Outdoorsmen cannot be len_____nt with themselves about staying in good
    physical condition.

11. My n_____ghbor took his n_____ce camping last summer.

12. Good fishermen have a talent for perc_____ving the good fishing holes.

13. When a fisherman does spot a good fishing hole, he tries to be very

    qu_____t.

14. Most backpackers rec_____ve great pleasure from enduring a twelve- or fif-
    teen-mile hike up and down mountain trails.

15. After you purchase your hunting license, be sure to keep the rec_____pt in
    case the tags get lost.

Copyright © 1985 by Harcourt Brace Jovanovich, Inc. All rights reserved.

16. If a climber slips while trying to pass a steep dropoff, the rope should catch her, much to her rel_____f.

17. Before each race, dedicated sailors rev_____w the course, the crew assignments, and crew performance in previous races.

18. Campers plan carefully so that their supplies will be suffic_____nt for the duration of the camping trip.

19. Fishermen report w_____rd occurrences in the Bermuda Triangle.

20. Inexperienced mountain climbers y_____ld the right to lead the group on a climb to the most experienced climber.

Study the list of words containing **-ie-** or **-ei-** to learn to spell the words you do not already know.

-ie-		**-ei-**
achieve	conceit	receive
belief	conceive	reign
believe	counterfeit	seige
chief	deceive	seize
convenience	eight	seizure
experience	either	sovereign
friend	foreign	stein
lenient	forfeit	surfeit
niece	freight	weigh
piece	height	weird
quiet	leisure	
relief	neighbor	
review	neither	
sufficient	perceive	
yield	receipt	

Copyright © 1985 by Harcourt Brace Jovanovich, Inc. All rights reserved.

Notes

UNIT SIX

WRITING

EXPANDED

6.1 GETTING STARTED BY READING

By planning for the future and learning to help shape the world you live in, you can live better with less effort. Planning for the future requires information. Useful planning is only possible after you have gained sufficient information and understanding to make informed judgments. Writers often make informed judgments on the basis of the information they have gathered by reading. For gathering such information, you will want to learn to read at a rate somewhat faster than the rate you will use for study, but the rate will be slower than the one you use for light reading.

Usually you will consider several different points of view by reading different sources before you decide which direction you will take even though there may be no clear-cut right or wrong choice. You can judge the direction you choose or the conclusion you reach as right or wrong only after you are able to look back and compare the result of your decision with other possible choices. Furthermore, the decisions you make will affect not only your own life but also the lives of your family, your friends, and your associates. When you read for information, your purpose is comprehending principles, understanding ideas, and learning concepts rather than studying specific facts. As you read for information, use a rate slower than the one you use for light reading. That is, you will try to see the whole elephant rather than to view its trunk, tusks, legs, sides, or tail separately.

As you read "Where Future Jobs Will Be," use your reading-for-information rate. For this speed you may at first have to force your eyes across the lines. While you do so, try to move ahead without returning to the beginning of the sentence. Develop the habit of moving forward without returning to reread. At first you may be thinking so much about how you are reading that you canot concentrate on what you are reading. With practice, however, you will no longer be bothered by that. When the subject matter you are reading appeals to you, you are less likely to be bothered by the mechanics of reading it.

Category	Information
Rate	Somewhat faster than the study rate but slower than your light reading rate
Purposes	To comprehend principles
	To learn concepts
	To understand ideas
Typical reading for information	A report in a newspaper that affects your welfare
	Reports on opportunities for summer employment
	Reports on scholarship offerings and student financial aid
	Articles on new car design
	Articles on decorating a dormitory room for under $100
	Articles on current legislation
	Tips on ways to save money
	Advice on what to do with aging parents
	Articles on financial planning
	Reports on futuristic predictions for employment
	Accounts of advances in social programs
	Accounts of scientific advances
	Presidential speeches
	Background materials on political candidates

You may be particularly interested in "Where Future Jobs Will Be" because it projects situations and events which will affect you. Although the title of the selection will help you focus on the information it contains, the three questions below will direct your attention to specifics.

1. What point of view does the article take toward jobs performed by blue- and white-collar workers?
2. What kinds of jobs are most likely to be available when you graduate from college?
3. How much and what kind of training will be necessary for the jobs of the future?

Copyright © 1985 by Harcourt Brace Jovanovich, Inc. All rights reserved.

6.2 *CAUSE AND EFFECT*

Anonymous   *"WHERE FUTURE JOBS WILL BE"*

Worries about unemployment are not new. Nineteenth-century steel barons fretted about what would happen to their businesses after the railways had been completed. One of their contemporaries talked of the "growing army of the unemployed." His name was Karl Marx. Today there are about 300 million unemployed people in the world.

In the slow-growing 1970s unemployment increased for four main reasons. The number of people wanting jobs rose faster than employment did—not just because of population growth, but also because there were proportionately more young people in the population and more women entering the job market. Inflation reached progressively higher peaks. Jobs that had once been the preserve of developed countries migrated to the less developed countries. The industrial countries, through their lack of innovation, did not fill the vacuum.

Looking at these causes of rising unemployment, the easiest trap to fall into is the "lump of labor fallacy"—the idea that there is a fixed amount of work to be shared among available workers. No country has ever satisfied all its wants and needs. Until the age of plenty arrives, there will be things to do. But the unemployed need to know where the prospects are brightest (and grimmest), and which countries are likely to do best (and worst) in the employment league.

The world's workforce is increasingly white-collar. The boiler-suited, oil-stained masses are a caricatured minority. Since 1950 their share of the job total has declined. Employment shifts in three stages—from agriculture to industry to services— a shift that has occurred everywhere, although in most poor countries agriculture is still the largest employer.

Within the turn-of-the-century workforce industrial countries will have a larger proportion of old people, and workers in less developed countries will be much younger. Nearly half the potential workers in Latin America, for example, will be under thirty.

Two other important differences will reinforce the white-collar trend. More women

Copyright © 1985 by Harcourt Brace Jovanovich, Inc. All rights reserved.

will hold paid jobs—because of smaller families, and because economic and social pressures will accelerate the entry of women into the labor force once two-breadwinner families become common. Emancipation has begun to affect even the less developed countries. Though most women there work as hard as men (and often harder), few are categorized as formally employed. But participation rates are rising except where religion or culture inhibits women from taking jobs, as in Saudi Arabia and Iraq.

Better education also supports the white-collar trend. Those who will be in their prime in 2000 are now on their way to becoming the best-educated generation the world has ever known. Young people in industrial countries have already found that too many are trained to do the clean jobs and too few the dirty (mainly service) jobs. This accounts for recurring anecdotes about plumbers earning more than teachers. The proportion of young Americans enrolled in higher education fell in the 1970s for the first time.

"Decline" has become the watchword in some fields—textiles, for example. From its cradle in England, that industry has migrated around the world in search of cheap labor. Between 1960 and 1969, Hong Kong quadrupled its employment in textiles. In 1979 its textile employment fell under the impact of competition from places like Mexico and Thailand. It will not be long before Mexicans and Thais feel the hot breath of competition from Bangladesh and Egypt.

The auto industry has recently become painfully aware of its growth limits. Motor manufacturers employ about 4 million people around the world and support 6 million more who make the components and materials that go into cars, trucks, and buses. A further 25 million depend on the industry—selling cars, driving trucks and buses, manning gasoline pumps, repairing vehicles, providing finance and insurance. So when auto manufacturers sneeze, the rest of industry sniffles.

America's motor manufacturers have caught a nasty bout of pneumonia. European firms have been infected, too, but not so badly. Sales of new cars will doubtless recover over the next couple of years, probably reaching a peak of about 42 million worldwide in late 1982. But the recovery will not restore employment in North America

Copyright © 1985 by Harcourt Brace Jovanovich, Inc. All rights reserved.

and Europe to its old level because technical changes in the industry will increase productivity.

A modern robot welder replaces three or four human workers. A new breed, equipped with "sight" and a sense of "touch," will be able to do many labor-intensive jobs [*Science*, Aug.]. A typical $40,000 robot can put in a double shift every day for about eight years. Allowing for servicing and depreciation, that works out to less than $5 an hour. Assembly-line workers in America currently cost $15 an hour in wages and benefits.

But the real scourge of jobs in the motor industry is market saturation. Each year fewer people come into the new-car market in America and Europe as first-time buyers. The annual growth of car sales in the world's two leading markets has slipped from the 12–13 percent associated with an expanding market of first-time buyers to 2–3 percent of a predominantly replacement market.

Shipbuilding is another industry undergoing drastic change. Its worldwide output reached a peak of 35 million gross registered tons in 1975, and fell to an estimated 10 million by 1980.

The real loser has been Western Europe. Japan's share has slipped only fractionally. The big winners have been a group of Third World countries (led by South Korea, Taiwan, and Brazil), which have benefitted from government-sponsored shipbuilding programs and an abundance of cheap labor.

While traditional manufacturing jobs are migrating from the industrial to the less developed countries, manufacturing is not necessarily on the slide in the developed world. In the engineering industries the number of jobs will expand in the 1980's, but the skills needed will change dramatically. In one sector—energy—engineers, will find work in their own backyard. Mining, chemical, and petroleum engineers; metalworkers for offshore-rig construction; and skilled labor for building synthetic fuels plants will be particularly in demand.

Another buoyant job market is the mining industry. Rising energy prices are good for coal—and gold. But before you rush down the pit, get a degree. The best opportunities will be for white-collar specialists; they will not have to compete with ma-

Copyright © 1985 by Harcourt Brace Jovanovich, Inc. All rights reserved.

chines. Job prospects for the largest mining employer—coal—have rarely looked brighter, thanks to OPEC.

The electronics complex is a dramatic growth area. The silicon chip has been a tremendous stimulus to innovation, inspiring new products like personal computers and transforming old ones like washing machines (which are now programmable) or telephone switchboards (now endowed with the ability to store messages). Some of these products have brought new jobs; others have displaced workers—in old-style telephone factories, for example. The chip has created enormous demand for programmers and electronics engineers, and for computer-skilled people generally (teachers and certain blue-collar workers).

Satellite-based telecommunications will be big business in the second half of the 1980s. Experts predict explosive growth in demand for cheap Earth stations—which will be used to pick up television programs in homes, and for electronic mail and other business communications. The manufacture of Earth stations is highly labor-intensive—essentially a matter of soldering together electronic components and chicken wire—so developing countries should claim their share of this.

There is a memorable cameo in the film *The Graduate* in which Dustin Hoffman is offered career advice by one of his father's friends: "I'm going to say just one word to you: plastics." Today's password is "information technology." Futurologists forecast that computers will put a Library of Congress in every home. Televised libraries will be playable on a video-cassette or disc, with controls for going forward or back.

Another industry still in its infancy is biotechnology, which encompasses genetic engineering and monoclonal antibodies. Initially only markets like medicine will be able to afford them. Then, as genes become cheaper to engineer, chemistry and agriculture will be affected.

The growth in the rich countries' job market will be mostly in occupations not yet formally categorized. It will be in small businesses and among the self-employed, providing specialized services with the help of machines. The computer industry is already beginning to mitigate the high cost and inconvenience of getting things repaired. If an IBM computer breaks down in Zurich, the engineer telephones a com-

Copyright © 1985 by Harcourt Brace Jovanovich, Inc. All rights reserved.

puter in New York, which consults its files and gives a diagnosis. The cure is effected not by someone tinkering for hours with wires, but by throwing out a faulty module and plugging in a replacement.

Recession and taxation have recently thrown the spotlight on the size of public employment, but the issue has been controversial for 100 years. Adolf Wagner, a late 19th-century German economist, held that increasing State activity was a function of rising income. In the opposite corner, California's Howard Jarvis in 1978 sponsored the celebrated Proposition Thirteen, which drastically cut property taxes, the first stage of ending ''government of the bureaucrats, by the bureaucrats, for the bureaucrats.''

The growth in government employment accelerated after World War II. By the early 1960s seven of ten new jobs in Sweden and Britain were in the public sector. Mr. Jarvis' Proposition Thirteen landslide victory does not necessarily mean the trend will be reversed, because two of the forces behind public-sector growth (political democracy and social liberalism) have not declined.

The only period when the trend in government employment was reversed was during the 1920s, in the economic slump and confusion after World War I. But that was followed by Roosevelt's New Deal in America, Hitler's National Socialism in Germany, and Britain's rearmament. There could be a still bigger army of State employees in the mid-1980s. The only certain way to cut public payrolls is by making fundamental changes in the provision of services like health and education, as well as (less controversially) refuse collection and roads.

The more money there is, the greater the task of managing it. The more uncertainty caused by inflation, the more investors and savers believe it pays to buy professional advice and insurance. Which means that the past thirty years of rapid growth and rising inflation have been fat ones for moneymen. The next thirty appear equally promising.

When you go into a bank you are increasingly likely to talk to a computer, not a clerk. That does not mean that employment in banking will shrink. Many countries are still ''underbanked,'' and the demand for new banking and related financial services is growing fast.

The job outlook is less rosy in the world's insurance industry, which has been al-

Copyright © 1985 by Harcourt Brace Jovanovich, Inc. All rights reserved.

most recession-proof in the past. There is currently a downturn in underwriting prof-
its, caused by fierce competition and overcapacity. Many companies plan to cut costs
in the near future. That could mean shedding staff.

Merchants are not much loved, but they can take comfort in numbers. Part-timers
abound—they are nearly 30 per cent of Britain's 2.5 million retail workers—and should
increase even more in future, as late-night shopping spreads. The real growth will be
in behind-the-scenes work like stock control and maintenance.

Franchising—getting local rights to market a big company's goods and services—
is a less risky way of running your own business. Hotels are one field where franchising is growing fast. The hotel business offers good job prospects, since all the
leading chains plan to expand.

The traditional professions—law, medicine, teaching, the church, the armed services—have prospered through centuries of industrialization, demographic change, war,
and peace. They will continue doing so, but there are a few points to bear in mind.
Born-again America offers plenty of jobs for shepherds of the soul; secular Britain
does not. At the other end of the spectrum, there should be plenty of jobs in the
armed forces. For teachers, demography dictates fortunes, which means many more
jobs in the less developed countries.

Doctors boom when population and the economy do; in Third World countries they
are still scarce. Training doctors is expensive, so less developed countries concentrate
more on nurses and paramedics. The potential for more medical jobs is enormous:
about 450,000 in Thailand, for example, if 100 years from now it were to achieve
today's British ratio of medical staff to population.

Global work patterns will undergo profound changes in the coming decades. In his
1936 film *Modern Times* Charlie Chaplin satirized the assembly line in the U.S. If
the film were made today it would be set in São Paulo or Seoul or even Gdansk,
where people are still coming out of rural poverty to work in industry.

If these comparatively poor countries become affluent, 21st-century locations for a
remake of *Modern Times* could be Lagos in Nigeria, or Dacca in Bangladesh, as the
more successful of today's developing nations become places where most people have
a high standard of living, clean jobs, and civilized hours.

Copyright © 1985 by Harcourt Brace Jovanovich, Inc. All rights reserved.

6.3 UNDERSTANDING WHAT YOU READ

1. List two positive and two negative features of your decision about preparation for employment after you consider the point of view the selection takes about future jobs.

   _____

   _____

   _____

   _____

2. How are the positive features of your decision likely to change? The negative features?

   _____

   _____

   _____

   _____

3. What kinds of additional information do you think you should look for before accepting or rejecting your decision about future employment?

   _____

   _____

   _____

   _____

6.4 DISCOVERING IDEAS FOR WRITING

1. Make a list of any work experiences you have had, paid and unpaid. If your list is very long, select the most significant experiences.

   _____

   _____

Copyright © 1985 by Harcourt Brace Jovanovich, Inc. All rights reserved.

_____

_____

_____

2. Make a list of expenses, if any, that you will pay from money you earn working part time.

_____

_____

_____

_____

3. Which of the experiences you listed above would you be willing to repeat or use to get a more responsible job in college?

_____

_____

_____

_____

4. After you consider your course load and other requirements, how much time do you think you can realistically devote to a part-time job?

_____

_____

_____

_____

5. If you have to adjust your class schedule or your course load to accommodate your job, what effect will that have on your education?

_____

_____

_____

Copyright © 1985 by Harcourt Brace Jovanovich, Inc. All rights reserved.

6. What part-time jobs could offer experience which will help you when you look for full-time employment after graduation?

_____

_____

_____

_____

Copyright © 1985 by Harcourt Brace Jovanovich, Inc. All rights reserved.

Notes

6.5 UNDERSTANDING WRITING

Most experienced writers report that in the midst of writing they periodically reread what they have written. If you, like experienced writers, reread what you have already written, you are more likely to keep from wandering from your topic because you will be reminded of what you intended to write in the first place. Another reason that you may want to reread frequently is to generate new ideas and insights which may help you continue to write. Perhaps the most important reason for rereading is that **rereading** helps you to **rethink** your original ideas; by rethinking them, you can sharpen them and present them more clearly to your reader. Rereading leads to rethinking, and rethinking leads to clearer writing.

6.6 WRITING—CAUSE AND EFFECT

Your responses to the questions in Section 6.4 will help you recognize a cause-and-effect relationship between your college education and employment. In this assignment you will learn to yoke together the results that stem from a definite cause. In writing your cause-and-effect paper you will answer the reader's question of why things are the way they are.

To answer the question ''why?'' and to emphasize a result or effect, you explain how a particular act or event causes or results in a particular effect. In other words, you examine the way things are at some moment in light of what happened before to make them that way. As you write, you will likely make use of narration, description, and comparison because all these modes will help you explain what something is like, how it happened, or why something exists.

WRITING ASSIGNMENT

Write a 500-word draft in which you explain how work that you have done or might do results in the choices you have made to finance your college education.

Reminder: Because you are writing a longer essay for this assignment, you can benefit even more than you did earlier from following the writing process summarized in 1.6. The value of being able to reenter your writing for revision increases as your writing lengthens. Your responsibilities to your audience are greater in a longer piece of writing because your reader will have to invest more time in reading what you have written. You may also find that a longer piece of writing forces a weakness you had not previously encountered to the surface. If a weakness does surface, your understanding of the writing process will give you confidence because you know how to reenter your writing to make any adjustments necessary to strengthen it. For instance, your essay may require a conclusion which a shorter essay did not.

In a 500-word essay, a weakness in any part of the essay—the introduction, the

Copyright © 1985 by Harcourt Brace Jovanovich, Inc. All rights reserved.

body, or the conclusion—will likely be more obvious than it might be in a shorter one. Unless you have all three parts carefully shaped and smoothly joined, your reader will likely experience uncertainty and dissatisfaction and may misunderstand your ideas. When you are not sure about your introduction or conclusion, ask your peer editor to comment on those parts particularly. If you are still not satisfied and cannot settle on a strategy yourself, explain your problem to your instructor and ask for a suggestion. Since it is your responsibility to solve your own writing problems, you should have at least one version and preferably several for your instructor to consider before you ask for advice. Conferring about a specific problem during the actual writing—which can usually be done briefly during a class period—will improve your writing without your instructor's having to read and reread false starts and unprofitable directions carried over from your early drafts.

When you write, you will first discover and plan ideas for writing, draft those ideas, revise your draft for your audience (your peer editor), revise after consideration of your peer editor's suggestions, proofread your paper to bring it to the required form, and finally submit all versions of your writing to your instructor. Of course, you are really working on your final copy from the moment you begin to discover ideas, so do not think you must finish one writing activity before you begin another. You can always return to any activity at any time.

6.7 THE WRITING PROCESS

People enjoy change and variety because change and variety create excitement and prevent monotony. When a sound, a word, a phrase, or even a pattern with different sounds, words, and phrases is repeated continuously, it often becomes meaningless, sometimes hypnotic, and eventually irritating. To avoid monotony, writers strive to vary their language (words, phrases, sentences, patterns) so that the language as well as the ideas the language carries are interesting and even entertaining to their audience.

A close look at the beginnings of each of your sentences in a draft of the essay you are currently writing will allow you to see if you use a variety of sentence openings or if you repeat a particular pattern. With a colored pencil, mark the subject in each of your sentences by placing brackets around the simple subject. If your simple subject is the first, second, or third word of your sentence, draw a circle around the bracketed simple subject. When you finish, look at the entire composition to see where you have put colored marks. What is the visual impact? Did you discover that more than half of your sentences contained a subject within the first three words? If not, you probably use a variety of sentence patterns in your writing, and your audience will likely not become bored with it. If half or more of your sentences do contain the subject in the opening words of the sentence, you can reduce monotony by choosing alternatives for the openings of some of your sentences. Of course, you would not

Copyright © 1985 by Harcourt Brace Jovanovich, Inc. All rights reserved.

want to change every sentence, for that could create a different kind of monotony. If more than half of your sentences begin with a noun or pronoun subject as one of the first three words, thoughtful selection from among these possibilities should help you achieve variety:

1. an introductory prepositional phrase

    In the slow-growing 1970s unemployment increased for four main reasons.

2. an introductory verbal phrase

    Looking at these causes of rising unemployment, the easiest trap to fall into is the "lump of labor fallacy."

3. an introductory dependent clause

    Until the age of plenty arrives, there will be things to do.

4. a modifier

    The *boiler-suited, oil-stained* masses are a caricatured minority.

5. a transitional word or phrase

    At the other end of the spectrum, there should be plenty of jobs in the armed forces.

Answering the following questions will lead you to discover other ways to begin sentences. You can reduce the possibility of boring your audience with the same old openings if you revise some sentences that have bracketed simple subjects in your essay.

1. How many sentences does your essay contain? _____

2. How many of those sentences contain introductory units before the subject? (*Hint*: Do not count words like *a*, *an*, *the*, *very*, *my*, *your*, or other common modi-

    fiers. _____

3. Can you move units such as prepositional phrases or dependent clauses in your sentences to the beginning of the sentence to help you relieve monotony?

    _____

4. Would it relieve monotony in your essay if you added some introductory prepositional phrases, dependent clauses, or other introductory units where they do

    not occur? _____

5. Can you combine some sentences in your essay so that you can make one of

Copyright © 1985 by Harcourt Brace Jovanovich, Inc. All rights reserved.

your ideas subordinate to another? _____

6. Can you add transitional words or connecting phrases to help guide your reader

    through your essay? _____

7. Do you think your reader will benefit from any of the changes you made?

    _____

8. Do you think your reader is more likely to accept your ideas after you have

    adjusted the openings of your sentences? _____

9. After your adjustments, how many sentences do you have that begin with a

    simple subject in the first three words of the sentence? _____

10. Have you created monotony by overusing any of the alternative openings? (*Hint*:
    You can use the same process of circling the target opening to see if you have

    done so.) _____

6.8 PARAGRAPH POWER

When you must answer a question such as "Why is it so hot in here?" or "Why did
you run the red light?" or "Why did she fall from the Ferris wheel?" you will need
to use the rhetorical mode of cause and effect. Like the modes of process and narration, the cause and effect mode presents a sequence of events in chronological time.
The chronological presentation allows your audience to notice that somebody (an agent)
or something (a force or action or decision) brought about (caused) something which
resulted in change (an effect). Any effect may have several causes, just as a particular cause may have several effects. In writing, you must select carefully among causes
and effects and present those to your reader. Otherwise, you will get bogged down
in unnecessary detail.

Although the following example does present a series of causes and effects, it shows
how boring writing can be to readers when the writer does not select causes and effects carefully.

If you touch a lighted match to newspaper crumpled under a grate in a fireplace

filled with wood, the paper will begin to burn. On *account of* the burning paper, the

wood reaches its kindling point and it too begins to burn. *Since* the wood is aflame,

it produces heat in the room that results from having ignited the match.

Copyright © 1985 by Harcourt Brace Jovanovich, Inc. All rights reserved.

No one would be surprised if you were irritated that the cause of the heat was attributed to igniting the match because you rightly attributed the heat in the room to the blazing wood. Attributing the heat to igniting the match demonstrates that a cause and effect paragraph or theme need not take into account every cause that results in a particular effect. If you were to write that way, you would never be able to explain anything efficiently. You can assume your reader understands, for example, igniting a fire is necessary before it can flame and eventually produce enough heat to warm a room.

When writing in the cause and effect mode, you explain how a particular cause resulted in a particular effect. To do so, you use your experience and reflect upon the most significant and important cause for your purpose in order to tie it together with the effect you are explaining.

Since you cannot include all causes that contribute to an effect, be selective in choosing those that you include. In scientific writing, of course, you would need to say that causes W, X, Y, and Z resulted in or caused effect E, but unless your purpose is to explain a scientific cause and effect relationship, you will usually find it more efficient to select one to three of the most immediate and important causes that produced a particular effect.

You can also focus on the several effects resulting from a particular cause. The same cautions apply when you focus on effects that apply when you focus on causes. Select only those effects that you judge most immediate and important to your purpose in discussing the cause.

Sometimes you will have several causes contributing to a single effect. If so, the T-R-I-I pattern will serve you well. First state the effect in your thesis sentence (T). Then present your primary cause as your restriction (R). Finally, show the other significant causes (I, I, . . .). The following example is written according to the T-R-I-I pattern.

The empty room startled the sponsors when they arrived at 10:00 P.M. to find the students had left the party an hour earlier (T). They probably left because the room had become unbearably hot (R). As the club's president had insisted, a roaring fire blazed in the party room fireplace even though the evening was unseasonably warm (I). After all one hundred members arrived with their dates and began dancing, the room became hotter moment by moment; even opening the windows did not help to cool the room (I).

In the preceding example, the first sentence (T) states the effect. The second sentence contains the primary cause (R). The third and fourth sentences present secondary causes (I, I).

Copyright © 1985 by Harcourt Brace Jovanovich, Inc. All rights reserved.

EXERCISE 1

Paragraph 2 of "Where Future Jobs Will Be" is an effective example of an effect-to-cause paragraph using the T-R-I-I pattern. Draw a box around the topic (the effect). Next, circle the restriction (the main cause). Finally, draw a continuous wavy line under each of the illustrations.

In the slow-growing 1970s unemployment increased for four main reasons. The number of people wanting jobs rose faster than employment did—not just because of population growth, but also [because] there were proportionately more young people in the population and more women entering the job market. Inflation reached progressively higher peaks. Jobs that had once been the preserve of developed countries migrated to the less developed countries. The industrial countries, through their lack of innovation, did not fill the vacuum.

EXERCISE 2

Plan the development of an effect-to-cause paragraph following the T-R-I-I pattern in which you explore the relationship between the yearly cost of a college education ($5,000 to $15,000) and part-time jobs for students.

EXERCISE 3

Select an audience that expects Standard English for which you intend to write a kernel paragraph using the material developed in Exercise 2. Describe that audience by listing specific features in the following categories:

Age _____

Sex _____

Education _____

Cultural, racial, or occupational characteristics _____

_____

Size of group (1 to many) _____

Copyright © 1985 by Harcourt Brace Jovanovich, Inc. All rights reserved.

Make a general statement about why many college students have to work.

T

Identify the main cause of college students having to work.

R

Support the topic and restriction with specific illustrations (details, evidence).

I		
I	I	I
Tuition	Supplies & equipment	Room & board

Copyright © 1985 by Harcourt Brace Jovanovich, Inc. All rights reserved.

Notes

EXERCISE 4

With the audience described in Exercise 3 in mind, write a kernel paragraph of four to seven sentences using the plan developed in Exercise 2. (*Hint*: Choose the appropriate variety of language for the audience.)

EXERCISE 5

Select an audience different from the one in Exercise 3. Describe that audience by listing its features:

Age _____

Sex _____

Education _____

Cultural, racial, or occupational characteristics _____

_____

Size of group (1 to many) _____

EXERCISE 6

Rewrite the paragraph in Exercise 4 for the new audience. (*Hint*: Think about how you need to change the variety of language you use for the new audience.)

EXERCISE 7

Revise your essay to include the paragraph you wrote in Exercise 6. Adjust your cause-and-effect essay (Section 6.6) for the audience you chose in Exercise 5.

Copyright © 1985 by Harcourt Brace Jovanovich, Inc. All rights reserved.

Notes

6.9 *SENTENCE POWER*

COORDINATION

In your study of writing you have learned to identify and to use compounds such as compound subjects, verbs, and sentences. Compounds are made by joining words, phrases, or clauses of equal importance. Effective use of compounds leads to coordination, parallelism, and balance in writing, closely connected concepts that can result in clearer writing.

The concept of coordination is important to learn because it allows you to link or join two or more items of equal importance which have the same grammatical form. Therefore, they are also parallel. If they are also of similar lengths, they are balanced. Your meaning and sense will be clearer to your reader when your writing is coordinate, parallel, and balanced. However, too much coordination can hinder effective writing, especially if several short sentences are strung together with the coordinate conjunction "and."

Simple coordination joins two items with a coordinate conjunction (*and*, *but*, *or*, *nor*, *for*, *so*, *yet*) and signals the reader that the items on either side of the conjunction are of equal importance. By linking coordinate items you emphasize the relationship between them for your reader.

SUBJECTS

1. a. **Employers *and* employees** want their companies to be successful.
   b. **Petroleum engineers *and* construction workers** have different kinds of skills.
2. a. **Studying in college *and* working after classes** keeps students busy.
   b. **To work *or* to play** is a choice you have to make every day.
3. a. **What you have to do *and* what you want to do** are often two different things.
   b. **That manufacturers want cheap labor *and* that laborers demand fair pay** point toward possible conflicts that negotiations reconcile.

Each of the preceding sentences contains coordinated subjects joined by a coordinating conjunction. Moreover, the subjects are said to be parallel because the items joined by the conjunction have the same grammatical form. In other words, a clause is joined to a clause, a phrase is joined to a phrase, and a word is joined to a word. While it is not necessary for items to be the same length for coordination and parallelism, the ones in these examples are. When coordinated items are of the same length and have the same grammatical form (parallelism), they are balanced.

Copyright © 1985 by Harcourt Brace Jovanovich, Inc. All rights reserved.

VERBS

1. The government **sponsored** *and* **organized** shipbuilding programs.
2. The computer **is keeping** records *and* **forecasting** the weather.

Both sentences contain coordinated verbs joined by a coordinating conjunction. In the second sentence, the helping verb *is* belongs to both *keeping* and *forecasting*. In other words, the compound verb has the sense of *is keeping* and *is forecasting*. Because the verbs are coordinate, repeating *is,* the helping verb, is not necessary.

OBJECTS

1. Object of verb
   a. Shipbuilders produce **aircraft carriers** *and* **submarines.**
   b. Engineers learn **to design products** *and* **to execute plans.**
   c. Manufacturers realize **that they must have contracts** *and* **that those contracts must be specific.**
2. Object of preposition
   a. Physicians answer questions for **patients** *and* **their families.**
   b. Medical specialists train many years before **diagnosing** *and* **operating.**
   c. Dentists instruct patients about **how they should brush their teeth** *and* **how they should care for their gums.**

In these examples, nouns, verbals, and clauses function as compound objects, as objects of verbs and as objects of prepositions; coordinating conjunctions join them. Notice that the compound objects in each case have the same grammatical form and are coordinate.

MODIFIERS

1. Adjectives
   a. The unemployed need to know where the prospects are **brightest** *and* **grimmest.**
   b. The **boiler-suited, oil-stained** masses are a caricatured minority.
      A comma separates coordinate adjectives if a coordinating conjunction does not join them.
2. Adverbs
   The auto industry has recently become **obviously** *and* **painfully** aware of its growth limits.

Like subjects, verbs, and objects, adjectives and adverbs can be coordinated. A comma, however, separates coordinate adjectives more frequently than a coordinate conjunc-

Copyright © 1985 by Harcourt Brace Jovanovich, Inc. All rights reserved.

tion. (Hint: To test if you have written coordinate adjectives, read your sentence and supply *and* between the adjectives. If *and* supplies the sense you mean, you can put a comma between the adjectives.)

FAULTY COORDINATION

There are five major reasons for faulty coordination.

1. Writers attempt to coordinate items that lack a logical relationship by using an imprecise or haphazard connection.

    Faulty   Do you walk to school or carry your lunch?
    Correct   Do you carry your lunch when you walk to school?

    Make the logical relationship between sentence elements clear.
    Here, subordinating one element to the other clarifies the relationship.
2. Writers leave out important information the reader needs in order to understand the relationship among the items.

    Faulty   Bob had scheduled an interview with the personnel officer, but he was delayed by a long-distance telephone call.
    Correct   A long-distance telephone call delayed Bob and caused him to be late for his scheduled interview with the personnel officer.

    The information that the long-distance call was responsible for the delay explains why Bob was late and makes clear that the call was to Bob rather than the personnel officer. The verbs *delayed* and *caused* are coordinated.
3. Writers attempt to coordinate items belonging to overlapping groups.

    Faulty   The meeting was attended by men, women, and parents.
    Correct   The meeting was attended by men and women, some of whom were parents.

    Since parents would be men and women, the correction shows that some of the men were parents and some of the women were parents, but that not all were parents. Other possibilities include that all were parents or that being a parent was irrelevant.
4. Writers treat all items as if they had the same level of importance when reason or common sense clearly show some are more important than others.

    Faulty   I went downtown to look for a job, and I found an employment agency, and there were several positions listed, and I was qualified for some of them, and I arranged an interview for tomorrow.
    Correct   I arranged an interview for tomorrow at a downtown employment agency which listed several positions I was qualified for.

Copyright © 1985 by Harcourt Brace Jovanovich, Inc. All rights reserved.

The correction reduces the length of the sentence by subordinating four of the five ideas to one. The reader understands that the writer emphasizes that he or she has arranged for an interview tomorrow.

5. Writers attempt to coordinate elements that are not grammatically parallel.

Faulty	Medical doctors spend much time in surgery, to diagnose patients, and examining x-rays.
Correct	Medical doctors spend much time diagnosing patients, examining x-rays, and operating.

The correction rearranges the order of the three non-parallel elements and makes them gramatically parallel: in the correction each verbal ends in an *-ing.* You can often make non-parallel elements gramatically parallel in more than one way. For example, consider another option.

Correct	Medical doctors spend much time in diagnosis, examination of x-rays, and surgery.

The five kinds of faulty coordination can occur with words, with phrases, and with clauses. You can find faulty coordination in subjects, verbs, objects, and modifiers. In other words, any time you join elements, faulty coordination can occur. The solution is to rewrite after you spot the problem and figure out what went wrong.

If your writing contains faulty coordination or faulty parallelism within your sentences or between your sentences, your reader will have difficulty knowing what you intend to focus on. On the other hand, if your writing overuses coordination, especially if your sentences are very long and have one independent clause connected to another with the conjunction *and,* then your writing will likely be ineffective. In coordination, avoid combining more than three or four items. Coordinating five or more items may create a humorous response which you do not intend. If you wish to include more than four items, look for some arrangement which will let you coordinate them in smaller groups.

EXERCISE 1

Identify the faulty coordination in the following sentences by writing *faulty* in the blank. If the sentence is correct, write *correct* in the blank.

1. _____ Nineteenth-century steel barons fretted about what would happen to their businesses, but the railways had been completed.

2. _____ In the slow-growing 1970s, crime, unemployment, and joblessness increased for four main reasons.

3. _____ Until the age of plenty arrives and all problems have been solved, there will be much to do.

Copyright © 1985 by Harcourt Brace Jovanovich, Inc. All rights reserved.

4. _____ Two other important differences will rein-
force the white-collar trend, and women will hold more important jobs.

5. _____ The counselor works with young people and
enthusiasm for his job.

6. _____ Workers in less developed countries will be
much younger and will have potential for greater earnings than their parents.

7. _____ The department's statistics were recently
released but unemployment continues to rise.

8. _____ Both countries support their work force and
their industry.

9. _____ A further twenty-five million depend on the
auto industry, and they sell cars, and they drive busses, and they man gasoline
pumps, and they repair vehicles, and they provide finance, and they sell insurance.

10. _____ The annual growth of car sales and a large
workforce have expanded the market of first-time buyers.

EXERCISE 2

The following sentences all contain faulty coordination. Identify the reason for the
faulty coordination and rewrite the sentence after you spot the problem.

Example   Do you walk to school or carry your lunch. *lacks logical relationship*
Do you carry your lunch when you walk to school?

1. Students work part time, and they go to school during the day. _____

_____

_____

2. Rising unemployment traps poorly educated employees, and food prices con-

tinue to climb. _____

_____

_____

Copyright © 1985 by Harcourt Brace Jovanovich, Inc. All rights reserved.

3. Future jobs will be found in high technology industries, services, and comput-

ers. _____

_____

_____

4. More women will hold paid jobs, and they will have smaller families, and the economic and social pressures will accelerate the entry of women into the labor

force. _____

_____

_____

5. Obsolete employees can retrain themselves or get to work on time. _____

_____

_____

6. The foreman arrived an hour late, and he was paid for a full day. _____

_____

_____

7. Aaron's favorite movies were *Star Wars*, *Return of the Jedi*, and watching the

football game. _____

_____

_____

8. To prepare for a job and getting there on time help you get a raise. _____

_____

_____

9. Sam got a new job and he had to have an operation. _____

_____

Copyright © 1985 by Harcourt Brace Jovanovich, Inc. All rights reserved.

10. That studying is important and you need to sleep regularly help a college student get good grades. _____

_____

_____

EXERCISE 3

Combine the following groups into a single sentence by using effective coordination.

1. Young people in industrial countries have already found that too many are trained to do the clean jobs.
   Employers in industrial countries have already found that too many young people are trained to do the clean jobs.

   _____

   _____

   _____

   _____

2. Some of these products have brought new jobs.
   Some of these products have displaced workers.

   _____

   _____

   _____

   _____

3. The computer industry seeks programmers.
   The computer industry seeks electronics engineers.

   _____

   _____

   _____

Copyright © 1985 by Harcourt Brace Jovanovich, Inc. All rights reserved.

4. The big winners have been Third World countries led by South Korea.
   The big winners have been Third World countries led by Taiwan.
   The big winners have been Third World countries led by Brazil.
   The winners have been a group.

   _____

   _____

   _____

   _____

5. Job prospects for young employees have never looked brighter.
   Job prospects for alert employees have never looked brighter.

   _____

   _____

   _____

6. That unemployment is increasing tends to create a conservative economic environment.
   That workers have difficulty changing jobs tends to create a conservative economic environment.

   _____

   _____

   _____

7. Investors believe that it pays to buy professional advice.
   Investors believe that the advice should be followed.
   Savers believe that it pays to buy professional advice.
   Savers believe that the advice should be followed.

   _____

   _____

Copyright © 1985 by Harcourt Brace Jovanovich, Inc. All rights reserved.

_____

_____

_____

8. Training doctors demands enormous commitments by Third World countries.
    Providing adequate hospital services demands enormous commitments by Third
    World countries.

_____

_____

_____

_____

9. An inflationary economy requires controlling the money supply to slow down
    inflation.
    An inflationary economy requires creating new jobs to slow down inflation.

_____

_____

_____

_____

10. The only certain way to cut public payrolls is by making fundamental changes.
    The only certain way to cut public payrolls is by providing reduced services.

_____

_____

_____

_____

Copyright © 1985 by Harcourt Brace Jovanovich, Inc. All rights reserved.

Notes

VARIETIES IN LANGUAGE

Since your childhood, you have been adding to the variety of language you use. For instance, you may have called your stomach ''tummy'' when you were a toddler; by the fifth grade, ''belly.'' By the time you left elementary school, you had your permanent teeth, so you could say ''stomach,'' pronouncing it ''stummik.'' In your science classes in high school, you probably learned ''abdomen.'' Now that you are in college, it would not be surprising if you know someone who has a ''beer gut.'' A tackle for a professional football team may complain about getting hit in the ''gut.'' One of your mother's friends may say she is going to lose a few inches from her ''mid-section,'' and her husband might complain of his ''spare tire.'' Most adults speaking in public would likely choose ''stomach'' or ''abdomen'' although they might use ''tummy,'' ''gut,'' ''spare tire,'' ''beer gut,'' or ''pot belly'' in other situations.

If you consider the choice of one of these words over another, you will see that language depends not only upon the speaker's age, education, and situation, but also upon other factors such as geography, cultural background, racial identity, and occupation. Recognizing that language appropriate in one situation is not necessarily appropriate in another is important. For this reason, educated people learn to use several varieties of language and to select the appropriate one for each situation.

Choosing appropriate language, however, involves more than just selecting a synonym. What is correct in spoken language is not necessarily appropriate in writing. The rich cultural variety of America extends to every person's language. For example, speech in different parts of the country varies so much that often you can recognize where people come from by the way they pronounce their words and by the words they choose.

All of us express ourselves by the personal ways we use language, and most develop tolerance towards differences among dialects. Even though such acceptance may be desirable, many public uses of language require Standard English. In public language there is little, if any, tolerance for different dialects. Every person, then, can benefit from having a public language, Standard English, as well as a private language—another dialect. Standard English is just one of the many varieties of English, but it is the variety used in business, government, journalism, and many other institutions. In other words, it is the dialect people expect, and indeed insist on, for public uses of language.

Because of the expectations of business, journalism, education, and other institutions, writers who speak a dialect other than Standard English often choose to write in Standard English. Sometimes, a writer may slip dialect forms into writing when Standard English is appropriate. Even though dialect forms are acceptable in speech in some situations, you should avoid them when writing Standard English as well as when you are in speaking situations where your audience expects Standard English.

Three particularly troublesome irregular verbs have common dialect forms inappro-

Copyright © 1985 by Harcourt Brace Jovanovich, Inc. All rights reserved.

priate when writing Standard English. These forms of *be*, *have*, and *do* are outlined in a chart for your convenience.

Some speakers, who do not use all of these troublesome dialect forms, incorrectly form the negative of *do*. They say *he don't like it* instead of *he doesn't like it*, or they might say *the car don't start* instead of *the car doesn't start*. *Don't* and *doesn't* require special attention.

EXERCISE 4

Circle the forms inappropriate in college writing, and write the Standard English forms in the blanks.

Example   _*makes*_   He ⟨make⟩ a big splash, ⟨don't⟩ he?
              *doesn't*

_____ 1. Electronic engineering be the highest paying profession.

_____ 2. He have traveled to the Third World countries.

_____ 3. Last week she were fired from the plant.

_____ 4. The computer have one disk drive broken and lacks the use of one terminal.

_____ 5. We was surprised that the economy have expanded in the second quarter.

_____

_____ 6. The surgeon done an operation to correct a trick knee.

_____ 7. Last quarter you was worried about the gross national product.

_____ 8. By the end of the second quarter, industry and manufacturing was growing at a fast rate.

_____ 9. We done what were necessary before we done the job.

_____

Copyright © 1985 by Harcourt Brace Jovanovich, Inc. All rights reserved.

Dialect (avoid in writing)		Standard English (use in writing)	
To Be			
Present Tense			
I be (or, omitted)	we be	I am	we are
you be	you be	you are	you are
he, she, it be	they be	he, she, it is	they are
Past Tense			
I were	we was	I was	we were
you was	you was	you were	you were
he, she, it were	they was	he, she, it was	they were
To Have			
Present Tense			
I has	we has	I have	we have
you has	you has	you have	you have
he, she, it have	they has	he, she, it has	they have
Past Tense			
I has	we has	I had	we had
you has	you has	you had	you had
he, she, it have	they has	he, she, it had	they had
To Do			
Present Tense			
I does	we do	I do	we do
you does	you does	you do	you do
he, she, it do	they does	he, she, it does	they do
Past Tense			
I done	we done	I did	we did
you done	you done	you did	you did
he, she, it done	they done	he, she, it did	they did

_____10. By the end of the month, I were learning to program the computer and were earning $1.25

_____ more an hour.

_____11. She don't ask my opinion when she be looking for a job.

_____

_____12. Car salesmen usually doesn't care to find financing for customers.

_____13. I be the best trained mechanic in the plant.

Copyright © 1985 by Harcourt Brace Jovanovich, Inc. All rights reserved.

_____14. They was expecting to increase the money supply.

_____15. They has more influence in the Third World than they has in other economies.

_____

Copyright © 1985 by Harcourt Brace Jovanovich, Inc. All rights reserved.

6.10 *PROOFREADING POWER*

When you become aware of a writing problem during proofreading, you figure out what the problem is before revising or correcting it. Some problems, such as spelling or subject-verb agreement errors, are easy to correct. Others require concentrated thinking first to figure what went wrong and then to revise your writing to make it right.

The writing problems in this proofreading exercise include faulty coordination and inappropriate language.

The auto industry have recently become painfully aware of its growth limits. Motor manufacturers employ about 4 million people around the world and support 6 million more who make the components and materials that go into cars, trucks, busses, and Cadillacs. A further 25 million depend on the industry—selling cars, drive trucks and busses, manning gasoline pumps, to repair vehicles, provide finance and insurance. So when auto manufacturers sneeze, the rest of the industry sniffles.

6.11 *DICTATION*

Your instructor will choose a passage of approximately 100 words and read it aloud. You are to write what you hear. As you listen to each sentence, concentrate and maintain silence. Do not ask your instructor to repeat because any sound other than the instructor's voice reading will break not only your concentration but that of others. Your instructor may repeat key words and phrases during the dictation, will allow sufficient time for you to write what you have heard, and will reread the entire passage a second time at a faster rate so that you can check what you have written and fill in any gaps you may have.

Write on every other line so that you will have space to correct your dictation upon the final reading in case you have made a mistake. Your instructor will show you the dictated passage and ask you to compare it to your version or perhaps a classmate's version. Be especially alert when you check the dictation because this exercise will help you develop your sentence sense by translating spoken into written language. It also tests your attention to the many mechanical details of writing.

6.12 *WORD POWER*

SOUND-ALIKES

Words that look or sound similar can be problems to write. The best way to sort out their meanings and usage is to learn them in context (the surroundings of a word).

Copyright © 1985 by Harcourt Brace Jovanovich, Inc. All rights reserved.

The words that have the same or similar sounds or forms appear in italics in these sentences for you to study.

1. a. Change will *affect* where jobs can be found.
   b. The *effect* of change will improve agriculture, industry, and service.
2. a. Park rangers warned the parents about the *bear*, the deer, and the turkeys in the park.
   b. An employer requires that an employee know more than the *bare* essentials about the operations.
3. a. Two other differences have *been* discussed in the meeting.
   b. The carpenter built another *bin* for storage.
4. a. If the bus fare is raised only a *cent*, it will be difficult to have correct change.
   b. When the *scent* of the baking bread filled the house, the baker had lots of visitors in the kitchen.
   c. The baker *sent* the kids back to the den to play.
5. a. When you apply for a job and you do not get it, you sometimes feel like a *loser*.
   b. The dancer should wear *looser* clothing than the tight ones of the model.
6. a. The secretary opens the *mail*.
   b. The *male* secretary typed over a hundred words correctly on his test.
7. a. To type that well, you have to keep your *mind* on the task.
   b. I hope the supervisor does not want to compare his test to *mine*.
8. a. The supervisor tried to keep *peace* and harmony among the arguing secretaries.
   b. Every *piece* of mail will be opened, read, and answered.
9. a. The *peak* of the work day happens when the afternoon mail arrives.
   b. The secretary *peeks* around the corner to see who is using the copy machine.
10. a. Sometimes secretaries shop during lunch if stores are having a *sale* that really reduces prices.
    b. The *sail* on the boat has a bright red emblem painted on it.
11. a. The secretary showed her friends the new ring *setting* that the jeweler had made for her diamond.
    b. She proudly displayed her new ring while *sitting* at her desk.
12. a. The *size* of her diamond, over a carat, made every other secretary envious.
    b. One secretary was so jealous that she would *seize* every opportunity she could find to mention her new fur coat.
13. a. Her *sole* reason for mentioning her fur coat was to take attention from the new ring setting.
    b. Her jealousy affected her inner being, her *soul*.
14. a. The secretary said that she would not have any trouble making dinner when she got married because her fiance would eat a *steak* and baked potato every night.

Copyright © 1985 by Harcourt Brace Jovanovich, Inc. All rights reserved.

    b.   The jealous secretary retorted that she hoped he had a *stake* that included a gold mine and oil wells.

15. a.   The frame for the secretary's old chair was made out of *steel*, but her new one was plastic.

    b.   Secretaries may argue among themselves, but they do not *steal* work because they have too much to do.

16. a.   The supervisor *taught* the office staff the new procedures for handling mail.

    b.   The two secretaries had created a tense, *taut* atmosphere for everyone in the office.

17. a.   Others in the office thought their behavior was less professional *than* it should be.

    b.   After a meeting with both employees, the supervisor could *then* understand the conflict.

18. a.   *Though* the supervisor could understand the conflict, she refused to allow it to interrupt the office routine.

    b.   After she *thought* about the problem, she decided to transfer one of the secretaries to another department.

19. a.   She interviewed the senior secretary to help her determine *which* was to be moved.

    b.   The supervisor learned that neither secretary was a *witch*, that both had admirable qualities, and that the conflict would probably end as soon as the other one got a marriage proposal.

20. a.   She was *right* in her evaluation of the situation because the conflict ended.

    b.   The supervisor decided to *write* a request for a raise for the senior secretary.

EXERCISE 1

Write your own sentences to show your mastery of the words studied in the preceding sentences. Strive to write sentences that will interest your reader and that have variety.

1. a.   affect _____

_____

   b.   effect _____

_____

2. a.   bear _____

_____

Copyright © 1985 by Harcourt Brace Jovanovich, Inc. All rights reserved.

b. bare _____

_____

3. a. been _____

_____

b. bin _____

_____

4. a. cent _____

_____

b. scent _____

_____

c. sent _____

_____

5. a. loser _____

_____

b. looser _____

_____

6. a. mail _____

_____

b. male _____

_____

7. a. mind _____

_____

b. mine _____

Copyright © 1985 by Harcourt Brace Jovanovich, Inc. All rights reserved.

8. a. peace _____

   b. piece _____

9. a. peak _____

   b. peek _____

10. a. sale _____

    b. sail _____

11. a. setting _____

    b. sitting _____

12. a. size _____

    b. seize _____

13. a. sole _____

Copyright © 1985 by Harcourt Brace Jovanovich, Inc. All rights reserved.

b. soul _____

_____

14. a. steak _____

_____

b. stake _____

_____

15. a. steel _____

_____

b. steal _____

_____

16. a. taught _____

_____

b. taut _____

_____

17. a. than _____

_____

b. then _____

_____

18. a. though _____

_____

b. thought _____

_____

19. a. which _____

Copyright © 1985 by Harcourt Brace Jovanovich, Inc. All rights reserved.

_____

b. witch _____

_____

20. a. right _____

_____

b. write _____

_____

EXERCISE 2

Supply the correct word to complete the meaning of the following sentences.

1. Technology will affect/effect _____ the size/seize

   _____ of the work force.

2. Though/thought _____ it is not the sole/soul

   _____ reason for learning to write/right _____ ,

   advancement in the world of work is one thing to bear/bare _____

   in mind/mine _____ .

3. Other reasons are that writing can help you sell yourself, give you peace/piece

   _____ of mind/mine _____ ,

   and help you stake/steak _____ your claim.

4. The scent/sent/cent _____ of success can steal/steel

   _____ reason from a looser/loser _____ .

5. Male/mail _____ in business had been/bin _____

   a way to increase sales/sails _____ since the days
   of the pony express.

Copyright © 1985 by Harcourt Brace Jovanovich, Inc. All rights reserved.

Notes

SPELLING

Words that end in a single vowel plus a single consonant sound double the final consonant when a suffix is added.

Example format + ed = formatted

EXCEPTIONS:

1. If a word ends in more than one consonant or more than one vowel, simply attach the suffix without doubling the final consonant.

   Example *form* + ed = formed

2. If the stress moves to the first syllable in the new word, do *not* double the final consonant when adding the suffix.

   Example refer + ed = referred
      but refer + ence = reference

EXERCISE 2

Using the preceding rule, combine the base word in the following list with the suffix. (*Hint*: Double the final consonant only when a word fits the rule.)

1. begin + er _____

         -ing _____

2. big + est _____

        -er _____

3. control + ed _____

         -er _____

         -ing _____

4. drop + ed _____

         -er _____

         -ing _____

5. equip + ed _____

Copyright © 1985 by Harcourt Brace Jovanovich, Inc. All rights reserved.

6. hop + ed _____

        -er _____

        -ing _____

7. occur + ence _____

        -ed _____

        -ing _____

8. omit + ing _____

        -ed _____

9. parallel + ed _____

10. plan + er _____

        -ed _____

        -ing _____

11. prefer + ed _____

        -ing _____

12. question + er _____

        -ing _____

13. refer + ed _____

        -ing _____

14. run + er _____

        -ing _____

15. step + ed _____

        -ing _____

Copyright © 1985 by Harcourt Brace Jovanovich, Inc. All rights reserved.

16. stop + ed _____

     -er _____

     -ing _____

17. sum + ary _____

18. swim + ing _____

     -er _____

19. win + er _____

     -ing _____

20. write + en _____

Copyright © 1985 by Harcourt Brace Jovanovich, Inc. All rights reserved.

Notes

UNIT SEVEN
WRITING
REFINED

7.1 GETTING STARTED BY READING

The slowest among the five reading rates identified in Unit Three is the one used for study. When you are reading at the study rate, your purpose is to have excellent recall of facts and specifics, and you should be able to analyze a process or to understand the intricacies of a blueprint or the subtleties of a poem. Sometimes you will use the study rate to read a class assignment or the sources you use to write a term paper. In fact, it is the rate you will likely use most in your college career. Because your goal is both to acquire specific facts and to understand principles and relationships, the information you gain in reading for study is important information which can help you change your behavior. For instance, you might need the information to pass an examination or to perform a significant part of your job, whether that job is in the marketplace, in the community, or in the home.

Category	Study
Rate	The slowest rate at which you have excellent comprehension and recall

Purposes	To learn specific facts
	To understand directions
	To read with analysis
Typical reading for study	How-to books
	Patterns
	Poetry
	Philosophy or religion
	Textbooks
	Government reports
	Scientific articles
	Professional articles
	Arguments for or against issues
	Health regimens
	Lecture notes
	Legal documents (deeds, wills, contracts)

''The Family Numbers Game'' reports sociological research that explores the possible influences of being first-born. You should use your study rate while reading this assignment. Probably, you will want to keep a pencil in hand to mark specifics that seem significant enough to you that an instructor might include them on an examination. The following three questions will guide you while reading this assignment.

1. How do youngest children behave? Middle children? Eldest children? Only children?
2. How does birth-order affect success in life?
3. Is it best to be the oldest, youngest, or middle child?

7.2 COMPARISON

Richard Wolkomir   *"THE FAMILY NUMBERS GAME"*

Were you the first-born child in your family? Number two? Number three? The caboose?

It may make a difference: Of the first 16 astronauts, 14 were eldest children or only children. So were John Paul Sartre, Robert Louis Stevenson, Leonardo da Vinci, Harry S Truman, Franklin D. Roosevelt, Abraham Lincoln, Gen. George Patton, Genghis Khan, Queen Elizabeth I, Joseph Stalin, and Geoffrey Chaucer.

So are a disproportionate number of the people named in *Who's Who*.

It's no wonder. Studies indicate that first-borns value achievement more highly than younger siblings do. Researchers also find that first-borns (a group that, by definition,

Copyright © 1985 by Harcourt Brace Jovanovich, Inc. All rights reserved.

includes only-children) have a penchant for "controlling and organizing the behavior of others." Two U.S. psychologists, who analyzed data on nearly all males born in the Netherlands from 1944 to 1947, found that—statistically—older brothers out-scored younger brothers on intelligence tests.

What gets into first-borns?

For one thing, say the psychologists, first-borns begin life as little stars, the only kids on the family stage. If attention were money, they'd be millionaires. For in-stance, two National Institutes of Mental Health researchers, Blanche S. Jacobs and Howard A. Moss, have found that mothers spend "less time in social, affectionate, and caretaking activities with their second-borns."

But that waning of maternal attention was greatest if number two was a girl. If number two was a boy—and the first-born child was a girl—the attention is practi-cally the same.

Why do girls get short-changed? Perhaps women find taking care of a boy more of a novelty, suggest Jacobs and Moss. "Not to be overlooked is the preferred status attributed to males in our culture," they add. But they also cite other studies with results less satisfying to the male ego: It turns out that infant boys are simply more demanding. In other words, a male number two gets extra attention simply because— let's admit it—the little dickens is more of a nag than his sisters.

Meanwhile other researchers have been getting the goods (also the bads) on those ambitious number ones. Here are some of their findings:

First-borns tend to have higher self-esteem than those born later. This is true es-pecially of first-born girls, who generally feel they have their fathers' approval. Male first-borns, on the other hand, are more conscious of having their peers' approval. In later life female first-borns are likelier to develop close relationships with authority figures, such as teachers or employers, while male first-borns continue to look to their peers for approval.

University of Virginia researchers have found that among criminals first-borns are the least likely to be repeat offenders.

Psychologists at the University of Connecticut report that first-born men tend to marry younger than later-born men. It may be because first-borns tend to seek the

Copyright © 1985 by Harcourt Brace Jovanovich, Inc. All rights reserved.

support of others in stressful situations. But first-born women marry neither earlier nor later than their younger sisters. No one knows why.

Researchers at the University of Maine have found that among neurotic people male only-children and female first-borns are "overrepresented." But male first-borns are "underrepresented."

Psychiatrist Alfred Adler theorized that male onlies are emotionally vulnerable because for them the normal father-son rivalry is undiluted by the presence of other children. Adler says that older children want to "be first, receive special attention, and emulate adults"—a golden opportunity for oldest sons, who get to "manage" their younger sisters and brothers. But female eldests have a special problem: As first-borns they're expected to be responsible and oversee their younger siblings. But society signals that girls should be passive and deferential. Thus they're caught in an emotional tug of war.

Number ones can have other disadvantages. For one thing, new parents are unsure of themselves and can transmit their stress to their first-born child. Studies do show that first-borns suffer more from anxiety than do their younger siblings. For instance, they tend to be more conformist, and they're less likely to try dangerous sports. Most ace fighter pilots are younger sons.

Do you crave popularity? Then don't be an oldest child. University of California researchers asked 1,750 grade schoolers which classmates they liked best. Results: Youngest children were the most popular, followed by middle-borns; first-borns were last.

Could this lack of popularity be because oldest children are bossy? In the early 1960's Helen L. Koch of the University of Chicago studied kindergartners and first graders. She found that first-borns tend to be "more quarrelsome, jealous, fault finding, exhibitionistic, and insistent on their rights."

What about only-children? Are they like the stereotype: spoiled, maladjusted, and dependent?

Gail Feldman of the University of New Mexico tested 75 women whose average age was 22. Those in the group who were only-children turned out to be the most confident, resourceful, and assertive.

Copyright © 1985 by Harcourt Brace Jovanovich, Inc. All rights reserved.

"They were the most independent, the least anxious, and [least] conventional,'' says Feldman.

She found that first-born women who had younger brothers were more responsible and more interested in men than the onlies and also more dependent. First-born women with younger sisters were even more conventional and dependent. But the study excluded middle and youngest children; how they would have rated is unknown.

One point on which psychologists seem to agree is the impact of family size. As Michael Olneck and David Bills of the University of Wisconsin reported: Regardless of their family's social position, "men from larger families tend to have lower test scores, less education, lower occupational statuses, and lower earnings than men from smaller families.''

They theorize that the reason may be economic. The larger the family, the fewer resources per member compared to smaller families with similar incomes. They also suggest that parents who *choose* to have large numbers of children "may socialize them in ways antithetical to high test performance.''

But scientists point out that all such findings are statistical trends in large groups. Individuals, as always, go their merry ways, despite both order and family size. Entertainer George Burns, for instance, who is enjoying a new turn in the spotlight, comes from a family of 12.

On the other hand, when it comes to marriage, you might be better off comparing birth orders than checking sun signs. German psychoanalyst Dr. Walter Toman says the marriages likeliest to succeed are between people with complementary family positions: an older sister of a brother marrying the younger brother of a sister, for instance. Or the older brother of a sister marrying the younger sister of a brother.

The most star-crossed marriage possibility, according to Toman, is when people marry their counterparts: older brother of brothers beware the older sister of sisters!

Toman's conclusions come from a 1963 study of 2,300 German and Swiss families in which the divorce rate was three times higher than the norm for such couples. Just as chancy (according to the statistics) are marriages between the younger brother of brothers and the younger sister of sisters.

According to Toman, birth order has a definite effect on personality. In his book

Copyright © 1985 by Harcourt Brace Jovanovich, Inc. All rights reserved.

The Family Constellation he notes that the youngest brother of sisters "is a girls' boy. They love him. They dote on him. He evokes all kinds of maternal instincts in them."

And the oldest brother of sisters? "He is a friend of the girls and ladies, whether sincerely or tongue in check," says Toman. "Love of the tender sex is the most important of all concerns to him, no matter how important his other engagements."

He says that the older brother of brothers "is the leader, the master of other men, whether he shows it by force or cunning. He is in charge. He is in control, not so much in a field or work or endeavor as he is of other people in that field."

Which is best: The oldest? The youngest? In the middle?

So far psychologists have no answer to that question. But columnist Abigail Van Buren recently polled readers of her Dear Abby column. She received some answers straight from life's battlefields:

"I think being the oldest child is definitely the hardest—especially when there are only two in the family and they're both boys," wrote Ricky in Kansas City. "They say, 'You're older and you should know better.' "

However, "A Middle Nothing" wrote in to say: "The middle child is second in everything, never first. If the oldest child accomplishes something, it's a big deal because it's the first time. Same with the youngest, because 'the baby is growing up.' When the middle does—nothing."

And then "Lucky In New Castle" wrote in: "My parents were more relaxed and made fewer mistakes raising me than raising the older ones," said Lucky. "I honestly can't think of any disadvantages in being the youngest."

Unfortunately, the issue is moot. Oldest, middle, youngest—that is one decision we do not get to make:

7.3 UNDERSTANDING WHAT YOU READ

1. List three or more traits of the youngest child. _____

_____

Copyright © 1985 by Harcourt Brace Jovanovich, Inc. All rights reserved.

of middle children. _____

_____

of eldest children. _____

_____

of only children. _____

_____

2. Which area has each most often been successful in? Identify particular successes

of youngest children. _____

_____

of middle children. _____

_____

of eldest children. _____

_____

of only children. _____

_____

3. Name one or possibly two advantages or disadvantages of being the youngest

child. _____

_____

a middle child. _____

_____

the eldest child. _____

_____

the only child. _____

_____

Copyright © 1985 by Harcourt Brace Jovanovich, Inc. All rights reserved.

7.4 *DISCOVERING IDEAS FOR WRITING*

1. Make a list of three to five advantages of your own birth position.

   _____

   _____

   _____

2. Make a list of three to five disadvantages of your own birth position.

   _____

   _____

   _____

3. How do the advantages of your birth order change at different times in your life?

   _____

   _____

   _____

4. How do the disadvantages of your birth order change at different times in your life?

   _____

   _____

   _____

5. How are your birth-order advantages and disadvantages similar to those of someone you are close to such as a roommate, a long-time friend, a boyfriend or girlfriend, or a spouse?

   _____

   _____

   _____

Copyright © 1985 by Harcourt Brace Jovanovich, Inc. All rights reserved.

6. How are your birth-order advantages and disadvantages different from those of the same person you analyzed in question 5?

    _____

    _____

    _____

Copyright © 1985 by Harcourt Brace Jovanovich, Inc. All rights reserved.

Notes

7.5 UNDERSTANDING WRITING

For most experienced writers, writing is a slow process. Writing takes time, more time than an inexperienced writer expects. Sometimes experienced writers work a full day and produce as little as three pages; sometimes, even less. Of course, at other times writing goes faster, but hardly ever as fast as an inexperienced writer thinks it should. As an inexperienced writer, you should expect to write no more rapidly than an experienced writer does.

Few writing assignments can be written in a single sitting. Because of the time needed to reread and reshape your writing and to rethink your ideas, allow sufficient time to complete your writing project. Even at those times when you are to complete an assignment in class, you can prepare for that writing well ahead of time by planning, rethinking, and perhaps drafting as much of your plan as possible. Even for an essay examination for which you do not know the questions, you can draft blocks of writing on those concepts you want to cover.

Experienced writers are constantly planning, rethinking, and drafting their ideas because they often have to write on short notice. Of course, rethinking, for them and for you, is more than simply musing about ideas. Rethinking begins before the actual drafting or writing of alternatives to your plan and continues through the selection of the most appropriate version from among those considered.

Another important principle is that good writing requires you to allow time for your ideas to incubate. When you have finished a draft of an assignment, you should leave it alone for a few hours or, better yet, overnight so that you can return to it with a fresh point of view. Sometimes you can turn your attention to something else for a time before you return to your writing. Most writers can discover ways to improve a draft after allowing an incubation period, and the inability to do so may signal that rethinking has not occurred.

Ordinarily a writer can work no more than four to six hours at a stretch on one project. You may find that, like most student writers, your efficiency decreases noticeably after only a couple of hours. When that happens, stop writing for a while and do something else. Later, return to your writing. You will then be surprised at your renewed energy and perception.

7.6 WRITING—COMPARISON AND CONTRAST

Your responses to the question in 7.4 helped you discover the advantages and disadvantages you may experience from having been born in the position you were. You also examined the ways in which your birth-order is similar to and different from that of a person you know well. These discoveries will allow you to compare or contrast your position to that of another person for your reader.

There are two ways to write a comparison and contrast essay. You can present all

Copyright © 1985 by Harcourt Brace Jovanovich, Inc. All rights reserved.

the features of one subject before you turn to the second to be compared or contrasted. If you develop your essay this way, you will write a whole-by-whole comparison or contrast. The second way to develop a comparison-contrast is to present a feature of one subject and then present the same feature of the second before introducing another feature. In this part-by-part development, the writer examines each feature for both subjects before examining any other feature.

For this assignment, if you choose to compare or contrast using whole-by-whole development, you will examine all of the features of yourself before you examine the same features in the same order of the other person. If you choose part-by-part development, you will examine a single feature of yourself followed by an examination of the same feature of the other person before moving to additional features. In other words you compare feature A of yourself to feature A of the other person before turning to features B, C, and so forth.

WRITING ASSIGNMENT

Draft a 500-word essay in which you compare yourself to the person you analyzed in Section 7.4.

Reminder: In your draft you will likely use some of the modes you have already learned—narration, analysis, description, definition, process, cause and effect. During revision of your draft, you may think of features you want to add to your comparison but that are not on your discovery list or in your draft. If so, make the effort to include them because writing often helps you discover something important you may have overlooked in planning. Don't hesitate to return to an earlier stage of the writing process than the one you are working on.

If you discover additional features, you may try them out by asking your peer editor to read a draft in which you have included the new features. Of course, you do not necessarily have to write a brand new draft. You can usually fit the new features into the old draft and most peer editors are willing to read a messy draft if it shows you are really working on your essay. Adding features may cause you to decide that some features you had included in your writing in your early drafts are not as effective as you thought they would be. If so, delete them. Remember that if you delete a feature about yourself, you must also delete the same feature about the other person you are comparing yourself to.

If you get stumped or cannot decide among the features you have identified, you may want to ask your instructor for help. To do so can keep you from heading down blind alleys or running in a circle. Sometimes you are so close to your subject that you cannot objectively decide which alternative is best. You can obtain that objectivity quickly by asking your instructor a specific question or by briefly showing your instructor your draft. Nevertheless, the responsibility for planning, drafting, revising—phrasing and shaping—and proofreading remain the writer's alone.

The writing process summarized in Section 1.6 can still help you produce an error-

Copyright © 1985 by Harcourt Brace Jovanovich, Inc. All rights reserved.

free essay. If necessary, review the procedures summarized there. It is likely that by now you remember that your instructor can help you more by answering questions about specific problems that surface while you are writing your essay than by meticulously marking all of them after you have finished. If you present a reasonably error-free final version (along with all of your drafts and Editor's Evaluations) for grading, your instructor can concentrate on the ideas and logic of your essay rather than mechanical errors and organizational problems. Discovering and correcting the mechanical errors and organizational problems are your responsibility. If your instructor has to focus on those faults, there will be little time left to focus on, or indeed even understand, your ideas. The more writing problems you can solve for yourself, the better writer you will become, and the more time your instructor will have to teach you how to write.

7.7 THE WRITING PROCESS

Sometimes repeating a word or phrase will help you achieve emphasis in your writing. At other times, repeating a word or a phrase will cause your reader (audience) to perceive your writing as dull and monotonous. Experience will teach you if repetitions in your writing are effective. Perhaps the first step in learning to judge the effectiveness of your repetitions is to become aware of how often you repeat words and phrases.

As you improve your skill and facility in writing you will become critical of the words you use to express your ideas. Already you strive for precise diction (selection of vocabulary) in your essays by writing synonyms near some of the imprecise words you wrote. At other times during writing you may have had second thoughts about a word or a phrase written and decided to change it because you thought of a more effective way to express your idea to your audience.

One systematic way to check if you are overworking a word or perhaps a phrase is to mark with a colored pencil those that occur more than once in the same sentence or in sentences next to each other. As you look over your markings do not be too hasty to change all your repetitions because sometimes intentional repetition can be effective.

In searching for repetitions in your comparison-contrast essay, limit yourself to nouns and adjectives, verbs and adverbs, and obvious phrases. Pay particular attention to *very*, *most*, *interesting*, *terrific*, *fabulous*, *a lot*, *in my opinion* because these are overused in general and have lost their original effectiveness. After having identified all your repetitions, you are ready to evaluate how effective your repetitions are. The questions below can guide you as you decide if some of your repetitions should be changed, or if, in some instances, you should increase their number. Repetition in writing can sometimes help you achieve a **momentum** which helps your reader move along, an **emphasis** which helps your reader get your point, and a **cohesiveness** which

Copyright © 1985 by Harcourt Brace Jovanovich, Inc. All rights reserved.

helps your ideas stick together. At other times, repeating a word or a phrase will cause your reader to perceive your writing as dull and monotonous. Conscious repetition can be effective; unintentional repetition can be dull and monotonous.

1. Can you increase your momentum by changing some of your repeated nouns to

   pronouns? _____

2. Can you emphasize a particular idea by increasing repetition? _____

3. Can you tighten a particular passage by repeating key words or phrases? _____

   _____

4. Should you rephrase any sentence to avoid ineffective repetition? _____

5. Can you substitute a synonym for an ineffective repetition? _____

6. How many times have you used *very*? _____ *A lot*? _____

   In my opinion? _____

   Other overworked words and phrases? _____

7. Can you combine any of your sentences or coordinate your ideas to avoid in-

   effective repetition? _____

8. Have you lengthened or shortened your sentences by avoiding ineffective rep-

   etitions? _____

9. Did you move any sentences from one paragraph to another to avoid ineffective

   repetition? _____ If not, could you improve your essay if you did?

   _____

10. Circle any of the following which describe your perception of the revising you
    did.
    a. My revisions improved my momentum.
    b. My revisions improved my emphasis.
    c. My revisions improved my cohesiveness.
    d. My revisions removed ineffective repetitions.
    e. I did not revise.

Copyright © 1985 by Harcourt Brace Jovanovich, Inc. All rights reserved.

7.8 PARAGRAPH POWER

The comparison and contrast mode provides an important way for you to express similarities and differences and to make decisions and evaluations. Because comparison is performed in two ways, you will view at least two objects or ideas part-by-part or whole-by-whole to identify or understand their similarities or differences. One way is to view entire objects or ideas (whole-by-whole comparison). The other is to view one dominant feature of each idea or object before considering another prominent feature of each idea or object (part-by-part comparison). Furthermore, the features examined in a comparison should reflect thoughtful, systematic analysis; otherwise, an audience will perceive the comparison as shallow and artificial.

In analyzing ideas or objects for comparison, strive to select those features of your subject which can logically be compared and which reveal significant similarities or differences. For example, if you wish to compare home computers, you might examine them by considering size of memory, ease of use, availability of programs, ability to perform desired tasks, and the relationship of cost to all of these *bases for comparison*. It would be silly to compare computers by considering the color of the cabinets because that feature has virtually no relevance to the uses of a computer. Furthermore, it would be superficial to compare computers solely on the basis of cost without considering what features you would get for your investment.

You can effectively organize either a part-by-part or whole-by-whole comparison into a T-R-I-I paragraph. Effective comparison paragraphs include the ideas or objects to be compared in the topic sentence (T). The basis for comparison serves as the restriction in the paragraph (R). The orderly examination of similarities or differences completes the paragraph as illustrations (I_1, I_2, I_3, I_4, I_5). In a part-by-part comparison you examine first one significant feature (I_1) of one of your ideas or objects before examining the same significant feature (I_1) of the other idea or object. Then you move on to examine the next significant feature (I_2) of both ideas or objects and continue to examine significant features in turn (I_3-I_5) until you have completed your comparison. Usually three illustrations are enough. It is rare to have more than five.

In the whole-by-whole comparison, you examine all the significant features of one idea or object before you examine the same features of the other idea or object. In other words, you should present the features of the second idea or object you examine in exactly the same order you used for the first.

For instance, if you are comparing automobiles to select the one you want to buy, you might be most concerned about body styles. To organize a whole-by-whole comparison, you would select three to seven of the most important features and examine those features of one model before you examine those same features in the same order on the next model. To organize a part-by-part comparison, on the other hand, you would examine body styles of the two or more automobiles under consideration by comparing the bumpers to the bumpers, the fender shape to the fender shape, the

Copyright © 1985 by Harcourt Brace Jovanovich, Inc. All rights reserved.

grills to the grills, and so forth. You would complete your comparison of bumpers before beginning your comparison of fender shapes. Furthermore, to make either kind of comparison complete, whether whole-by-whole or part-by-part, you should include no fewer than three and no more than seven of the most important features.

EXERCISE 1

An examination of the parts of the following paragraph from ''The Family Numbers Game'' will help you observe how a comparison-contrast paragraph can be arranged to insure that it is cohesive (holds together).

First-borns tend to have higher self-esteem than those born later. This is true especially of first-born girls, who generally feel they have their fathers' approval. Male first-borns, on the other hand, are more conscious of having their peers' approval. In later life female first-borns are likelier to develop close relationships with authority figures, such as teachers or employers, while male first-borns continue to look to their peers for approval.

By answering each of the following questions, you will gain further understanding of how you can arrange paragraphs carefully so that the ideas are logically presented to your reader. This paragraph illustrates the principles of constructing a T-R-I-I comparison-contrast paragraph.

1. Which sentence states the topic in the preceding paragraph? _____

    _____

2. Which sentence or sentences restrict the topic? _____

    _____

3. Which sentence or sentences provide illustration of the topic? _____

    _____

4. What two groups are compared in this paragraph? _____

    _____

5. What is the order in which these two groups are compared in the restriction?

    _____

    In the illustration? _____

Copyright © 1985 by Harcourt Brace Jovanovich, Inc. All rights reserved.

6. How does this arrangement affect the structure of the paragraph? _____

    _____

7. Are the groups compared whole-by-whole or part-by-part? _____

    _____

8. How many illustrations are contained in the last sentence of the paragraph?

    _____

    _____

9. How many sentences are in the paragraph? _____ How many words?

    _____ What is the average number of words in each sentence? (*Hint*:

    Divide the total number of words by the number of sentences.) _____

    _____

EXERCISE 2

Using the T-R-I-I pattern, plan a paragraph comparing who you are at the moment to who you intend to be ten years from now.

EXERCISE 3

Select an audience for which you intend to write a paragraph using the material developed in Exercise 2. Describe that audience by listing specific features in the following categories:

Age _____

Sex _____

Education _____

Cultural, racial, or occupational characteristics _____

_____

Copyright © 1985 by Harcourt Brace Jovanovich, Inc. All rights reserved.

Size of group (1 to many) _____

(*Hint*: Consideration of these features will help you choose the appropriate variety of language for your audience.)

EXERCISE 4

With the audience described in Exercise 3 in mind, write a paragraph of four to seven sentences using the plan developed in Exercise 2. Try to use an arrangement that will hold your paragraph together. Use the T-R-I-I pattern as you imitate the arrangement used in the paragraph in Exercise 1 (part-by-part).

EXERCISE 5

Adjusting the arrangement, rewrite your paragraph from Exercise 4. For example, you have used a part-by-part comparison in Exercise 4. Will a whole-by-whole arrangement be effective in a different situation? Will rearrangement of your illustrations produce a different effect? As you consider these points and others, write a whole-by-whole comparison paragraph.

EXERCISE 6

Choose the paragraph from Exercise 4 or Exercise 5, and revise it so that you can include it in your comparison-contrast essay. You may have to revise your essay if your audience is different from the one you originally wrote for. In addition, you may have to add a transitional paragraph or make other adjustments to include this paragraph.

Copyright © 1985 by Harcourt Brace Jovanovich, Inc. All rights reserved.

Make a general statement about who you are *now* and who you will be in ten years.

T

State what you will have to do to achieve the goal stated in the topic.

R

Develop illustrations comparing your *now* and your *then* in these categories.

I		I		I	
Personal life		Public life		Inner psychological and/or spiritual life	
Now	Then	Now	Then	Now	Then

Copyright © 1985 by Harcourt Brace Jovanovich, Inc. All rights reserved.

Notes

	T
Make a general statement about who you are *now* and who you will be in ten years.	

	R
State what you will have to do to achieve the goal stated in the topic.	

Develop illustrations comparing your *now* and your *then* in these categories.

I		I		I	
Personal life		Public life		Inner psychological and/or spiritual life	
Now	Then	Now	Then	Now	Then

Copyright © 1985 by Harcourt Brace Jovanovich, Inc. All rights reserved.

Notes

7.9 SENTENCE POWER

COMPLEMENTS

Complements complete the meaning of sentences. Their function is easy to remember because a complEment complEtes. Not all sentences require a complement because their subjects and verbs and perhaps modifiers supply complete meanings. The subject and verb in the following sentences are complete within themselves regardless whether they have modifiers.

> **subject   verb**
> Only-children play.

or

> **subject   verb**
> Only-children play by themselves.

Sometimes the subject and verb in a sentence require more to give a sense of completeness or wholeness. Do you sense an incomplEteness when you read the following two examples?

> **subject   verb**
> The first-born finally *found*. . .

or

> **subject   verb**
> The family *birth order is* . . .

For you to have a sense of completeness or wholeness when you read the preceding examples, you would need to add a complement. Consider the sentences with a complEment.

> The first-born finally found **happiness**.
> The family birth-order is **important**.

These two examples let you see that a complement is a word, or a group of words, that completes the meaning of the verb in a sentence.

English sentences use five different kinds of complements: *direct object*, *indirect object*, *objective complement*, *predicate nominative*, *predicate adjective*. Predicate nominatives and predicate adjectives belong to a different class of complements than the other three and are often called "subject complements."

DIRECT OBJECTS

Direct objects complete the meaning of action verbs. They are usually nouns or pronouns, but sometimes they are clauses or phrases that function as nouns. An example of each appears in boldface type in the following sentences.

Copyright © 1985 by Harcourt Brace Jovanovich, Inc. All rights reserved.

Noun	The first-born discovered **happiness**.
Pronoun	The first-born discovered **it**.
Phrase	The first-born discovered **eating fish and chips**.
Clause	The first-born discovered **that success changed his life**.

In each of the sentences the direct object answers the question *What?* For instance, in the first example above **happiness** answers the question "The first-born discovered *what?*" If you repeat the question for each of the other three examples, the answer to the question will be the direct object. Follow the same process to locate the direct object in any sentence. First find the subject and the verb in the sentence; then ask "what?" or "whom?" after the subject and verb. The answer to the question will be the direct object. It is possible to have more than one answer to the question. If you do, you likely have a compound direct object. If there is no answer to the question "what?" or "whom?" when it follows your subject and verb, the group of words has no direct object. If the sentence makes sense without an answer, you have a verb which does not have a direct object.

EXERCISE 1

Some of the sentences in this exercise contain direct objects; some do not. Circle the verb of each sentence, and draw an arrow to the subject. Then test for a direct object. If there is a direct object in the sentence, draw a box around it. (*Hint*: Some of the sentences contain compound direct objects.)

Example   First-borns (establish) significant [relationships] with adults.

1. Only-borns play difficult and entertaining games by themselves.

2. Middle children develop communication skills.

3. The eldest child often helps the youngest with homework.

4. Sociologists have not yet solved the relationship between birth-order and success.

5. Parents catch the youngest and the eldest in mischief.

6. Older brothers introduce their sisters to classmates.

7. Children often wait patiently for their parents' attention.

8. Sociologists believe that research will help them understand children.

9. Parents' responsibilities include educating children and preparing them for adult life.

10. Informed scientists hope that their research will improve educational systems and that it will solve many problems for parents.

Copyright © 1985 by Harcourt Brace Jovanovich, Inc. All rights reserved.

INDIRECT OBJECTS

A sentence can have an indirect object only if it also contains a direct object. An indirect object is a noun or a pronoun which follows an action verb such as *ask, bring, buy, give, lend, make, promise, show, teach, tell, or write.* To locate an indirect object, first find the direct object; then ask yourself the questions "to whom?" or "for whom?" or "to what?" or "for what?" The answer will be the indirect object.

i.o.   **d.o.**
Barbara gave Brian a new schedule.

i.o.   **d.o.**
Steve brought Janie a list of clients.

The position of the indirect object is important. Never the object of a preposition, it comes between the verb and the direct object.

d.o.   **obj. prep.**
Collene sent the order to Stuart.

i.o.   **d.o.**
Collene sent Stuart the order.

i.o.   **d.o.**
Collene sent him the order.

Indirect objects may also be compound.

i.o.   **i.o.**   **d.o.**
Richard lent Stephen and Jain the report forms.

EXERCISE 2

Identify the italicized words by writing *i.o.* (indirect object), *d.o.* (direct object) or *obj. prep.* (object of the preposition) over the word.

i.o.   *d.o.*   *o.p.*

Example   Younger sisters bring older *brothers* a *sense* of *responsibility*

1. Older brothers outscore younger *brothers* on intelligence *tests.*

2. They are caught in an emotional *tug* of *war.*

3. New parents buy their *babies* presents.

4. Female eldests often send younger *brothers* and *sisters gifts* on *birthdays.*

5. Psychologists give *parents help* with large *families.*

6. First-born women lend *sisters* their *clothing.*

Copyright © 1985 by Harcourt Brace Jovanovich, Inc. All rights reserved.

7. The author of the *study* wrote *it* for the *board*.

8. The scientist brought *him* her *keys* to the *laboratory*.

9. Sociologists send *parents* the *results* of their research.

10. Popularity makes younger *children* the *center* of *attention*.

Copyright © 1985 by Harcourt Brace Jovanovich, Inc. All rights reserved.

OBJECT COMPLEMENTS

Object complements, like indirect objects, appear only in sentences that contain a direct object and complEte the meaning of the direct object. An adjective, a noun, or a group of words functioning as a noun that follows a direct object and rename or describe it will be an object complEment. Object complements can occur only in sentences which have such verbs as *appoint*, *call*, *color*, *consider*, *declare*, *elect*, *judge*, *label*, *make*, *name*, *paint*, *think*.

d.o.   **o.c.**

Every fourth year we elect someone president.

d.o.   **o.c.**

The firm appointed Patricia manager.

d.o.   **o.c.**

The parents named the child Elaine.

d.o.   **o.c.**

Marshall painted the fence white.

A close examination of the sentences above shows that the object complement renames or describes the first object. To discover if a sentence has an object complement, find the subject, verb, and direct object; then, ask "what?" after you say the verb and the direct object. For example, "named the child what?" gives you the answer "Elaine" which is the object complement. Object complements, like other parts of sentences, may be compound.

d.o.   **o.c.**   **o.c.**

The scientist labeled her research original and exciting.

EXERCISE 3

Identify the object complement by writing *o.c.* over them.

Example   *o.c.*
The parents named the child Eric.

1. The teacher thinks the students smart.

2. The judge appointed Sam sheriff.

3. Joe nominated himself chairman.

4. Karen considers Betty intelligent and charming.

5. The seasoning in the veal makes the sauce spicy and fragrant.

6. The class elected George sergeant-at-arms.

Copyright © 1985 by Harcourt Brace Jovanovich, Inc. All rights reserved.

7. The team named the mascot Butch.

8. Julie called Jim and Lynne friends.

9. Paula designates that area off-limits.

10. Andrea thought the designation useful.

EXERCISE 4

Use the verb indicated to write sentences that contain object complements. Include at least two sentences which have a compound object complement.

1. (appoint) _____

_____

_____

2. (call) _____

_____

_____

3. (consider) _____

_____

_____

4. (declare) _____

_____

_____

5. (judge) _____

_____

_____

6. (label) _____

_____

Copyright © 1985 by Harcourt Brace Jovanovich, Inc. All rights reserved.

7. (make) _____

8. (name) _____

9. (paint) _____

10. (think) _____

Copyright © 1985 by Harcourt Brace Jovanovich, Inc. All rights reserved.

Notes

SUBJECT COMPLEMENTS

There are two kinds of subject complements: predicate nominatives and predicate adjectives. A predicate nominative is a noun or pronoun that follows a linking verb (such as *appear*, *be*, *become*, *feel*, *grow*, *look*, *remain*, *seem*, *smell*, *sound*, *stay*, *taste*, *turn*) and that renames the subject of the sentence. A predicate adjective is an adjective that follows a linking verb and that describes the subject of the sentence.

1. Predicate nominatives

   subject   **p.n.**
   Ellen is the regional manager.

   subject   **p.n.**   **p.n.**
   Barry seems a good choice and a reliable candidate.

   subj.   **p.n.**
   I am she.

2. Predicate adjectives

   subj.   **p.a.**
   He feels happy.

   subj.   **p.a.**   **p.a.**
   The sauce tastes salty and greasy.

Notice that subject complements may be compound.

EXERCISE 5

Each of the following sentences contains a subject complement; some are compound. Identify each complement by writing *p.a.* for predicate adjective and *p.n.* for predicate nominative.

                                p.n.
Examples   Barry seems a reliable candidate.

                        p.a.
             Barry seems reliable.

1. Raoul appears confident.

2. Michael looks dashing in his new suit.

3. Marjorie turns livid over injustices.

4. Laurie became the block supervisor and the leader in the neighborhood.

5. David seems a reasonable person for the job.

6. The employees grow weary after hours at a computer.

Copyright © 1985 by Harcourt Brace Jovanovich, Inc. All rights reserved.

7.   Lyn feels successful and proud.

8.   Scott is being helpful when he stays late.

9.   Mike and Mickey are active in the community.

10.   The orchestra sounds disciplined to Craig.

EXERCISE 6

Identify complements in the following sentences by writing d.o. (direct object), i.o. (indirect object), o.c. (object complement), p.a. (predicate adjective) or p.n. (predicate nominative) over each.

1.   I labeled the container safe.

2.   We wrote the Senator and the President letters.

3.   They still introduce boys and girls at social functions.

4.   The roses grow tall.

5.   The trombonist seems a skillful musician.

6.   The characters on the computer screen appear faint.

7.   The student will become either an engineer or a systems analyst.

8.   The policeman ticketed the red Volkswagon camper, the battered Toyota pickup, and the shiny Mercedes.

9.   The pianist taught herself Mozart's concerto.

10.   The city council named the auditorium Orchestra Hall.

Copyright © 1985 by Harcourt Brace Jovanovich, Inc. All rights reserved.

SUBORDINATION

The writer's attitude toward the material and the particular effect to be achieved determines which idea is to be subordinated to another. Subordination establishes relationships between ideas making one of them grammatically dependent upon the other. It is possible that ideas which are grammatically subordinate may be the most important in the sentence. Subordination successfully used in writing creates tension between ideas, and the writer's meaning becomes more precise as a result of that tension.

Effective writing uses subordination to emphasize relationships between ideas. When you choose to subordinate one idea to another, you establish a specific and important relationship between them. By establishing this relationship you guide and control your reader's perception of your meaning. The decision of which idea to subordinate depends upon your meaning and the effect you wish to create. Most often, when you are subordinating ideas, you will write complex sentences.

Ordinarily, the less important idea will appear in a subordinate clause.

> *When I last saw her*, Judy had lost 25 pounds.

Sometimes, the subordinate clause carries the primary idea.

> The tornado tore through the school yard ***while*** *the children were playing at recess.*

Frequently, the relationship between the ideas is strictly grammatical. In such cases, it is not unusual for the subordinate clause to contain the most important idea in the sentence.

> The newscaster reported *that someone had gained access to the computers at NORAD.*

In the above example, the main clause, "the newscaster reported" contains relatively unimportant information. The important idea in the sentence is found in the subordinate clause.

Three important principles should guide your use of subordination.

1. Choose the correct subordinating word to emphasize the precise relationship you intend. (See Section 3.9.)

   Faulty   Tom kissed his wife goodbye after he left.
   Clear   Tom kissed his wife goodbye before he left.

2. Be certain that you subordinate logically.

   Faulty   I saw my college roommate again after fifteen years when I was surprised to see how much she had changed.
   Clear   I was surprised to see how much my college roommate had changed when I saw her again after fifteen years.

Copyright © 1985 by Harcourt Brace Jovanovich, Inc. All rights reserved.

3.   Limit the clauses in your sentences to a reasonable number.

Faulty	My college roommate gave me a book which her uncle had presented to her seventeen years ago which was nearly coming apart and a raccoon coat which still keeps me warm when I go to a football game when they have them in our area when it is very cold and when the wind blows straight out of the north.
Clear	My college roommate gave me a tattered book which her uncle had presented her seventeen years ago and a serviceable raccoon coat which I enjoy wearing to football games in extremely cold weather.

EXERCISE 7

Identify which of the following sentences are independent clauses and which are dependent clauses. Connect the independent clauses after you decide which subordinating word to use. Circle all subordinating words that you use. (*Hint:* You may want to review Section 3.9.)

1.   First-borns begin life as little stars.
     First-borns are the only kids on the family stage.
     The second-born changes that.

     _____

     _____

     _____

     _____

2.   Some first-born women have younger brothers.
     They are responsible.
     They are interested in men.
     Only-born women are not as responsible as first-born women.
     They are not as interested in men.

     _____

     _____

     _____

     _____

Copyright © 1985 by Harcourt Brace Jovanovich, Inc. All rights reserved.

3. George Burns came from a family of twelve.
   He enjoyed a return to the spotlight at 80.
   He is an entertainer.

   _____

   _____

   _____

   _____

4. You may be better off checking birth-order.
   You may not be better off checking sun signs.
   You may want to get married.

   _____

   _____

   _____

   _____

5. The oldest child accomplishes something.
   It is a big deal.
   It is the first time.
   A middle nothing reports.

   _____

   _____

   _____

   _____

6. Older children want to be first.
   Older children receive special attention.
   Older children emulate adults.
   Older children manage their younger sisters.
   Older children manage their younger brothers.

   _____

Copyright © 1985 by Harcourt Brace Jovanovich, Inc. All rights reserved.

_____

_____

_____

7. A male number two gets extra attention.
    A male number two is a little dickens.
    A male number two is also a nag.
    A male number two nags more than his sisters.

_____

_____

_____

_____

8. The family has two children.
    Number two was a boy.
    The first-born child was a girl.
    Both receive attention.
    The attention is the same.

_____

_____

_____

_____

9. New parents are unsure of themselves.
    New parents can transmit their stress to the first-born child.

_____

_____

_____

_____

10. Ricky in Kansas City thinks.
    Being the older child is harder.

Copyright © 1985 by Harcourt Brace Jovanovich, Inc. All rights reserved.

There are only two children in the family.
Both children are boys.

_____

_____

_____

_____

Copyright © 1985 by Harcourt Brace Jovanovich, Inc. All rights reserved.

Notes

APPOSITIVES

An additional way to subordinate ideas and to achieve economy in your writing is to use appositives. Appositives are words or word groups that rename or explain the meaning of a subject, complement, indirect object, or object of a preposition. They follow the sentence element they rename or explain and can function in the sentence in the same way.

> George Burns, **an entertainer**, returned to the spotlight at eighty.
> The audience gave George Burns, **the entertainer**, a standing ovation.
> *Going in Style* starred George Burns, **the entertainer**.
> All of us have enjoyed George Burns, **the popular entertainer**.
> The man on the stage is George Burns, **the entertainer**.

If you can remove the appositive from the sentence without confusing the meaning of the sentence, it is usually set off from the rest of the sentence by commas, one at its beginning and one at its end. If, on the other hand, you cannot remove the appositive without confusing the meaning of the sentence, you should use no punctuation.

> Burns's film *Going in Style* has a happy ending.

Appositives may be phrases, and if they are, the noun and all of its modifiers make up the appositive. Appositives may also be compound as in this example.

> The man on the stage is George Burns, **the noted celebrity and energetic entertainer**.

EXERCISE 8

Combine the pairs of sentences by turning one sentence into an appositive.

Example George Burns is an entertainer.
George Burns returned to the spotlight at eighty.
George Burns, an entertainer, returned to the spotlight at eighty.

1. First-borns and only children are the only kids on the family stage.
They are little stars.

_____

_____

_____

2. In his book, Toman noted that the youngest brother of sisters is "a girl's boy."
Toman wrote a book called *The Family Constellation*.

Copyright © 1985 by Harcourt Brace Jovanovich, Inc. All rights reserved.

_____

_____

_____

3. Toman is a German psychoanalyst.
   He concluded that the divorce rate was three times higher than the norm for such couples.

_____

_____

_____

4. Scientists are researchers of sociological principles.
   They point out that all such statistical trends in large groups vary.

_____

_____

_____

5. Neurotic people are overrepresented.
   Male only children and female first-borns are overrepresented.

_____

_____

_____

Copyright © 1985 by Harcourt Brace Jovanovich, Inc. All rights reserved.

7.10 PROOFREADING POWER

As you proofread your paper, look for any problem with your writing that you should correct or revise. When you spot a problem, correct it so that your reader will be able to focus on your ideas instead of stumbling over your errors, mistakes or slips of the pen. All writing problems, especially subordination, create barriers between you and your reader. To help you identify with your reader as closely as possible, revise all errors in your writing before giving it to your reader. Proofreading requires that you read your own writing from the point of view of your reader. When you read with your reader's eyes, you may discover gaps that you might not otherwise find.

In actual writing, any writing problem might surface during proofreading. In this exercise, the writing problems are limited to subordination problems, faulty coordination, and improperly used sound-alike words.

Psychologists agree on one point. The point is the impact of family sighs. As Michael Olneck and David Bills of the University of Wisconsin reported: Regardless of there family's social position, men from larger families tend to have lower test scores and men from larger families are less educated, and they have lower occupational statuses, and they have lower earnings than men from smaller families.

7.11 DICTATION

Your instructor will choose a passage of approximately 100 words and read it aloud as you write what you hear. As you listen to each sentence, concentrate and maintain silence. Do not ask your instructor to repeat because any sound other than the instructor's voice reading will break not only your concentration but that of others. Your instructor may repeat key words and phrases during the dictation, will allow sufficient time for you to write what you hear, and will reread the entire passage a second time at a faster rate so that you can check what you have written and fill in any gaps you may have.

You will want to write on every other line so that you will have space to correct your dictation upon the final reading in case you have made a mistake. Your instructor will show you the dictated passage and ask you to compare your version, or perhaps a classmate's version, to the original. Be especially alert when you check the dictation because this exercise will help you develop your sentence sense by translating spoken into written language.

Copyright © 1985 by Harcourt Brace Jovanovich, Inc. All rights reserved.

7.12 WORD POWER

VOCABULARY

As you gain confidence and facility in your writing, you will create many combinations that you have not used before. As you grow in your ability to convey your ideas and to persuade your reader, you will need a greater vocabulary. The most effective way to increase your vocabulary is to read. In addition to reading, carefully designed vocabulary exercises can assist you in developing your vocabulary.

One of your goals as a college student undoubtedly is to gain control of as much of the language as you can so that you can communicate as effectively as possible. To build your power with language, you need to learn as many subtleties about the language as possible.

In this unit you are to learn more of the troublesome words that sound alike or have similar sounds. By isolating these words that cause so many slips in diction for so many writers and by focusing your attention on their meanings and spellings, you can take a giant step toward eliminating spelling errors and diction errors from your writing. As you read your assignments for other classes or the newspaper or your favorite magazines, notice these words, most of which appear in the selections in this text.

1. a.   We must *accept* our place in the family birth order and try to stress its positive rather than its negative qualities.
   b.   Among neurotic people, only-children were represented in greater numbers than any other group *except* female first-borns.
2. a.   We cannot *alter* our birth order in a family.
   b.   The way some families treat the television set as a family *altar* disturbs many sociologists.
3. a.   Most people choose *blue* as their favorite color.
   b.   The wind last night *blew* so hard that lots of shingles flew off the roof.
4. a.   First-born girls are *caught* in an emotional tug of war.
   b.   When a girl goes to camp, she often must sleep on a small bed called a *cot*.
5. a.   Parents who *choose* to have large numbers of children may socialize them in ways contrary to high test performance.
   b.   Mr. and Mrs. Barnes *chose* to have four children.
6. a.   The marriages likeliest to succeed are between people with *complementary* family positions. (*Hint*: When the the word has the sense of "complEtE," spell it with an "e.")
   b.   The good qualities shared by first-born males who have younger brothers draw *complimentary* remarks from psychologists. (*Hint*: When the word has the sense of "praIse," spell it with an "i.")

Copyright © 1985 by Harcourt Brace Jovanovich, Inc. All rights reserved.

7. a. Psychiatrist Alfred Adler *discussed* his theory about why male only-children show greater emotional vulnerability.

   b. Imagine my *disgust* to learn that first-borns suffer more from anxiety than do their younger siblings!

8. a. Many Roman soldiers died because they cooked in pots made of *lead*.

   b. Julius Caesar, a great Roman general, *led* his legions against the Gauls and brought Vercingetorix back to Rome. (*Hint*: Sometimes you will see *lead* as a verb. When it is, it rhymes with *seed*. When *lead* and *led* sound the same, the first is a noun or adjective, and the second is a verb.)

9. a. Individuals, as always, go their *merry* ways, despite birth order and family size.

   b. The most star-crossed marriage possibility occurs when people *marry* their counterparts.

10. a. Female only children *meet* challenges with confidence and assertiveness.

    b. The only kind of *meat* I dislike is liver.

11. a. The older of a *pair* of brothers usually becomes a leader.

    b. A ripe, golden *pear* makes a delicious dessert, particularly if accompanied by cheese.

    c. Many prefer to *pare* the skin from an apple before eating it.

12. a. Religious people *pray* for world peace.

    b. The American bald eagle, a magnificent bird of *prey*, is an endangered species.

13. a. When you *read* about the importance of birth order, did you find out anything about yourself?

    b. Marriage between two first-borns will likely make one or the other see *red* because of the possibility of a power struggle.

14. a. Love of the tender sex is *seen* as the most important of all concerns to the oldest brother of sisters.

    b. First-borns begin life as little stars, the only kids on the family stage playing a *scene* for Mom and Dad.

15. a. Psychologists agree that family *size* contributes to the success a person may achieve in later life.

    b. *Sighs* and groans won't help much in getting a difficult task finished.

16. a. When it comes to marriage, you might be better off comparing birth orders than checking *sun* signs.

    b. The oldest *son* in a large family may tend to have lower test scores than a male from a smaller family.

17. a. The oldest brother of brothers ought to be able to advertise his birth order on his business *stationery*. (*Hint*: "Envelopes" are station**E**ry.)

    b. First-borns have a tendency to control and organize the behavior of others to keep relationships *stationary*.

Copyright © 1985 by Harcourt Brace Jovanovich, Inc. All rights reserved.

18. a. Terry Bradshaw *threw* four touchdown passes and led the Pittsburg Steelers to victory during Sunday's game. (*Hint: threw* is the past tense of *throw*.)

    b. In the last 1983 game against the Dallas Cowboys, Washington Redskin player Dave Butts charged *through* their line repeatedly.

19. a. The extremely low temperatures during December 1983 broke many *weather* records.

    b. The frigid weather caused many people to wonder daily *whether* they had enough fuel to stay warm and *whether* they could get their cars to start. (*Hint: Whether* indicates that alternatives are possible.)

20. a. A surprisingly large number of the people named in *Who's Who* are first-born children. (*Hint: Who's* is a contraction for *who is*. The apostrophe replaces the ''i'' in ''is.'')

    b. Most ace fighter pilots are younger sons *whose* parents were relaxed and confident.

EXERCISE 1

Write the correct word in the blank.

1. People have no choice but to accept/except _____ their birth order.

2. The troops escaped through/threw _____ the mountain pass.

3. An older brother of a sister marrying the younger sister of a brother creates a

    complimentary/ complementary _____ relation-ship.

4. Charles Martel lead/led _____ troops against the enemy.

5. I can never decide who's/whose _____ winning an argument.

6. The police caught/cot _____ Paul's sun/son _____

    trying to altar/alter _____ his driver's license.

7. When men merry/marry _____ happily, they can

Copyright © 1985 by Harcourt Brace Jovanovich, Inc. All rights reserved.

expect their lives to be merry/marry _____ rather than full of sighs/size and sorrow.

8. "Why the Sky Is Blue/Blew _____ " is the title

   of an article I red/read _____ while I was waiting

   to meat/meet _____ my friend at the station-

   ary/stationery _____ store.

9. Have you ever felt discussed/disgust _____ when

   you have scene/seen _____ a pare/pair/pear _____

   of larger children pray/prey _____ upon a smaller
   child?

10. Does it matter to you whether/weather _____ you
    are the oldest or youngest child in your family?

Copyright © 1985 by Harcourt Brace Jovanovich, Inc. All rights reserved.

Notes

SPELLING

When you wish to add a suffix to a word ending in "e," if the suffix begins with a vowel, drop the final "e" before adding the suffix. Keep the "e" if the suffix begins with a consonant.

Example   produce + -ing = producing   ("e" is dropped)
                 refine + -ment = refinement   ("e" is kept)

Several *exceptions* to the rule should be memorized:

Example   argue + -ment = argument
                 courage + -ous = courageous
                 dye + -ing = dyeing
                 notice + -able = noticeable
                 true + -ly = truly

EXERCISE 2

Combine the base word with the suffix to make a new word.

1. accommodate + -ion _____

2. achieve + -ment _____

3. affectionate + -ly _____

4. aggravate + -ion _____

5. announce + -ment _____

6. argue + -ment _____

7. assassinate + -ion _____

8. compete + -ition _____

9. complete + -ly _____

10. consist + -ent _____

11. definite + -ly _____

12. entire + -ly _____

Copyright © 1985 by Harcourt Brace Jovanovich, Inc. All rights reserved.

13. extreme + -ly _____

14. imagine + -ary _____

15. imitate + -ion _____

16. manage + -ment _____

17. please + -ant _____

18. sense + -less _____

19. sincere + -ly _____

20. sure + -ly _____

Copyright © 1985 by Harcourt Brace Jovanovich, Inc. All rights reserved.

UNIT EIGHT
WRITING
PERSONALIZED

8.1 GETTING STARTED BY READING

Research confirms that the faster you read with understanding, the more you will understand. Further, experience bears out that the purpose you have while reading determines your reading rate. Even though your initial purpose may be to study when you begin to read, you may alter your rate to a faster rate, perhaps the rate you use for information or even light reading when you encounter a portion of your text that does not require your slower rate. Conversely, you may begin to skim and later discover that there are portions of the text you need to study or which have facts you wish to remember or which bring you pleasure. Remember that your reading speed is relative and that your goal is to read as fast as you can in any of the five categories: skimming, modified skimming, reading for pleasure or recreation (light reading), reading for information and ideas, reading for study. Remember to be flexible and to alter your rate as the text requires instead of slavishly reading at a single rate when you can accomplish your purposes more easily by modifying it.

An illustration will give you an understanding of how to adjust your reading rate. You may use all five speeds in reading your school newspaper. You may skim the calendar to decide which activities you will attend over the weekend or an article to locate information about where you will buy tickets for a concert or sporting event, or the classified ads to see if a cheap apartment is available. Perhaps you belong to a club whose functions the paper reports. Since you were probably at the function, you know what went on, but you read the news article for the pleasure of reliving the event. Because your club's event conflicted with the time of a major sports event between your school and a traditional rival, you read the sports page for information about the game. If your school is considering a change in the graduation requirements, you may read a news article about those changes at a rate that allows you to consider and study the effects such a change will have on you personally.

In addition to learning to adjust your reading rate, you need to train your eyes to see larger and larger units. If you now read single letters, push yourself to read an entire word; if you now read words, push yourself to read phrases; if you now read phrases, push yourself to read half a line or more. Once you can read at this rate, you can begin to read several lines at a time. Then you will read a page in the same length of time you formerly took to read a line.

Remember that reading takes concentration and alertness, practice and effort—and most of all *time*—to develop skillful reading habits. In order to learn these habits you must be willing to monitor yourself as you read. By following the advice given here, you will improve your reading skills. Perhaps your school offers a special course in reading that can help you. Remember you can make significant improvement on your own by following these techniques. A full application of the reading techniques you have learned will increase your enjoyment, add to your knowledge, and improve your performance not only in college, but for the rest of your life.

3 Steps to Effective Reading

1. Practice reading regularly
2. Adjust reading rate according to purpose for reading
3. Strive to read units larger than words

As you read "Getting Down to Business: How Personal Computers Can Aid the Professional," try to note when you change your reading speed. Also, keep the following questions in mind to guide you and to help you establish your purpose for reading. You may want to monitor your change in reading speed by putting a mark when you realize that a change has occurred. When you finish reading, review the record to see how often you recognized you varied your reading speed.

1. What do computers offer to make doing business easier for professionals?
2. How will the computer change habits of professionals?
3. In what ways do the uses of the computer for the four kinds of professionals differ?

Copyright © 1985 by Harcourt Brace Jovanovich, Inc. All rights reserved.

8.2 CLASSIFICATION

Danny Goodman   *"GETTING DOWN TO BUSINESS: HOW PERSONAL COMPUTERS CAN AID THE PROFESSIONAL"*

The idea of having a personal computer in your office may be intimidating. But if you are a professional or a manager, avoiding what may be the inevitable only gives the edge to competitors who have already overcome their fear of the desk-top monster. To give you a hint of what the other guys are doing with their computers while you push a pencil, here are some typical applications used by four different professionals: a sales executive, an attorney, an educator, and an insurance agent. Although the people aren't real, their computers, specific software programs, and business and professional requirements are.

The Sales Executive

Jonas Johns manages a team of 12 salespeople. One of his most time consuming tasks is completing sales forecasts. Each month, he must submit detailed reports on each product in the company's line, each customer, and each salesperson. The report includes not only forecasts for the next month, quarter, and year, but also figures showing how well each category performed the previous month when compared with an earlier forecast.

Before Johns had a computer, he had to produce several spread sheets—columns with endless rows of numbers, subtotals, totals, and grand totals. Once he had computed all of the figures with pencil and pocket calculator, his secretary then typed up the sheets for presentation. Often the deadline for submission forced them to begin the typing session long before all the figures were complete. And needless to say, many overtime hours went into making last-minute corrections when subtotal C had to be recalculated back through sheets A and B.

Enter the personal computer—a Digital Equipment Corporation (DEC) Rainbow 100, to be precise. Johns has added an electronic spread-sheet program called Multiplan (developed by Microsoft and distributed by DEC) to take care of the figures. Johns no longer tediously enters and erases subtotals and totals; now the computer maintains all of the charts simultaneously. Johns sets up the definition of each entry

Copyright © 1985 by Harcourt Brace Jovanovich, Inc. All rights reserved.

in plain English ("Widget No. 245 Sales") only once. Now, every month, subtotals are automatically carried over to predefined summary charts.

Checking up on his staff's performance is easier, too, because as Johns enters the previous month's results, Multiplan flashes a message on the screen if actual sales are either below or above projections. And because each month's forecasts are stored in the computer's memory, they won't have to be re-entered when he prepares next month's chart.

With the computer, a final printout of the finished spread sheet can be produced at the last minute without a single eraser smudge. In fact, with the computer, Johns also can now outshine his rivals because the Graphwriter business graphics program for the Rainbow allows his secretary to reply to questions on the screen with figures from the finished spread sheets. Out of a plotter or graphics printer come full color, detailed bar graphs, trend lines, and pie charts of his territory's performance. Eventually, the Graphwriter will be able to read data directly off the Multiplan storage disk for entry into the graphs.

Sales in Johns's territory are booming because he also uses the Rainbow to gain access to more sales leads for his staff than other managers can. With a telephone modem attached to his Rainbow, and a telecommunications program, Johns dials up the Electronic Yellow Pages on the DIALOG data base. By specifying zip and standard industrial classification (SIC) codes, Jonas can enter into his computer all of the prospective customers for his staff.

To cut travel expenses for his territory, Johns is now equipping his staff with computers capable of running Multiplan. Johns has them "telecommunicate" monthly forecasts, rather than making the company pay for staff transportation to the regional office each month.

The Attorney

Contracts, briefs, pleadings, and persuasive, if not threatening, letters are the universe of the legal profession. For an attorney, one of the most powerful applications for a computer is word processing. A large law firm, of course, is likely to have a

Copyright © 1985 by Harcourt Brace Jovanovich, Inc. All rights reserved.

big computer with several word processing stations or perhaps a complete word processing department. But a small firm doesn't have the resources to justify such a large expenditure. A personal computer, such as the IBM Personal Computer XT, however, was ideal for the two-person office of Adams & Bailey, Attorneys-at-Law. Catherine Bailey convinced her skeptical partner that the word-processing computer would save time and increase productivity.

Now, a contract, which formerly had to be retyped in full every time a client wanted even a minor change, is assembled on the computer from a permanently stored library of complete contracts and clauses. Using WordStar and its companion program MailMerge, Bailey's secretary simply needs to know which sections, paragraphs, and clauses are to be included in the contract. The secretary types into the IBM PC a very short list of names previously assigned to each piece. The program automatically summons each segment from the PC's internal hard-disk storage device and prints out a completed contract. Where a name or other specific data are to be entered, the computer halts the printer and prompts the secretary in plain English for the required information.

Furthermore, drafts of briefs can be reviewed by both Adams and Bailey before an important case. Because only changes need to be typed, corrections or additions can be made up to the last minute. As new research turns up an important precedent or argument, the brief can be completely reorganized by moving sections or paragraphs around electronically. SpellStar, another program that works with WordStar, checks the entire brief against a built-in dictionary of 30,000 words for any typing errors. If there appears to be a mistake, the computer asks the secretary whether the spelling offered is correct. If not, the secretary can easily change it.

But the computer has yet another function in this busy office. Few small firms can afford to keep a law library updated. With all the decisions in Federal and state courts, plus the reporting services for the firm's specialties, the monthly bill is hard to justify. And having to go to the nearest law library is time-consuming and downright inconvenient. The computer comes to the rescue again with its telecommunications powers. What is essentially an entire law library is now available on-line from a data

Copyright © 1985 by Harcourt Brace Jovanovich, Inc. All rights reserved.

base called WestLaw. Although not inexpensive, WestLaw presents full texts of cases on request. Cases can be read directly from the computer screen or from a printed copy for study away from the computer.

A further research aid of WestLaw is called Insta-Cite, which removes the drudgery of locating citations to cases. With those citations, further texts can be retrieved. All of these legal aids are available practically 24 hours a day, and thus they are especially useful if lawyers need information when libraries are closed.

The Teacher

At the Ogilvy Elementary School, Hilary Thomas is causing quite a stir. Thomas is part of a program to test the possibility of using the computer not just as a simple tutor for her fourth-grade students using canned programs, but also as an extension of the teacher's lesson plan.

On an Apple IIe computer, Thomas uses The Learning System by Micro Lab to create customized lessons and tests for her students. She constructs lessons by typing in textual material. At the end of each lesson, she gives the students one of three kinds of quizzes based on the material. Thomas can write multiple-choice, fill-in-the-blank, and matching-column quizzes. The Learning System program prompts her through all phases of the creative process, so that she doesn't have to be a programmer to enter the material.

In the case of fill-in-the-blank tests, Thomas can enter both the preferred and alternate answers for each question, giving her students more leeway in finding the right answers. In multiple-choice and matching-column quizzes, the order of the answers is mixed up if the student takes the quiz again. This reduces the likelihood that a student will squeak through a retest by memorizing the sequence of answers.

At the end of each quiz, the student's results are recorded on a special Records Disk. From this disk, Thomas gets a summary of each student's performance, along with the number of times the student has taken each quiz and the average score for the entire class. She can then determine how well the class is learning from her lesson material.

Copyright © 1985 by Harcourt Brace Jovanovich, Inc. All rights reserved.

The Insurance Agent

Larry Wilkins is an independent insurance agent who had a real need for a computer to help him and his secretary manage the reams of paperwork and files that, at times, seemed to smother the operation. Wilkins opted for the Radio Shack Model 12 professional computer because he liked the Profile Plus electronic filing software that runs on the machine.

With this combination, Wilkins has now placed all his client and prospect records on a hard disk tied into his Model 12. The hard disk drive has a considerable memory—it can store up to 12 million characters—and an additional drive can be added if the need arises. All relevant client information is available at the press of a few keys. For example, if a new policy should become available that is of special benefit to married males under 45 years of age with two or more children, the program will search the entire file for all clients who fit that mold. To do this manually would require perhaps hours of thumbing through files in a cabinet or the maintenance of separate sorted lists as each client file folder was created. But the computer can handle the search in less than a minute, completely unattended.

Moreover, in concert with Radio Shack's Scripsit word-processing software, a personally addressed letter can be printed using the information stored in the file of each target client. A client's coverage, the expiration date of his policy, and other data can be mentioned within the letter as if it had been specially prepared just for him. And yet, with a letter-quality printer, tractor feed attachment, and micro-perforated continuous-form letterhead, the entire mailing campaign can be typed up during lunch.

Furthermore, Wilkins keeps extensive prospect files on his computer. Full records of every contact, its results, and the date to contact the prospect again are maintained. Every Friday afternoon, he has the computer search through the prospect file for the records of each person he should contact the following week, thus helping him schedule his work. Periodic mailings go off to all prospects. Depending on the type of insurance plan Wilkins is recommending, one of several canned letters is matched to each record and customized with information from that record.

Wilkins now also has the time to give more personal attention to his bigger clients.

Copyright © 1985 by Harcourt Brace Jovanovich, Inc. All rights reserved.

Each week he has the computer search his records for all clients who have policies exceeding a particular limit and who have birthdays coming up the next week. Every client meeting those criteria gets a birthday greeting from Wilkins and his agency. The signing of the card, however, is one task that Wilkins easily manages by hand.

None of these four professionals knew a bit from a byte before they bought a personal computer. They still might not know. If you buy a personal computer, it's not all that important for you to understand the technical pieces of the personal computer puzzle. It is important, however, to be aware of how your work habits can be made more efficient and professional.

For these four people, the first couple of months entailed a bit of learning and frustration while they were getting to know the powers and limitations of their wonder machines. But their investments in money and time soon started paying off as they gained increased productivity and an edge over their noncomputerized colleagues or competitors.

8.3 UNDERSTANDING WHAT YOU READ

1. Are there ways that others use a computer that could help you as a college student? _____

   _____

   _____

2. If you had a computer and could use it, how would your college experience be different? _____

   _____

   _____

3. In what ways do you think understanding and using a computer could help you

Copyright © 1985 by Harcourt Brace Jovanovich, Inc. All rights reserved.

succeed in the future. _____

_____

_____

8.4 DISCOVERING IDEAS FOR WRITING

1. Make a list of activities and routines that govern your daily schedule. If your list

is very long, select the most important ones. _____

_____

_____

_____

2. Which of the routines control the morning? _____

_____

The afternoon? _____

_____

The evening? _____

_____

The night? _____

_____

The entire day? _____

_____

Other categories? _____

_____

3. Which four of the categories you listed above have the most influence on your

Copyright © 1985 by Harcourt Brace Jovanovich, Inc. All rights reserved.

schedule? _____

_____

_____

The least influence? _____

_____

_____

4. If you had to move one from the "most influential" category to the "least influential" category, which would you move? _____

_____

If you had to move one from the "least influential" category to the "most influential" category, which would you move? _____

_____

5. How do outside controls dictate the routines that govern your life? _____

_____

6. How do you think you can influence those outside controls to make your life easier? _____

_____

_____

Copyright © 1985 by Harcourt Brace Jovanovich, Inc. All rights reserved.

8.5 *UNDERSTANDING WRITING*

You may be surprised to learn that you likely have something in common with many well-known writers: Many writers admit that they really do not like to write. Despite that, almost all writers experience a feeling of satisfaction and accomplishment when they complete a piece of writing. Have you felt the same way?

The reactions of three famous writers may help you resolve any negative feelings you may hold toward writing. A well-known American short story writer, Eudora Welty, declares that she had rather do almost anything than write. A renowned music scholar and critic, Jacques Barzun, once lamented that he would not write unless ''there was a gun at his head.'' John Kenneth Galbraith, a famous economist and writer, dislikes writing so much that he makes excuses daily to avoid writing; yet he has published a dozen or more books.

Though few people really enjoy writing, the satisfaction they feel when they have completed a piece of writing drives them on. Writing exposes your inner self to others, and the very thought of doing that frightens most people. When you write, your thoughts and ideas become concrete; they also become public. After they become public, anyone can read and evaluate your thoughts and ideas. Despite the vulnerable position writing places you in, you will still write because your job will likely require it. Furthermore, you may write because writing is satisfying to the ego and because it will help you understand yourself, those around you, and your world. When you complete a piece of writing, you will experience satisfaction, and once you have experienced the satisfaction that writing brings, you will do it again in spite of the pain writing may cause.

Writers often find writing painful. Yet they write. Why? The rewards of having written overshadow any pain of writing.

8.6 *WRITING—CLASSIFICATION*

Your responses to the exercises in 8.4 will help you identify classes of routines you use in ordering your life. Arranging your routines into groups that have a common feature is part of the organization necessary before you write your classification essay. When you include routines in a group, be sure you do not include any that lack the common feature. In other words, if you are arranging your routines according to the time of day, you should not include one that occurs in the evening in the morning group.

WRITING ASSIGNMENT

Draft a 500-word essay in which you classify the routines of your surroundings that help you regulate the way you live your life.

Copyright © 1985 by Harcourt Brace Jovanovich, Inc. All rights reserved.

Reminder: While drafting your classification essay, you may make use of all the other modes. The integration of modes in writing is normal and helpful. To explain one class, you may write a definition paragraph while description may be appropriate for another. It is almost certain that you will use analysis and description too. In this particular assignment, you may find you need to use process to explain one of your routines. Nonetheless, your overall organization of the essay should be classification if you have well-defined and carefully arranged classes or categories and if each one of them focuses upon a single feature.

Once you have completed your draft, let your peer editor read it so you can be sure that the classifications you have used are clear and readily understandable. Consider your peer editor's suggestions before you revise your classification essay, and choose those that are most helpful.

A frequent problem with classification essays is that the writer establishes classes that overlap. Sometimes, if you have overlapping classes, it is difficult to see how to rearrange them so that they are logical. If this happens, analyze your categories again. If you are still uncertain of how to rearrange your categories or where to include details and features, check with your instructor who can give you objective advice. Indeed, before you finish this essay, you may find it necessary to describe your categories to your instructor briefly so that you can be sure you have classified them logically. Unless your categories are logical, you will not be able to write an effective classification essay.

When you are satisfied with your categories, check the organization of your essay. You will probably begin with an introduction establishing the classes, develop each class as a separate paragraph, and end with a direct or indirect conclusion. When you have all three parts of your classification essay shaped into a whole and have proofread it to make it error-free, you will have fulfilled your responsibility as a writer and will be ready to submit all of your versions and your Editor's Evaluations to your instructor.

Since this is your final essay in this course, strive to make this the best essay you have ever written. Perhaps you can measure your improvement as a writer not only in your ability to achieve an error-free version but also in your ability to handle many of the revision procedures on your own. Recognizing your limitations and knowing when to seek advice are also important as measures of your improvement as a writer. But you will want to be responsible about how you seek advice. As a writer, you are the one who performs; while others are willing to help, you will need to develop the confidence to work on your own and to know when your writing is finished.

8.7 THE WRITING PROCESS

The sections on the writing process help you recognize that when you have completed your first draft you have more writing to do. Professional writers realize that

Copyright © 1985 by Harcourt Brace Jovanovich, Inc. All rights reserved.

when their first draft is done, the writing process has just begun. Their experience and skill allow them to enter and reenter a draft when they notice a weakness. You have learned some of the ways experienced writers use to enter and reenter their writing. As yet, no one has listed all of the ways writers use to revise their drafts. Nevertheless, as you gain experience entering and reentering your writing by using proven ways, you will learn to test your writing for weaknesses and develop additional ways to improve its effectiveness. Until you do, use the questions in the list at the end of this section to guide you.

Good writers do more than state and rewrite their ideas. They identify differences between their ideas and those of their audience, and in their writing they strive to bridge that gap. To build a bridge across a gap requires more than simply collecting materials. It requires that the writer use the materials according to a plan designed with the function of the bridge in mind. If you think of your ideas as materials and your writing as the bridge, you will have completed your bridge when it spans from the bank on which you are standing to that of your audience and when it will support traffic between the two.

If there is a weakness in your writing bridge and it will not support the traffic, you correct the construction fault before anyone in your audience can be allowed to cross your writing bridge.

Ideally, you will reread your writing several times and revise it as you answer different questions from the list each time you work through your writing. When you have a satisfactory answer to one of the questions, you are ready to move to the next question. With experience, you will read your essay fewer times because you will keep more questions in mind as you read. Sometimes you will not be able to revise your writing to your satisfaction even though you try. At such times, move along to another question or perhaps even to another section of the list. You can always go back later when you have time to the part you had trouble with. Also, by going on to other questions, you may discover a way to fix what was troubling you, or occasionally you may find that fixing something else will correct the problem you were having. There may also be times when, under the pressure of getting an assignment in on time, you will find the time available for revision severely limited. When that happens, it is better to use a part of the list than to ignore the revision process altogether. Any attention to revision improves writing.

Effective writing is rewriting, and to rewrite, you enter and reenter your writing.

QUESTIONS FOR REENTERING WRITING

A. Content and organization
   1. Is your essay interesting enough that your audience will want to read it?
   2. Are the ideas and content of your essay appropriate for your audience?
   3. Does your essay satisfy the purpose for which you have written it, for instance, for the specific requirements of a class assignment?

Copyright © 1985 by Harcourt Brace Jovanovich, Inc. All rights reserved.

B. Paragraphs
   1. Does your introductory paragraph contain your main idea or thesis?
   2. Is your introductory paragraph proportional in length to the rest of your essay?
   3. Do you have a conclusion?
      a. One paragraph?
      b. More than one paragraph?
      c. Less than one paragraph?
   4. What kind of conclusion do you have?
      a. Delayed?
      b. Direct?
   5. Is your conclusion proportional in length to the rest of your essay?
   6. Are all the paragraphs in the body of your essay well-developed?
      a. Do they have a T(opic)?
      b. Do they have an R(estriction)?
      c. Do they have one I(llustration)?
      d. Do they have other I(llustration)s?
      e. Do they follow some other pattern?
C. Sentences
   1. Have you used any fragments instead of sentences?
   2. Is your coordination effective?
   3. Are compound sentences punctuated properly to avoid comma splices and run-ons?
   4. Are coordinate constructions parallel?
   5. Have you used sufficient subordination?
   6. Are your sentences too short? too long?
      a. How many sentences under twelve words do you have?
      b. How many sentences over twenty-seven words do you have?
   7. Do you use a variety of sentence patterns?
   8. Can you convert any short sentences to appositives?
D. Verbs
   1. Do your subjects and verbs agree?
   2. Do you need to check the forms of any of your verbs?
   3. Have you followed proper tense sequence?
   4. Have you used too many *to be* verbs?
E. Language
   1. Have you used the appropriate level of language for your audience?
      a. Have you used any slang?
      b. Have you used any common dialect?
      c. Have you used any trite expressions?
      d. Does your essay have any vague words? (Hint: Words like *area*, *thing*, *fact*, *point* are often vague.)

Copyright © 1985 by Harcourt Brace Jovanovich, Inc. All rights reserved.

e.   Does your essay have any overused words or expressions?
2.   Do you need to check the meaning of any word you have used?

F.   Mechanics
1.   Does every sentence begin with a capital letter?
2.   Does appropriate punctuation end every sentence?
3.   Are all of your words spelled correctly?

8.8 PARAGRAPH POWER

Classification, a fundamental thought process, means systematically arranging your material into categories or groups. During your study of writing, you have learned to use modes that can now help you classify. *Definition*, for instance, requires that you label every item defined according to class. An *analysis* separates a whole into particular parts or divisions. A *comparison* depends upon the classification of items into similar groups. Recognizing that classification uses the modes you have already studied may make it easier to understand.

You can classify any group (ideas, objects, people, animals, etc.) in which the members share a common feature. When your purpose in writing is to classify, you first identify the single feature common to every item to be included in a class; you use this single feature as your *basis of classification*. As a basis of classification, you might use color, size, taste, cost, or perhaps frequency, usefulness, noise-level, or reasonableness. In other words, you can classify according to color or size or taste or cost. You cannot, however, classify according to color and cost or frequency and noise-level at the same time.

To begin to classify your material, you arrange or sort the items into groups. Before you finally label your groups as classes, you may arbitrarily sort items into Class One, Class Two, and Class Three. During the process of classifying your material, you may discover a second common feature that you believe would make your classes more useful. If so, refine your classes as many times as you want.

For example, if you want to establish a class of round, soft, cheap items, you must first identify round items. Then you must identify those round items that are also soft. Finally, you will select only those round, soft items that are also cheap. In this process of refining classes, you will establish others. Obviously, in identifying round items, you will also identify non-round items, and so forth.

As you refine classes, strive to identify at least three classes, but no more than seven. If you have only two classes, your classes might seem simplistic unless they are absolute. If you have more than seven, your audience may perceive the classes as unreasonable or perhaps humorous. Too many classes will also be hard to remember.

Ordinarily, your purpose in writing will help you select the bases for classification most appropriate for your audience and situation. Establishing arbitrary classes with-

Copyright © 1985 by Harcourt Brace Jovanovich, Inc. All rights reserved.

out considering the interests and expectations of your audience is pointless. If you are writing for fashion designers, for instance, they may be most interested in color, weight, and texture of fabric, whereas if you are writing for dry cleaners, they are more likely to be concerned about the fabric's durability, its fiber content, and its sensitivity to chemicals.

It may be instructive to compare classification to analysis. In analysis your divisions depend on differences. In classification divisions or classes depend on similarities. A further difference between analysis and classification is that you analyze a single item (a motor, a process, a contract), whereas you classify a group of items (NFL teams, computers, colognes). When you analyze, you have a single item; when you classify, you have several (at least two) similar items.

Classification paragraphs model easily on the T-R-I-I paragraph pattern. In your topic sentence (T), state the basis (the common feature) of your classification. In the restriction (R), list the groups, classes or types in your classification. In the following sentences, explain or define each group, class, or type and include examples of each (I_1, I_2, . . . I_5). Usually three illustrations will serve your purpose (I_1, I_2, I_3).

EXERCISE 1

An examination of the parts of the following paragraph from "Getting Down to Business: How Computers Can Aid the Professional" will help you observe each part of a T-R-I-I classification paragraph. By answering each of the questions below, you can identify the divisions of these paragraphs and observe how they are arranged.

1. Contracts, briefs, pleadings, and persuasive, if not threatening, letters are the universe of the legal profession. **2.** For an attorney, one of the most powerful applications for a computer is word processing. **3.** A large law firm, of course, is likely to have a big computer with several word-processing stations or perhaps a complete word-processing department. **4.** But a small firm doesn't have the resources to justify such a large expenditure. **5.** A personal computer, such as the IBM Personal Computer XT, however, was ideal for the two-person office of Adams & Bailey, Attorneys-at-Law. **6.** Katherine Bailey convinced her skeptical partner that the word-processing computer would save time and increase productivity.

1. Which sentence states the topic in the paragraph? _____

2. Which sentence or sentences restrict the topic? _____

3. Which sentence or sentences provide illustration of the topic? _____

Copyright © 1985 by Harcourt Brace Jovanovich, Inc. All rights reserved.

4. What two classes can you identify in this paragraph? _____

    _____

5. What is the basis for the classification? _____

    _____

6. Describe your reaction to the presentation of the classes side-by-side. _____

    _____

7. Do you think the paragraph would be better if there were a class between the

    two extremes illustrated in the paragraph? Why or why not? _____

    _____

    _____

8. If you decided in question 7 that one or more additional classes is necessary,

    where would you put it? Before? Between? After? Why? _____

    _____

    _____

    _____

EXERCISE 2

Using the T-R-I-I-I pattern on page 389, write a paragraph in which you classify the ways in which the world around you helps you regulate your time.

EXERCISE 3

Select an audience for which you intend to write a paragraph using the material developed in Exercise 2. Describe that audience by listing specific features in the following categories:

Age _____

Sex _____

Copyright © 1985 by Harcourt Brace Jovanovich, Inc. All rights reserved.

Education _____

Cultural, racial, or occupational characteristics _____

_____

Size of group (1 to many) _____
(*Hint:* Choose appropriate variety of language for the audience.)

EXERCISE 4

With the audience described in Exercise 3 in mind, write a paragraph of four to seven sentences using the plan developed in Exercise 2. Try to use an arrangement that will hold your paragraph together. Use the T-R-I-I pattern as you imitate the arrangement in the paragraph in Exercise 1.

Copyright © 1985 by Harcourt Brace Jovanovich, Inc. All rights reserved.

Make a general statement about how many ways your surroundings help you regulate time.

T

State how these ways cause you to follow your schedule.

R

Support the topic and restriction with specific illustrations (detail, evidence).

I		
I	I	I
Mechanical	Sensory	Established routines

Copyright © 1985 by Harcourt Brace Jovanovich, Inc. All rights reserved.

Notes

8.9   ORGANIZING AN ESSAY

Each of the three parts of an essay, the introduction, the body, and the conclusion, deserves special attention. You examined paragraphs appropriate for introductions and the body in earlier chapters. It is now time to focus on conclusions. Conclusions or endings are of two kinds, direct or delayed (indirect). Both help your audience understand that you have finished your writing, and they provide a psychological sense of finality and closure.

The direct ending most often summarizes, restates, or evaluates the information in the essay. The delayed (indirect) conclusion may introduce a question for further thought or suggest directions for future study of the topic before actually ending an essay.

A conclusion is not limited to the last paragraph. Nonetheless, the amount of space that a conclusion occupies should be in proportion to the length of your essay. Just as two or three paragraphs are too much space for an introduction to a five paragraph theme, so two or three paragraphs of four to seven sentences are too long for the conclusion to a five-paragraph theme.

Ideally, the ratio of 1:7:1 is the least amount of space that you should allow for an introduction or a conclusion. In other words, if you intend to write an essay that will have nine paragraphs, you should have at least one paragraph for your introduction and another one for your conclusion if your body will have seven paragraphs. If your essay will have more than nine developed paragraphs, then you may decide to expand a conclusion for a particular effect. In such cases, you may decide to use the delayed ending (conclusion). The greatest amount of space that you will want to allow for your introduction or conclusion is 1:2:1. In other words, if you write a four paragraph theme and if all paragraphs are of equal length, you would have one paragraph as an introduction, two paragraphs as body, and one paragraph as a conclusion. In an essay this short, you might have the ratio of 1:2:0. In other words, you might choose to omit the conclusion. Remember that the ratio of the essay that conforms to the ''rule of seven'' are 1:2:1 (1:2:0), 1:3:1 (1:3:0), 1:4:1, 1:5:1, 1:6:1, 1:7:1. (*Hint*: Most successful writers choose the option of the conclusion as the length of the essay increases.) You should think of these suggested proportions as guidelines only. They are suggested to help you develop a sense of balance in constructing your essay.

8.10   SENTENCE POWER—MECHANICS

To make your writing look the way your audience expects it to look, use established rules for mechanics such as those for capitalization, abbreviation, and punctuation. The rules for mechanics are conventions that writers and readers generally agree upon, but they change as needs and expectations change. If you follow the rules given here, few readers will have difficulty reading your writing.

Copyright © 1985 by Harcourt Brace Jovanovich, Inc. All rights reserved.

A. Uses of capital letters
   1. First word of a sentence

      It rained. **The** water flooded the street.

   2. First word of a direct quotation

      The mother shouted, "**Stop!**"
      "**Stop** playing in the mud," the mother shouted, "before you ruin your new shoes!"

   3. Proper names
      a. Names and titles of people

         Eric and **N**ancy are in my class.
         Ethel **S**trobeck taught me manners.
         President **H**uey is the president of the university.
         Dr. Longoria is a popular professor.

      b. Relatives

         Aunt **E**sther is my favorite aunt.
         I wrote **M**om.   *Compare*: I wrote my mother.

      c. Geographical locations and nationalities

         Austin, **T**exas, is a popular resort city.
         The **R**ed **R**iver separates **T**exas and **O**klahoma.
         Mexico borders the **U**nited **S**tates of **A**merica.
         My mother lives at 860 **S**outh **R**oss **A**venue.
         It's a real treat to eat **M**exican or **C**hinese food.

      d. Regions and directions

         I lived in the **W**est for ten years.   Compare: He rode the motorcycle west.
         I went to school in the **M**idwest.   Compare: The school is on the southeast side of town.
         She travelled in **E**astern **E**urope.   Compare: She travelled east in Europe.

      e. Historical periods and events

         We studied the **R**evolutionary **W**ar, the **C**ivil **W**ar, and **W**orld **W**ar **O**ne.
         Many historians consider the **Y**alta **C**onference a sell-out.
         The **S**herman **A**nti-**T**rust **A**ct still governs businesses.

Copyright © 1985 by Harcourt Brace Jovanovich, Inc. All rights reserved.

An interesting event of our early history was the **W**hiskey **R**ebellion.
American political philosophy developed during the **A**ge of **R**eason.

f. Races and religions

The Bureau of the Census records each person's race as **C**aucasian,
Hispanic, **N**ative American, **N**egro, **O**riental or **O**ther.
My teacher's mother is **P**rotestant and her father is **R**oman **C**atholic.
To learn about **G**od, people read sacred writings such as the **B**ible, the
Torah, and the **K**oran.

g. Schools and buildings, businesses, and organizations

Dunbar **H**igh **S**chool won the championship.
I plan to visit the **W**orld **T**rade **C**enter and the **E**mpire **S**tate **B**uilding.
This shopping center has **S**ak's, **B**loomingdale's, **M**arshall **F**ield's, and
    Neiman **M**arcus.
The **K**nights of **C**olumbus use the hall on Monday; the **K**iwanis, on
    Tuesday; the **M**asons, on Wednesday; the **L**eague of **W**omen **V**oters,
    on Thursday; and the **C**ity **C**ouncil, on Friday.

h. Titles of such items as student essays, books, magazines, films, and
songs

I wrote my term paper, ''**H**uck's **J**ourney down the **R**iver,'' after I had
    read *The Adventures of Huckleberry Finn*.
You can look up the time for *Monday Night Football* in *TV Guide*.

i. Brand names

I eat **C**ampbell's **S**oup and drink **C**oca **C**ola.

j. School subjects and courses, languages

We speak **S**panish during **I**ntroduction to **S**panish **L**iterature.
I am taking **W**estern **C**ivilization, **C**alculus for **T**eachers, and two
    chemistry courses.

k. Dates, holidays, and special events

The holiday that celebrates the end of summer is **L**abor **D**ay.
We always celebrate **C**hristmas on **D**ecember 25.

l. Government bodies

The largest world organization is the **U**nited **N**ations.
During January, the **C**ongress begins a new session.

Copyright © 1985 by Harcourt Brace Jovanovich, Inc. All rights reserved.

4. Pronouns. Capitalize "I" and pronouns referring to God.

   Michael and **I** will travel this summer.
   Some prophets have been especially close to God and have known **H**is will.

B. Italics

   To indicate italics in typing or longhand, underline the words to be italicized. (Italic letters are *slanted print*.)

   1. Italicize titles of such items as books, films, magazines, plays, record albums, TV shows, works of art, and names of ships.

      a. of books

         The Adventures of Huckleberry Finn

      b. of films

         Casablanca

      c. of magazines

         People

      d. of plays

         Julius Caesar

      e. of record albums

         Greatest Hits of the Fifties

      f. of TV series

         Monday Night Football

      g. of works of art

         Mona Lisa
         the *Mona Lisa*

      h. of names such items as ships, and airplanes.

         the *Queen Elizabeth II*
         the *Spirit of St. Louis*

   2. Italicize foreign words that have not become common.

      Como se llama? in Spanish and *Comment vous appelez-vous?* in French mean "What's your name?"

Copyright © 1985 by Harcourt Brace Jovanovich, Inc. All rights reserved.

3. Italicize words, letters, and numbers used as examples.

   The word *catsup* comes from the Malaysian word for a spiced fish sauce, *kechap,* and can be spelled *ketchup.*

4. Italicize words for emphasis.

   The computer is *dominant* in the workplace.

   (*Note:* Italicizing words for emphasis is the least effective way to show their importance. Compare "The computer dominates the workplace." Most of the time repetition or placement will serve your purposes better. Italicize very rarely.)

C. Quotation marks
   1. Use double quotation marks to enclose the exact words of a speaker or writer.

      Mark Twain opens *The Adventures of Huckleberry Finn* with "You don't know about me, without you have read a book by the name of *The Adventures of Tom Sawyer.*"

   (*Note*: Quotation marks are always used in pairs; if you open them, you must close them.)

   2. Use single quotation marks to enclose quotations within quotations.

      My teacher said, "Mark Twain said, 'The coldest winter I ever spent was August in San Francisco.' "

   3. Use quotation marks to enclose titles of short works.

      a. of poems

         "My Last Duchess"

      b. of short stories

         "The Telltale Heart"

      c. of songs

         "Hey Jude"

      d. of TV shows and radio programs

         "The Dallas Cowboys vs the Washington Redskins" on *Monday Night Football*

   (*Note*: Commas and periods always go inside quotation marks.)

Copyright © 1985 by Harcourt Brace Jovanovich, Inc. All rights reserved.

D. Abbreviations

Avoid using abbreviations in your writing. A few abbreviations are all right and you can use them. Punctuate most abbreviations with a period. A few require no punctuation.

1. Titles used before a person's name are abbreviated.

Mr. James E. Dobkins
Mrs. Martha Willingham
Ms. Shirley Trevino
Dr. Betty Lindsay
Rev. Karl Allemeier

2. Titles or degrees used after someone's name are abbreviated.

Glenda Vasicek, **M.D.**
Phyllis Stier, **Ph.D.**
Walter Ward, **D.D.**
Robert E. Lee Capps, **Jr.**

3. Some companies, government agencies, and organizations are known primarily by their abbreviations.

CBS (Columbia Broadcasting System)
FBI (Federal Bureau of Investigation)
NATO (North Atlantic Treaty Organization)
UNESCO (United Nations Educational Scientific and Cultural Organization)
IMF (International Monetary Fund)

4. Words used with numbers are abbreviated.

9:00 A.M. (**a.m.** or **am**)
6:30 P.M. (**p.m.** or **pm**)
43 B.C., but A.D. 1066
No. 3301 or **no.** 3301

E. Numbers

1. Spell out numbers that take no more than two words.

two thousand chickens, but **2003** chickens
ten dollars, but **$10.19**
one-fourth acre, but **40¼** acres
twenty-five, but **101**

2. Spell out any number that begins a sentence.

Sixteen cows grazed in the field.
(*Hint*: Rewrite your sentence if the number is one like 4938.)

Copyright © 1985 by Harcourt Brace Jovanovich, Inc. All rights reserved.

3. Spell out very large numbers unless you want to emphasize their size.

    fifteen million dollars or **15 million** dollars or **$15 million** or **$15,000,000**

4. Use numbers for street addresses. If the name of a street is a number below 100, some spell the number out.

    67 East **Thirty-Third** Street, but **2654** West **115th** Avenue

5. Use numbers for telling time.

    3:30 P.M., 12 noon, but **three o'clock** in the afternoon

6. Use numbers for dates.

    November **22**, 1937 (NOT November 22**nd**, 1937)
    January **1**, but the **first** of January

7. Write out numbers such as fir**st**, seco**nd**, thi**rd**, four**th**, etc.

    The nin**th** lap was the hardest.

8. Use numbers to show parts of a book.

    Read pages **7** to **12** in Chapter **10** and answer questions **4** and **5**.

F. Punctuation
    1. End marks

        a. Use a period to show the end of a sentence that makes a statement.

            The kite is hung in the tree**.**

        b. Use periods after most abbreviations.

            Mr**.** Ehrstine, Dr**.** Schimel, 9 P.M**.**

        c. Use a question mark after direct questions.

            When will we finish**?**
            How do birds fly**?**

        d. Use an exclamation point to emphasize strong emotion.

            Get out**!**
            Leave me alone**!**

            (*Hint*: Avoid overusing the exclamation point to show emphasis.)

    2. Apostrophes

        a. Use an apostrophe to show missing letters of a contraction.

            don't, for **do not**

Copyright © 1985 by Harcourt Brace Jovanovich, Inc. All rights reserved.

I'm, for **I am**
he'll, for **he will**

(*Hint*: Four contractions cause many problems: they're, it's, you're, who's. They're means *they are*; it's means *it is*; you're means *you are*; and who's means *who is*. Do not confuse them with possessive pronouns.)

b. Use an apostrophe to show possession or ownership

Audrey's dog
child's shoe

(*Hint*: Do not use an apostrophe to show possession for pronouns: their book, its importance, your ticket, his lampshade, whose coat.)

3. Commas

Use commas in your writing only when you have a specific reason. In other words, you should not use a comma unless you are following a specific rule. The old saw that says to insert a comma when you pause in speech or to make the sentence read more clearly can trap you more often than it will help you. A better old saw to remember is "When in doubt, leave it out."

a. Use a comma before coordinating conjunctions (**and**, **but**, **for**, **nor**, **or**, **so**, **yet**) that join independent clauses.

Technology will change the world of work, **but** machines will not replace people.

(*Note:* Experienced writers often omit the comma before a coordinating conjunction that joins independent clauses if the clauses are very short. College students should remember their audience likely expects a comma before a coordinating conjunction.)

b. Use a comma to set off introductory material.

Finally, the check arrived in the mail.
Having left the check on the counter at the bank, I wondered if the teller would deposit it.
Just to find out about the check, I called the bank.
For your information, I had filled out the deposit slip and clipped it to the check.
Although I had filled out the deposit slip and clipped it to the check, I forgot to give it to the teller.

(*Note:* If introductory material is short, you may omit the comma.)

Copyright © 1985 by Harcourt Brace Jovanovich, Inc. All rights reserved.

c. Use commas to separate items in a series.

> **Banks, savings and loans, and stock brokers** offer different ways to invest your money.
> They are located **in shopping malls, in investment centers, and at airports**.
> Banks are **trustworthy, dependable, financial** institutions.

(*Note*: The comma that comes before *and* in a series may be omitted.)

d. Use commas on either side of appositives and non-essential information. To find out whether the information is non-essential, read your sentence aloud leaving it out. If the sentence still makes sense, put commas around the information you left out when you read the sentence aloud.

> "Getting down to Business," **a report on the personal computer,** contains four case studies.
> Hilary Thomas, **who teaches at Ogilvy Elementary School,** uses the computer to keep class records.
> The computer, **especially the personal computer,** can be used to customize lessons and tests for students.

Two other possibilities:
(1) Use dashes to emphasize nonessential material separated from the rest of the sentence.

> Teachers can use the computer—**especially the personal computer**—to customize lessons and tests for students.

(2) Use parentheses to separate from the rest of the sentence nonessential material that you do not want to emphasize.

> Teachers can use the computer **(especially the personal computer)** to customize lessons and tests for students.

e. Use commas to set off direct quotations from the rest of the sentence.

> "Learning to use the computer," the consultant said, "will reduce your time on task."
> The consultant said, "Learning to use the computer will reduce your time on task."

(*Note*: Commas and periods go inside quotation marks.)

f. Use commas for the following special uses.
(1) Use a comma to separate street address, city, and state.

Copyright © 1985 by Harcourt Brace Jovanovich, Inc. All rights reserved.

The company is located at 624 Castle Court, Pullman, WA 98701.

(*Note*: A comma does not separate the state from the zip code. The post office prefers that abbreviations be used for states.)

(2) Use a comma to separate the day from the year and the year from the rest of the sentence.

My mother was born on May 12, 1942, during World War II, but my father was born May 10, 1937.

(3) Use a comma to set off the name of a person addressed (spoken to).

Terry, please give Justin the box of disks.
I plan, **Terry,** for you to write a program.
Please turn off the power when you finish, **Terry**.

4. Semicolon
    a. Use a semicolon to separate independent clauses which lack coordinating conjunctions.

    Technology will change the world of work; however, machines will not replace people.
    Machines will ease the workload; they will not replace people.

    b. Use semicolons to separate items in a series if those items contain commas.

    On our vacation we visited San Francisco, California; Anchorage, Alaska; and Honolulu, Hawaii.

EXERCISE 1

Where needed, add capital letters or make letters lower case, underline material to be italicized, and make corrections in the use of numbers and abbreviations.

1. charles played the barbara streisand album color me pink on his stereo.

2. He set his turntable for sixteen and a half Revolutions per minute.

3. his sister, melinda, wanted to watch the beverly hillbillies because her friends were there to watch TeleVision.

4. international business machines produces the international business machines personal computer and the international business machines personal computer junior.

Copyright © 1985 by Harcourt Brace Jovanovich, Inc. All rights reserved.

5. the address of the french embassy is ninety-six ten embassy row, Wash. district of columbia.

6. i often eat linguine when i go to the restaurant, ciao, but when i go to The Palms, i order in french—c'est magnifique.

7. the play blood wedding was written by federico garcia lorca.

8. we walked down broadway to times square before we took the subway out to one hundred and tenth street.

9. the agency accepted applications between eight A.m and four fifty-nine pM.

10. the college lib. contains four hundred thousand volumes in the gen. collection and another six thousand twenty seven in special coll., three hundred fifty-five in the faculty collection and seventy-two in the rare book rm.

EXERCISE 2

Where needed, add quotation marks, commas, dashes, parentheses, apostrophes, and end punctuation. Add capitals where necessary.

1. Vivian answered Can you expect me can you even imagine it to complete this assignment before the assembly

2. closing the book the teacher replied abruptly I most certainly do and if you dont you wont go to the assembly

3. with that answer Vivian settled against the desk crossed her legs twirled her hair and stared out the window

4. two minutes later vivian opened her notebook and began to write hastily first without making corrections then with real concentration and effort

5. eureka I finished cried vivian and its ten minutes before the assembly starts

6. ruth Ive lost my comb vivian whispered looking anxiously at the teacher

7. did i hear you say Ive lost my comb vivian the teacher said as she picked a comb up from the floor

8. oh no thats not my comb vivian said rudely before adding it belongs to chip I think

9. after handing the comb to chip the teacher wrote on the chalkboard the assign-

Copyright © 1985 by Harcourt Brace Jovanovich, Inc. All rights reserved.

ment for wednesday: read the rest of chapter seven pages 117–32 and the be-ginning of chapter eight pages 133–41.

10. in other words I want you to finish part three of chapter seven and read the introduction to chapter eight

EXERCISE 3

Supply commas, semicolons, and end punctuation.

1. Even though the number of majors in high technology fields is increasing university officials foresee the need for even greater numbers of high technology graduates in the future

2. High technology graduates can expect to find jobs easily but they should recognize that their training can become obsolete quickly

3. For a well-rounded educational program many students choose electives in the liberal arts

4. Advisors usually recommend to students courses in literature drama or art

5. Sometimes advisors recommend psychology and sociology or history and government as electives however these courses are often required

6. Psychology emphasizes the individual behavior sociology stresses group behavior

7. Often students enjoy the demanding organized courses the concentrated precise work and the changing developing ideas that training in computer architecture affords

8. Until you learn about microcomputers and laser technology you are not likely to find employment in high technology fields

9. Computer technology requires that you understand physics and that you know mathematics

10. When the graduates from the 1980s become the executives of the 1990s and when their children are college students the high technology of the 1980s may appear as obsolete as the technology of vacuum tube electronics appears now nonetheless to have a perspective on changes in any field requires the passage of time

Copyright © 1985 by Harcourt Brace Jovanovich, Inc. All rights reserved.

8.11 DICTATION

Your instructor will choose a passage of approximately 100 words and read it aloud. You are to write what you hear. As you listen to each sentence, concentrate and maintain silence. Do not ask your instructor to repeat because any sound other than the teacher's voice reading will break not only your concentration but that of others. Your instructor may repeat key words and phrases during the dictation, will allow sufficient time for you to write what you hear, and will reread the entire passage a second time at a faster rate so that you can check what you have written and fill in any gaps you may have.

Write on every other line so that you will have space to correct your dictation upon the final reading in case you have made a mistake. Your instructor will show you the dictated passage and ask you to compare your version, or perhaps a classmate's version, to the original. Be especially alert when you check the dictation because this exercise will help you develop your sentence sense by translating spoken into written language.

8.12 WORD POWER

VOCABULARY

In this unit you are to learn still more of those words that have the same or similar sounds and forms. If you pay particular attention, you may find that you will use them correctly and avoid slips in diction whenever you encounter them. As you read for school or for pleasure, the newspaper or your favorite magazines, notice these words.

1. a. Sales in Johns's territory are booming because he uses the computer to gain *access* to more sales leads for his staff than other managers can.
   b. Even a computer, however, can be used to *excess* if you ignore human relations.
2. a. Sales, law, teaching and insurance benefit from using a computer to *aid* organization.
   b. The attorneys' legal *aide* probably operates most of the computer's word processing program.
3. a. When Leroy entered college, he could *already* run the mile in less than 4 minutes.
   b. Leroy is *all ready* to train for the U.S. Olympic team.
4. Renting skis and boots is *all right* until you learn to ski.
   (*Hint*: Most consider it incorrect to spell *all right* as one word.)
5. a. Billy Jack and his buddies sat *all together* at Friday's game.

Copyright © 1985 by Harcourt Brace Jovanovich, Inc. All rights reserved.

    b.   Every time the team scored, Billy Jack and his buddies made *altogether* too much noise.

6. a.   You do not have to know a *bit* from a byte to operate a computer.

   b.   Eight binary digits (bits) make up a *byte* which represents a single letter or number in a computer.

   c.   To understand that computers don't *bite*, you almost have to work with one for a while.

7. a.   A first-time computer user may fear that the computer will *break* if he pushes the wrong key.

   b.   Computers, unlike automobiles, do not require a *brake* to slow down.

8. a.   Each computer has its own *serial* number which identifies it.

   b.   Today, children can learn about computers by reading *cereal* boxes at breakfast.

9. a.   A *fourth* kind of professional businessman, an insurance agent, also found a computer helped to organize his business.

   b.   Expecting a computer to give *forth* information of better quality than the information fed into it ignores the hacker's maxim, "garbage in, garbage out."

10. a.   No matter what you may have *heard* about computers, they cannot think for you.

   b.   Don said in amazement, "Look at that old man *herd* that Cadillac around the corner!"

11. a.   Features that one computer *lacks* another probably will have.

   b.   People who recognize the computer as a servant rather than as a master will not become *lax* about maintaining their own mental agility.

12. a.   If you can, always purchase a computer from a *local* company to insure that you will have service when you need it.

   b.   "Silicon Valley" is the name given to a special *locale* near San Francisco, California, where the highest concentration of computer companies carries out research and development.

13. a.   A really good computer usually has a *metal* cabinet.

   b.   The high quality of some computer designs should merit a *medal*.

14. a.   Programs will often transfer from one kind of computer to another with only *minor* adjustments.

   b.   In one of its coal mines Japan has a new computer-operated system designed to keep the *miner* as safe as possible.

15. a.   Manufacturers of some of the plastic parts for a computer use an injection *mold*.

   b.   Cheese manufacturers can use computers to measure the amount of *mold* present as cheeses ripen.

   c.   If you discover a *mole* on your body, you should let a dermatologist look at it.

16. a.   *None* of the computers on the market today can actually think, but scientists

Copyright © 1985 by Harcourt Brace Jovanovich, Inc. All rights reserved.

are developing artificial intelligences to be used in the next generation of computers.

b. Our local Catholic hospital has a head nurse, a *nun*, who knows computer programming.

17. a. Some baseball teams use computer analysis to help their *pitcher* improve his speed and accuracy.

b. The computer graphs a *picture* of the path the ball takes after the pitcher has thrown it.

18. a. The CAT scanner, a sophisticated hospital computer, analyzes a series of X-rays of the body each of which shows a different *plane*.

b. Jonas Johns sets up the definition of each computer entry in *plain* English only once.

19. a. Many college students remember their high school *principal* as their pal. (*Hint:* Notice the last three letters of princiPAL.)

b. The rules of the organization represented *principles* accepted by all the members.

20. a. Jonas Johns manages a *team* of twelve salespeople.

b. With the aid of a computer microscope scientists can see how drops of ordinary water *teem* with tiny organisms.

EXERCISE 1

Write the correct word in the blanks.

1. Some 16 bite/bit/byte ———————— computers process information in two

   bits/bytes/bites ———————— of eight bits/bytes/bites ———————— each.

2. The teem/team ———————— of programmers which writes software pro-

   grams for use in personal computers all ready/already ————————

   has access/excess ———————————— to the most popular brands
   on the market.

3. Students who use computers and calculators often become lacks/lax ————

   about their math skills and need to brake/break ————————————

   themselves of the habit of using that calculation aid/aide ————————.

4. The principal/principle ———————— that makes a computer work is diffi-

   cult to state in plane/plain ———————— English.

Copyright © 1985 by Harcourt Brace Jovanovich, Inc. All rights reserved.

5. Altogether/all together _____, thousands of soft-

   ware programs are available to computer users for a miner/minor _____ investment of cash.

6. Nun/none _____ of the students enrolled in the

   programming class had ever herd/heard _____ of COBAL, a computer language used frequently by businesses.

7. The daytime cereal/serial _____ told the heart-

   breaking tale of a locale/local _____ family.

8. If you leave bread in the wrapper too long, it will mold/mole _____.

9. A computer monitor looks a lot like a television picture/pitcher _____ tube.

10. If gold, silver, and platinum are the three most popular metals/medals _____

    for making jewelry, what is the forth/fourth _____?

Copyright © 1985 by Harcourt Brace Jovanovich, Inc. All rights reserved.

SPELLING

Change the "y" to "i" when adding a suffix to a word ending in "y":

1. if the letter before the "y" is a consonant;
2. if the prefix to be added does not begin with "i."

Otherwise, leave the "y" alone.

Example   apply + -ed = applied
but,   play + -ed = played, or try + -ing = trying

EXERCISE 2

Combine the base words with the suffixes following the plus mark. Spell the combined word properly in the blank provided.

1. accompany + -ed _____

2. beauty + -ful _____

3. carry + -ing _____

4. family + -ar _____

5. forty + -eth _____

6. happy + -ly _____

7. hungry + -er _____

8. luxury + -ous _____

9. ordinary + -ly _____

10. pity + -ful _____

11. privy + -lege _____

12. secretary + -al _____

13. stay + -ed _____

14. strategy + -c _____

Copyright © 1985 by Harcourt Brace Jovanovich, Inc. All rights reserved.

15. study + -ing _____

16. vary + -ous _____

17. study + -es _____

18. quantity + -es _____

19. controversy + -al _____

20. buy + -ing _____

Copyright © 1985 by Harcourt Brace Jovanovich, Inc. All rights reserved.

Editor's Evaluation

Writer's Name _____

Title _____

I liked . . .
1.

2.

3.

I think you could improve if . . .
1.

2.

3.

Editor _____

Date _____

Copyright © 1985 by Harcourt Brace Jovanovich, Inc. All rights reserved.

Notes

Editor's Evaluation

Writer's Name _____

Title _____

I liked . .
1.

I think you could improve if . . .
1.

2.

2.

3.

3.

Editor _____

Date _____

Copyright © 1985 by Harcourt Brace Jovanovich, Inc. All rights reserved.

Notes

Editor's Evaluation

Writer's Name _____

Title _____

I liked . . .
1.

2.

3.

I think you could improve if . . .
1.

2.

3.

Editor _____

Date _____

Copyright © 1985 by Harcourt Brace Jovanovich, Inc. All rights reserved.

Notes

Editor's Evaluation

Writer's Name _____

Title _____

I liked . .   I think you could improve if . . .
1.   1.

2.   2.

3.   3.

Editor _____

Date _____

Copyright © 1985 by Harcourt Brace Jovanovich, Inc. All rights reserved.

Notes

Editor's Evaluation

Writer's Name _____

Title _____

I liked . . .
1.

I think you could improve if . . .
1.

2.

2.

3.

3.

Editor _____

Date _____

Copyright © 1985 by Harcourt Brace Jovanovich, Inc. All rights reserved.

Notes

Editor's Evaluation

Writer's Name _____

Title _____

I liked . .
1.

I think you could improve if . . .
1.

2.

2.

3.

3.

Editor _____

Date _____

Copyright © 1985 by Harcourt Brace Jovanovich, Inc. All rights reserved.

Notes

INDEX

A 4
B 5
C 6
D 7
E 8
F 9
G 0
H 1
I 2
J 3